Shooting the Civil War

Cinema and Society series

GENERAL EDITOR: JEFFREY RICHARDS

SHOOTING THE CIVIL WAR

Cinema, History and American National Identity

Jenny Barrett

I.B. TAURIS
LONDON · NEW YORK

Published in 2009 by I.B. Tauris & Co Ltd
6 Salem Road, London W2 4BU
175 Fifth Avenue, New York NY 10010
www.ibtauris.com

In the United States and Canada distributed by Palgrave Macmillan,
a division of St. Martin's Press, 175 Fifth Avenue, New York NY 10010

ISBN   (Hb) 978 1 84511 775 7
         (Pb) 978 1 84511 776 4

A full CIP record for this book is available from the British Library
A full CIP record for this book is available from the Library of Congress
Library of Congress catalog card: available

Typeset in Garamond by Dexter Haven Associates Ltd, London
Civil war rifle detail illustrated by Hallie Stiller at Dexter Haven
Printed and bound in India by Thomson Press (India) Limited

Contents

Foreword

In the heady days of early cinema, the humourist Will Rogers announced, 'There is only one thing that can kill the Movies, and that is education.' Historical films, it seems, might be most vulnerable to such a prophecy. And of the myriad sub-genres of those, films of the American Civil War – a subject so minutely and tirelessly pondered by professional, popular and amateur historians for well over a century – may top the list. From 1915's *The Birth of a Nation* to 2003's *Cold Mountain*, critics have rarely refrained from lamenting the often wanton ahistoricity of these movies, yet popular films depicting the Civil War have steadfastly resisted scholars' most zealous efforts to turn them into history lessons.

This should come as no surprise. Popular feature films, after all, are not meant to be history lessons. Rather, they are cultural products, designed to profit their producers by crafting or recapitulating captivating historical mythologies. Historical films thus pretend to something far different from mere scholarship. As film analyst Gene M. Moore puts it, 'We live in an age in which film has replaced literature as the main channel through which cultural values are transmitted.' Standing at the apex of a multi-billion-dollar worldwide entertainment industry, popular feature films are one of the most culturally influential media forces in the modern world. How necessary, then, that we understand how film works, especially in relation to the past it claims to represent.

The distinction between the kind of recollection that happens in popular feature films and the kind that happens in scholarly books has become the stuff of intense analysis in recent years, and languages for discussing the difference are emerging. Historian David Blight tells us:

> Memory is often owned; history is interpreted. Memory is passed down through the generations; history is revised. Memory often coalesces in objects, sites, and monuments; history seeks to understand contexts in all their complexity. History asserts the authority of academic training and canons of evidence; memory carries the often more immediate authority of community membership and experience.

In short, popular feature films do not purport to partake of the past in the ways that scholars do. Instead, they engage in the formulation and reformulation of historical memory. When harnessed to the profit incentives of a titanic media industry, they are a potent cultural force, shaping viewers' collective understanding of the past, and in the process moulding their very identities.

None of this is to denigrate popular films on the Civil War, many of which offer landmarks in both cinema history and national mythmaking. It is simply to highlight the well-worn shibboleth that historical films seldom make good history. But even this insight may not be exactly true. The motion picture industry – 'Hollywood', if you will – *does* follow the academy in important ways, if only belatedly and haphazardly. Major scholarly revisions of the Civil War era have come to be accepted in film, just as at its nascence film embodied accepted scholarly views of the period. No one, of course, could today credibly pass off a film of *The Birth of a Nation's* racial sensibilities. And though *Gone With the Wind* remains the top-grossing film of all time, even the lingering fans of its outdated romantic racialism understand that, thankfully, its sentiments lie squarely outside the mainstream of accepted public discourse. Even those who remain unoffended by Butterfly McQueen's portrayal of Prissy can appreciate that in the first decade of the twenty-first century, it is most decidedly not 'politically correct'.

Rather than simply neglecting the scholarly state of the art, Hollywood's depictions of the Civil War era have always trailed it, serpentining in its wake, sometimes near the scholarly consensus and sometimes farther off, sometimes embracing elements of it whilst simultaneously rejecting other components. And it is here – in the pulsating divide between memory and history so deftly occupied by cinema – that the real value in understanding Civil War film lies. For it is precisely here that we see these films doing their cultural work – of continually constituting and reconstituting race, class, gender and region, as well as the roles of these in shaping national identity in an intensely market-driven world of mass media. It is perhaps only in understanding this role of film as cultural work that we can stand apart from the ideological projects of the films themselves, and decide for ourselves what lessons of the past we choose to learn.

This book is an enormous step in that direction. It is a valuable contribution to a burgeoning scholarship on the Civil War in film, yet stands apart for its interest in film *as* film. It is time to move beyond direct equations between social context and the content of films. Dr Jenny Barrett does just this, by examining cinematic depictions of the Civil War under rubrics that meld both film studies and history. In challenging us to consider these depictions in light of existing film genres and the ideological work they do, she offers us a vision of the inchoate, variable nature of the Civil War as a distinct category of film. In exploring the ways the Civil War inflects existing film genres, as well as how particular genres encapsulate specific understandings of the conflict itself, she reveals the historical memory of the Civil War as a cultural phenomenon deeply engaged in a process of imagined (but nonetheless powerful) nation-making.

Will Rogers probably had it wrong, then, at least with respect to Civil War films. Education – well, not the college-bred variety we so often associate with the word – is in no danger of killing the movies. For, as Dr Barrett shows us, movies have always found a fertile niche in the ever-shifting gulf between historical memory and historical scholarship, between the authority of popular mythology and the authority of the professoriate. It is a different sense of 'education' that Civil War films impart, for movies teach historical lessons with a kind of cultural sanction far different from, and increasingly alienated from, that of the education offered by the academy. If we are to appreciate this divide and its significance, we can do no better than with an effort such as this one.

Patrick Rael
Associate Professor of History
Bowdoin College
Brunswick, Maine USA

General Editor's Introduction

In Billy Wilder's *Sunset Boulevard* a hapless Hollywood producer, played by Fred Clark, laments the fact that his biggest career misjudgement was turning down *Gone With the Wind* with the immortal line: 'no-one wants to see another Civil War picture'. If he had had the opportunity to read Jenny Barrett's book, he would not have made this mistake. For she reveals that there have been over seven hundred Civil War films to date, suggesting a continuous audience demand. But what is new and fascinating in her study is that she rejects the idea of the Civil War as a distinct cinematic genre and instead argues that Civil War films can be found across a range of different generic forms, the domestic melodrama, the Western, the combat film, for instance. Each genre has highlighted a different aspect of the Civil War experience and she examines these aspects with great subtlety and insight through a selection of filmic examples spanning the whole history of Hollywood from early silent days to the present.

Thus, she argues that the domestic melodrama, such as *Gone With the Wind, So Red the Rose* and *Friendly Persuasion*, focuses on the war as a threat to the unity and permanence of the family. The Western, such as *Escape from Fort Bravo, How the West Was Won* and *The Undefeated*, explores the themes of race, land and authority. The combat film, represented by *The Red Badge of Courage, The Horse Soldiers* and *Glory* looks at codes of masculinity, rites of passage and male bonding. The idea of national identity runs through all her chapters and she quite properly devotes a chapter to the epoch-making but highly contentious *The Birth of a Nation*. This innovative and stimulating study makes a remarkable suggestion, that no Civil War film yet made has had a central black character who survives the war, fathers the children of the future and stands as representative of the whole American people and not solely its ethnic population. To that extent, the American Civil War remains unfinished business.

Jeffrey Richards

Introduction

American Civil War films are amongst some of the most notorious and well-known films of western cinema's history. It is a story that continues to fascinate directors and audiences alike. Taking a single year as a case study, 2003 alone saw three films released in the USA in which the Civil War was, if not the dominant narrative factor, then at least a historical backdrop for the action. These included Ronald F. Maxwell's *Gods and Generals*, the prequel to his previous Civil War film *Gettysburg*, starring respected actors such as Robert Duvall and Jeff Daniels. Anthony Minghella's *Cold Mountain*, starring Nicole Kidman and Jude Law, was released in the same year, as was Martin Scorsese's *Gangs of New York*, set during the time of the Civil War but concerning itself with the life of Irish immigrants and city life. Clearly, the American Civil War is a narrative topic and historical milieu that, almost one hundred and fifty years after the conclusion of the war, still attracts some of the most respected and popular of directors and actors, and this has been true throughout the history of American cinema since its earliest years. Prominent directors including D.W. Griffith, John Ford, John Huston and Clint Eastwood have all chosen to explore this period of American history on screen. Actors as diverse as John Wayne, Elvis Presley, Shirley Temple and Morgan Freeman have starred as, respectively, soldiers, farmhands, Southern belles and ex-slaves, characters that face the threats and trauma of a war that famously saw more Americans die than all previous US military conflicts put together.

The American Civil War of 1861 to 1865 deserves continuing critical attention as one of the single most significant events in the making of the modern United States and in the beginning of emancipation for African-American slaves. Regularly, a single year will see several hundred books published on far-ranging topics including the private lives of military figures, detailed renditions of single battles, revisionist histories of the war and the wartime experiences of women, slaves and politicians, not to mention the continuing publication of novels concerned with these same matters. It is a landmark historical event that, according to some writers, is very much an ongoing conflict today.[1] Other scholars have pondered on the possible consequences of an alternate history in which key moments of the war might have turned in favour of the Confederacy, such as Peter Tsouras' *Dixie Victorious: An Alternate History of the Civil War* (2006). What is it, then, that leads to such a persistent fascination with this conflict? Perhaps the answer to this question is that not only did this war see the death of 620,000 Americans, it also led to the freedom of four million slaves and, subsequently, the elevation of America's arguably most charismatic and significant leader, Abraham Lincoln, to an iconic status currently unsurpassed. It was recorded through the press, through diaries, letters, new legislation, and the arts, including theatre, literature and sculpture. It also stands alone as the first military conflict to be consistently documented through photography, meaning that not only was its impact translated into a visual form and distributed by the press throughout the globe, but its images also remain accessible to those who strive to understand its significance and meaning today.

According to popular historian and novelist Shelby Foote in Ken Burns' television documentary of 1989, *The Civil War*, to truly understand the American nation, one must understand this particular civil conflict. Foote adds, 'the Civil War defined us as what we are, and it opened us to what we became, good and bad things'. What Foote expresses here is that this period of history saw the birth of the American nation and, as such, any history of the Civil War is a history of national origins. He is stating that not only is the Civil War a time of beginnings ('it opened us to what we became'), but also it is an indication of identity ('it defined us as what we are'). It is a historical event, therefore, that speaks of what it means to be American today, as well as being a sign of American ancestry. What exactly the nation is in those terms can be found through a reading of historical accounts of the Civil War, some of which will posit America as the land of the free, others of which will argue, however overtly or covertly, that genuine freedom and equality still remain unachieved. One historian may understand the Civil War as a necessary evil in the construction of a permanently unified nation, whilst another may suggest that the war is still effectively being fought in the minds of many Americans who continue to harbour the sectional allegiances of North and South. Most will refer to the conflict as the 'American Civil War', imagining the conflict as within a single nation, whilst others name it the 'War Between the States', which implies the concept of two nations at war. What these different histories and vocabularies reveal is the diversity of worldviews at play in discourses on the Civil War. What lies behind them are distinct and opposing ideologies of the American nation and national identity governing the agendas and questions of historians, cultural commentators and the general public. For some more in-depth discussions of attitudes towards and histories of the Civil War, a wide range of texts are available, including Catton (2004), Grob and Billias (1982), Pressly (1962), and the host of publications from the likes of James McPherson, Shelby Foote and others.

The one abiding source of knowledge about the Civil War, however, is not the historical textbook, nor even the novel, but the cinema. This is particularly true in Britain, where Civil War scholarship is not as prominent a component of historical research or of education as it is in the United States. It can be estimated that there are now currently more than seven hundred Civil War films, documentaries, shorts and animations, with the number slowly but consistently rising. According to historian William C. Davis, the reduction in the frequency of Civil War productions is down to a public demand for historical accuracy. He writes 'we become a nation of critics and letter writers whenever a Confederate soldier's jacket has the wrong buttons', concluding '[a]s a result, moviemakers avoid the subject in part to avoid its scholars and buffs'.[2] Yet the films continue to be made, and they contribute to an even wider field of popular cultural representations of the war since the late nineteenth century including poetry, novels and art. What is different about the Civil War in film, as opposed to another public medium, is that it is able to reach millions of individuals in America and beyond, and has the potential to be regularly and effortlessly re-consumed through broadcast, satellite and cable television, video and other digital technologies over subsequent years, thereby reiterating particular cultural representations of history.

As well as this kind of public consumption of Civil War films, some appear regularly as the subjects of debate within film studies as examples of technological breakthrough, racism in film, or the manipulation of history, with those particular films gaining in the process an academic history of their own. Civil War films constitute an aspect of American cinema that deserves serious scholarly attention. Despite this, consideration of Civil War films has been intermittent, and has tended to concentrate on individual instances. Since the Civil War is, as Foote suggests, inherently about the making of a nation and its identity, it is necessary to question whether and how the kind of nation represented in Civil War films indicates some kind of coherent national identity, or a range of identities, representing the United States of America. If the Civil War is a historical event so vital to the formation of an American's sense of self, and if audiences continue to watch Civil War films with such consistency, then it is essential to explore the likelihood that these films play a part in constructing identity. It is now vital, with the continuing production of Civil War films, to reflect upon the relationship between this war and cinema. This goes beyond the many publications that are, quite rightly, designed to highlight the historical inaccuracies found in many films of this category.

My own personal interest in American Civil War films began with an investigation into genre, particularly the Western. Like many generations before me, I spent countless hours as a child watching Saturday matinees which were invariably Westerns, often starring John Wayne, Alan Ladd, William Holden and Audie Murphy. As an undergraduate student I found the arena to explore these films from an academic perspective, and took the opportunity to examine the gradual adaptation of genre conventions over time in the Western. It was in this task that I became aware of regular references to the war. I noticed, for example, that it would be used for narrative economy, to suggest a character's history or to explain his behaviour, even after the war was over. The title character of *The Outlaw Josey Wales* (1976) is typical. Clint Eastwood plays a man who continues to fight the war long after the Confederacy's surrender because he is driven to avenge the murder of his wife and child at the hands of Union guerrillas, the so-called 'Red Legs'. Through further investigation I discovered that Civil War references and narratives were by no means restricted only to the Western genre; it was present in the epic melodrama *Gone With the Wind* (1939), in the silent comedy *The General* (1927) and even in the science fiction film *The Supernaturals* (1986).

This discovery was set aside until, on reading Scott Simmon's account of the career of D.W. Griffith,[3] I found the phrases 'Civil War genre' and 'the Civil War film'. Although Simmon refers here to a period of filmmaking history when Civil War films were common, during the silent era of American cinema, from my experience Civil War narratives appeared to be present across multiple genres throughout the twentieth century, and so could not be labelled as a film genre in their own right. This belief also appeared to be shared by Steve Neale in his overview of the war film genre, where he writes that the Civil War films of early cinema came to develop certain 'alliances' with other genres, such as the Western and the war film.[4]

From this position, seeing Civil War films as having generic alliances, I formulated a hypothesis: there is no such thing as 'the Civil War film', or at least, there is no such genre as the Civil War genre, unlike the Western or the science fiction film. There are, however, Civil War films, in the plural, that can be found across the range of generic output from the US film industry. They are predominantly American films, although occasionally exceptions may be found, such as Sergio Leone's *The Good, the Bad, and the Ugly* (1966), an Italian film that uses the Civil War as a device to spur the action and interaction of the central characters. This example, although not an American film, is a Western, one of the most common genres to make use of the Civil War in its development of characters and plot. Each of these genres is an established film category that is usually easily recognisable and able to channel the expectations of an audience. The Civil War appears, to put it crudely, to be slipped into a genre, and once there follows the rules of narrative and style that apply within that form. Thus, the Civil War film does not exist; instead, there are Civil War films that are in fact Westerns, war films and so forth.

Given that one Civil War film can be distinguished from another by dint of its genre, it seems logical to approach a study from a generic perspective, taking one genre at a time and searching for consistencies in the construction of a sense of the war and of American national identity. There is, however, a difficulty in categorising Civil War films in terms of their generic allegiances. As Steve Neale states, Hollywood genres are each 'hybrid and multi-generic'.[5]

1. *The Outlaw Josey Wales* (Clint Eastwood, 1976): Josey Wales metes out justice to the Red leg aggressor.

Genres do have certain peculiarities and characteristics, but generic boundaries cannot be seen as fixed and clear; in practice they are dynamic, changeable and vague. Certainly today it is increasingly difficult to identify a film as one single, pure example of a genre, if in fact this was ever truly possible. This dilemma is partly to do with the variety of generic labels that can be given to individual films, offering up a problem in the categorisation of Civil War films. Firstly, almost every film that deals with concerns or events of the Civil War, bar *The Supernaturals*, which is science fiction, can be labelled a 'historical film', since the content of the narrative reconstructs an event or period from the distant past. Although this category does not constitute one single genre, it is nevertheless a way in which the films can be collectively recognised by audiences and film industry alike on the grounds of their difference from films with a contemporary setting. Secondly, a high proportion of the films include a romance element that is present in almost every genre, meaning that they could be described as 'historical romances'.

Thirdly, because each to a certain degree contains narrative reference to the American Civil War, they can legitimately be termed war films. The central problem with this step, however, is that the war film category carries connotations of actual combat, which might not be a narrative element within the film under consideration. Instead it may demonstrate features indicating an affinity with another genre, perhaps the Western or the thriller, or even both. Robert Ray's list of the conventions of the World War II combat film, which can also be found in films representing other American wars, may not necessarily be present in Civil War melodramas or comedies. Where, for example, is the isolated, all-male group 'involved in a life-and-death task'[6] in *Gone With the Wind* beyond one single brief excursion into a shanty town that is not even shown on screen? In this film, the narrative's concern is with one central protagonist, a woman. To label *Gone With the Wind* as a combat film, or perhaps even as a war film, would be to ignore the dominant generic allegiance towards domestic melodrama that it displays.

Taking the presence of the Civil War as a prerequisite, this book identifies films according to their dominant characteristics of genre, style and narrative content. In some cases, films that initially seem safe to categorise as, for example, war film, have been relocated to another genre, such as melodrama, by virtue of certain overriding narrative elements. Most of the film texts, however, have been chosen because of their distinct generic identity for the purpose of discovering how that particular genre treats the historical period of the Civil War. The aim of this approach is to ascertain the range of uses of the Civil War in film and some of the possible ideological projects in play in both a reconstruction of the war and a construction of American national identity.

Very few published studies deal with the Civil War's relationship with film genres, although many consider the war's representation in cultural products and the resultant expressions of national identity. One notable recent study is Bruce Chadwick's *The Reel Civil War: Mythmaking in American Film* (2002). Chadwick is particularly concerned with historical distortion, or the 'mangling' of history,[7] found in Civil War films. Through an exploration of the rise of the Southern myth in American literature, he traces the presence of the Southern 'heroic underdog', the absence of political comment on slavery and the ideology of national reconciliation. Chadwick proposes that the history of the Civil War had to be re-written as a 'tidy legend' without winners or losers, slavery or blame, in order to reinforce the unity of the nation. It is a fascinating and well-researched study, but Chadwick focuses particularly on narrative themes and formulas without

2. *The General* (Clyde Bruckman, Buster Keaton, 1927): Buster Keaton gives the Civil War a comic treatment.

giving any extended attention to one of the most enduring of conventional structures – the genre – one means by which ideologies are made material. Chadwick does consider the post-Civil War Western in one chapter, but views it more as a narrative category that re-writes the Civil War. He does not interrogate the genre's conventions and their stability or alteration in the face of the war narrative. Chadwick is concerned with how true to history the films are and the meaning of their myths in terms of American national identity. My study, however, aims to investigate how true to *genre* the films are, and how this relationship reflects ideologies of American national identity. Of course, generic conventions, like films, cannot be legitimately regarded as windows upon some kind of truth. However, as this book highlights, many filmmakers have proclaimed their reconstructions of the Civil War as representative of historical truth and reviews have often reasserted this claim. My study is concerned with the extent to which those 'truths' conform to the requirements and conventions of genre, as well as investigating the resultant assertion of national identity.

Another significant publication is Jim Cullen's 1995 book *The Civil War in Popular Culture: A Reusable Past*. Cullen examines the uses to which the Civil War has been put, including chapters on one film (Edward Zwick's *Glory*, 1989), one novel (*Gone With the Wind*, 1936, by Margaret Mitchell), Southern rock music and Civil War re-enactment. Like Chadwick, he considers how history has been 're-written' at particular moments in time, and how the process has been inflected by historical contexts, identifying a certain sense of national communion engendered by these cultural products. He quotes Shelby Foote's comments from Ken Burns' *The Civil War* documentary series at length, including Foote's statement referred to at the beginning of this introduction. Cullen's point is that an understanding of Civil War films, novels and so forth, reveals as much about the American nation and what it considers its identity to be, as does a knowledge of the historical event itself. Cullen's book argues that historical, cultural and social contexts are vital in the analysis of Civil War cultural products but, like Chadwick, he does not consider the place of genre and generic convention in the construction of ideological viewpoints in the films, novels and other products.

The influence of genre has been consistently overlooked in literature about Civil War films. Paul C. Spehr's encyclopaedic list of films, *The Civil War in Motion Pictures: A Bibliography of Films Produced in the United States Since 1897* (1961), is a valuable resource to the historical film scholar, encompassing over six hundred narrative and documentary films about the war, but it is designed only as a reference manual. Roy Kinnard's book *The Blue and the Gray on the Silver Screen: More Than Eighty Years of Civil War Movies* (1996) is similarly descriptive, although less comprehensive. It is a useful introduction to the study of Civil War films, but again it is a reference book that offers little in the way of interpretation or argument and is not concerned with questions of genre.

Perhaps some of the most striking and important work on Civil War films has been conducted by Thomas Cripps, whose meticulous research into the reception of *The Birth of a Nation* and of the representation of race in Civil War films, is groundbreaking. His 1963 article 'The Reaction of the Negro to the Motion Picture *The Birth of a Nation*' is one of the first scholarly articles to delve into a range of primary sources to remind film scholars that *Birth's* racist ideology was far from condoned by the whole viewing public of the United States.[8] He concludes that controversy over the film proves that cinema not only reflects worldviews but also creates, or draws out, opinions on key issues such as identity, racism and political bias, and so by stating this he brings these issues squarely into the arena of film studies. More recently, Cripps' article 'The Absent Presence in American Civil War Films' concerns the 'structured absence' of African Americans in the films, a strategy to ignore slavery and the politics of race in the creation of a unified white nation on screen.[9] It is an approach developed by a film industry that remembers the controversy of *The Birth of a Nation* yet continues to attempt to appeal, through its mostly white protagonists, to the white majority in cinema audiences.

What Cripps, Cullen and Chadwick each achieve is the raising of the profile of Civil War films in film scholarship. They demonstrate how films that depict the war appeal to notions of American national identity with their roots in a moment in time that is of deep significance to the American nation. The authors identify that the Civil War is put to use in films in the service of a small range of agendas revolving around, particularly, the ideological project of constructing what I term a 'white American ancestry'. However, as important as these publications are, none deal with the role played by genre and generic convention in the process of constructing these ideas of identity.

Possibly the most significant work that establishes a basis upon which all Civil War films should be understood is Benedict Anderson's *Imagined Communities*. Anderson is concerned with the way in which a nation is imagined by its members, and he writes that there is an entire 'pedagogical industry' endeavouring to make Americans 'remember/forget the hostilities of 1861–65 as a great "civil" war between "brothers" rather than between […] two sovereign nation-states'.[10] Anderson is proposing that it is part of the American education of its citizens to make them forget the truth and imagine instead another version of history, one in which the 'enemy' as such is forgotten. This is an ideological scheme that helps to remind Americans that the Civil War resulted in the re-forming of a national family. Instead of being understood in any way as an enemy, the American ancestor, both Northern and Southern, can thus be remembered as a man or woman enduring a necessary process towards national unity. Bruce Chadwick's study of Civil War films follows this same understanding of America tidily re-writing its history in order to conform to an ideology of national reconciliation after the war.

My study takes Anderson's imagination of the American Civil War as a starting point from which to assess the construction of a national identity through a range of film genres. Chapters 2 to 4 explore the relationship between the Civil War and film genre, and attempt to discover the resultant ideologies and imaginings of American identity in the combination of generic conventions with the war. Chapter 2 considers domestic melodrama and asks if the conventions of this genre are either sustained or challenged by an interaction with the Civil War, what ideologies appear to be propagated and what version of American national identity is imagined. It also asks what melodrama and the melodramatic form achieve in the films, suggesting that a strong relationship exists between the melodramatic and the Civil War. Chapter 3 turns attention towards the Western to see if similar generic strategies are in use. It suggests that the presence of the Civil War in the Western narrative modifies the iconic Western hero, and identifies changes of emphasis in representations of the conflict, as dictated by certain generic requirements. Chapter 4 then analyses examples of the war film's combat sub-genre, considering military representations of the war. This chapter, again, looks for challenges to convention introduced by the war itself, and recognises the particular imagining of masculine identity that is constructed in the films.

The films themselves, four from each genre, are chosen with certain criteria in mind. Firstly, all of the films were produced and funded in the USA. The validity of this choice is clear; the films are American constructions of American history, produced predominantly for American audiences. Secondly, each is also representative of their particular genre and is therefore an acceptable starting point for productive generalisations to emerge. Lastly, and importantly, most are frequently transmitted on American and British broadcast and satellite television channels, making them the most regularly consumed of Civil War films in these countries. Although there are many Civil War films that require analysis in terms of their articulations of American national identity, the films chosen here are representative of the enduring fascination that America has with this aspect of history.

Chapter 5 goes on to examine an individual film more closely, perhaps one of the most controversial films of Hollywood's history, D.W. Griffith's *The Birth of a Nation*. More space is given here to production context and close textual analysis, in order to draw conclusions about its particular imagining of nation. Chapter 6 then brings the study more up-to-date with an examination of two more recent Civil War films, Ron Maxwell's *Gods and Generals* and Anthony Minghella's *Cold Mountain*, noting similarities and differences from key films of the study, particularly *Birth*, asking if the concerns and ideological imperatives of one are reproduced in the other. The concluding chapter, finally, returns to Benedict Anderson's notion of the ideological project to remember/forget the Civil War, an approach to the war that imagines the nation of America in ways that exalt its ancestors and its origins.

However, before the analysis of individual films can be conducted, it is necessary to interrogate certain key concepts, such as 'nation'. Understandings of this concept are diverse and varied, so it is important to put some markers in place before going on to use the term throughout the book. It will also be useful to survey some of the more recurrent and established elements of American national identity by briefly looking back at particular historical pronouncements such as the Declaration of Independence and Abraham Lincoln's 'Gettysburg Address'. This will help in the search for ways in which the chosen genres imagine American identity in the weight they give to values such as equality and liberty. Chapter 1 explores these areas of nation and national identity, and recognises that this study is thus ideological in nature. The importance of this is compounded when it is remembered that American film genres have traditionally demonstrated certain ideological imperatives. What will be asked in subsequent chapters is how one expression of ideology, the genre, feeds into and interacts with another, that of the imagining of the American Civil War. Chapter 1 therefore surveys the relationship between ideology, American film genres and the imagining of national identity.

My deepest thanks in the research and writing of this book go to colleagues who have supported and advised me throughout the process, Paul McDonald, Peter Wright and Andrea Wright, as well as friends Louise

Livesey and John Scott. I am indebted to the kind help of Jeff Shaara and the guiding hand of Philippa Brewster at I.B.Tauris, and most of all to the love and support from Jacquie Barrett, David Barrett and Kevin Chambers.

NOTES

1   See for example Horwitz, Tony, *Confederates in the Attic: Dispatches from the Unfinished Civil War* (New York, 1999).

2   Davis, William C., *The Lost Cause: Myths and Realities of the Confederacy* (Kansas, 1996). p. 200.

3   Simmon, Scott, *The Films of D. W. Griffith* (Cambridge, 1993). p. 116.

4   Neale, Steve, *Genre and Hollywood* (London, 2000). p. 125.

5   Neale: *Genre and Hollywood.* p. 51.

6   Ray, Robert, *A Certain Tendency of the Hollywood Cinema, 1930–1980* (Princeton, 1985). p. 115.

7   Chadwick, Bruce, *The Reel Civil War: Mythmaking in American Film* (New York, 2002). p. 4.

8   Cripps, Thomas, 'The Reaction of the Negro to the Motion Picture *The Birth of a Nation*', *Historian*, no. 25 (1963). pp. 344–62.

9   Cripps, Thomas, 'The Absent Presence in American Civil War Films', *Historical Journal of Film, Radio and Television*, vol. 14, no. 4 (1994). pp. 367–76.

10   Anderson, Benedict, *Imagined Communities*, 2nd edition (London, 1991). p. 201.

1

National Identity, Ideology and American Film Genres

The object of this book is not to compare American Civil War films to historical accounts of the war itself. Rather, it is to ascertain their generic nature (their genre), to compare them to one another and to question what is being 'said' about America as a nation, and so not to judge or read them according to an external referent (the war itself), but to look at the internal workings in the films in constructing a sense of the war. What the structure of genre reveals here, through textual analysis, are ideologies of American national identity found in their representations of the American ancestor. American national identity cannot, however, be considered without making clear what is meant by the term. The meanings of 'nation' and 'nationalism' must not be left to assumption, but should be investigated at the outset. 'Nation' is not easily defined, so theorists have tried to work around the problem by exploring the meaning of common metaphors of nation, such as family or brotherhood. Additionally, the assertion that a nation has a single, homogeneous identity, particularly a nation that is constituted of multiple ethnicities, should be challenged.

When the French philosopher and historian, Ernest Renan, posed the question 'What is a nation?' in 1882, he concluded that it was not a matter of dynastic origins, race, language, religion or geography. He believed that it was in fact a 'soul, a spiritual principle'.[1] Renan's own religious background may have contributed to this definition, but it indicates the vagueness of the concept of nation. He also introduced the idea of nation being ambivalent, what Bhabha calls 'Janus-faced',[2] since it is made up of two elements: past and present. The idea of national identity is based on a nation's history, its glories, sufferings and stories, and also on its common will, or aspiration towards the 'great deeds' of the future and the sacrifices the people would be prepared to make for their nation. Both Renan and Bhabha, over a century apart, are stating that the idea of nation and national identity is something that corresponds to a collective state of mind.

Similarly, Benedict Anderson's conception of the nation as 'imagined community' sees it existing not in a tangible, material sense, but in the minds of the nation's members,[3] imagined as a community, a 'fraternity', 'a deep, horizontal comradeship'.[4] Looking at nation in this way makes it less a matter of geography or race than of a collective concept, often unconsciously accepted by individuals. Although this is a collective identity, it is linked closely to the individual's identity, much as gender or religious identity may be. The use of 'fraternity' as a descriptive term is an example of the common familial metaphors used for nation, many of which are regularly found in historical films, including Civil War films. Anderson writes that the language, or vocabulary, of nationhood links the people to the land in which they live (or once lived) in familial terms – motherland, fatherland, homeland – each carrying a sense of natural ties.[5] Whilst a family can be comprehended and represented physically and tangibly, a nation can only exist at a conceptual level because of its vastness and fluidity. The importance of Anderson's idea is that it foregrounds the necessary imaginative process in the understanding of national identity. The nation is a community that is effectively formed in the imagination. This is a crucial point when examining the construction of national identity through cinema. Since cinema is a medium that appeals to the imagination, a film narrative that recounts a national story such as the Civil War is stimulating an imagining of nation. Cinema thus plays an active role in imagining the American nation, helping to create a sense of belonging and identity for Americans who consume it.

Anthony D. Smith's perspective on nation follows similar lines. He writes of nation as a combination of many elements such as ideology, politics and culture, but is again conceptual by nature. Smith's definition draws strongly on what is held in common: mass culture, myths, memories, laws, economy and territory.[6] He investigates nationalism as an ideology, which conceives of unity and loyalty as primary allegiances to be held by the nation's members, the metaphorical bond between them, again, being that of the family or the brotherhood.[7] This ideology, Smith writes, is made tangible or visible in its national, cultural symbols, customs and ceremonies, each of which operates at an emotional level for the individual. In other words, it appeals to the individual's sense of identity, reinforcing a sentiment that one's identity owes its make-up fundamentally to one's home and forefathers. Thus history is a vital component in the construction of the individual's identity.

Since national identity, according to Smith, is most easily identified through a nation's cultural symbols and customs, it makes sense to turn to those aspects of the American nation in order to draw a picture of its character and its self-image. What aspects of American identity circulate in symbolic forms should reveal a common sense or imagining of American-ness. Certain historical, political documents are pertinent in this exercise, and they also demonstrate a shift in the conception of American national identity. The Declaration of Rights, for example, written by the American colonists to the British monarchy in 1774, describes England as the 'mother country'. The authors named themselves 'English colonists' not 'Americans'.[8] The whole tenor of the document is that the colonists desired to re-establish their sameness or brotherhood with all other English people, and their rights as English people.

Abraham Lincoln's dedication of the National Cemetery in 1863, known as the Gettysburg Address, transferred the notion of parenthood from England to the first generation of independent Americans: 'Fourscore and seven years ago our fathers brought forth on this continent a new nation'.[9] Lincoln was speaking of America as a nation in its own right, with its parentage dating back to the Declaration of Independence in 1776, not the European colonies of the seventeenth century or the countries from whence they hailed. Lincoln was placing the 'birth' of the nation at the moment of their independence, a political and cultural condition that is essential to an understanding of American national identity. It is evident that the United States places much significance on independence, Independence Day itself of course being an annual ritualised remembering of the past as much as a celebration of identity.

Before his election as president of the United States, Lincoln used another metaphor for nation, one that corresponds to a sense of home. In an atmosphere of sectional unrest across the nation and the threat of Civil War, he made reference to the Bible stating that '[a] house divided against itself cannot stand'.[10] Although the Biblical meaning may have been intended to refer to an individual and his or her allegiances spiritually, Lincoln was using the metaphor of house to refer to the nation. In his mind, America would no longer be a nation if it was divided, it could only exist in the future if it was 'all one thing, or another'. What this seems to suggest is that Lincoln's own concept of nation was of a unity of values, holding the states of the Union together like cement between the bricks of a house. When those values are compromised or rejected, to prevent the house from falling, it must reinforce one set of values or another, since it cannot hold both. The differing values in this case were held so strongly by its separate sections that it led to Civil War. When that war was finally won by the Union, the values of liberty and unity survived, and still survive as aspects of a national ideology.

Lincoln himself is often represented as a father figure of the American people. One very popular image of Lincoln during the Civil War was a Mathew Brady photograph of the president reading with his son Tad, symbolic of Lincoln's paternal relationship with the nation. See also the portrayal of Lincoln in D.W. Griffith's film *The Birth of a Nation* (1915). Since Griffith places the birth of America at the time of the Civil War and Reconstruction period, the father of the new nation is the man who made that birth possible: Abraham Lincoln. The idea of president as father is equally connoted by the term 'Mr President', the father of the United States with his 'First Lady'. All sorts of associative metaphors could be followed from these terms, including that of the first man and the first woman, Adam and Eve, from whom the earth is populated. Interestingly, Lincoln used the marriage metaphor himself in reference to the nation. His first Inaugural Address in 1861 at the beginning of the Civil War, stated that a husband and wife may divorce themselves from one another, but a nation cannot. To Lincoln, America could not continue to exist as a nation if it was divided. The guiding principle behind this aspect of American national identity is that of unity: a binding agreement of national communion at political, legal and social levels.

These two metaphors employed by Lincoln are fundamental imaginings of American national identity and they both play an important role in Civil War films, as this study will go on to show. Civil War domestic melodramas, examined in Chapter 2, place the fate of the family and the home at the centre of their re-writing of the conflict. It is thus through these national metaphors that the Civil War can be imagined by the films' viewers. The unity of the family and the survival of the home become direct correlatives of the unity and survival of a single nation.

Returning again to the Declaration of Independence, two more aspects of American identity can be found. The document states: 'We hold these truths to be self-evident, that all men are created equal, that they are endowed by their Creator with certain unalienable Rights, that among these are Life, Liberty and the pursuit of Happiness [...]'.[11] The twin values of equality and liberty are, according to Liah Greenfeld, 'the national commitment' of America.[12] As a nation composed largely of immigrants it sought to appear to uphold the rights of the individual to expect equality with his or her fellow countrymen and the freedom of religion and speech. It is all the more poignant then that some were held to be 'more equal than others' by dint of race, an inconsistency that Greenfeld notes. Although some argued that American slaves were treated better than slaves in other countries, 'their slavery appear[ed] more oppressive, because they were slaves of people dedicated to freedom'.[13] The 'self-evident' value of liberty seemed to reach only as far as those who could trace their parenthood back to the first independent Americans. Even after emancipation, it took another seventy years and more for African Americans to enjoy any true level of equality with their white compatriots. In that time, and still in today's more liberal environment, America's national identity was conspicuously white.

The inconsistency of aspiration and achievement in this aspect of American history is reproduced in the majority of Civil War films. Slavery is regularly given only passing mention or is ignored. There are several reasons for this which shall be explored in later chapters, but it is important to note that what this achieves is a particular imagining of American history that excludes one of its most vital elements. It can be recognised as part of the project to remember/forget that Benedict Anderson exposes: if slavery is forgotten, the nation that is imagined is one free of guilt. The dependence of the Southern states, and ultimately the entire nation, on the institution of slavery can be safely overlooked.

A form of Southern nationalism, adapted from the Confederate vision of a separate nation, thrived after the Civil War, fuelled by popular cultural products such as the plantation novel. The myth of the Southern plantation with its pillared porches, contented slaves and honourable owners, hailed the old Southern way of life and its values as positive attributes lost forever. It was an effort to regain validity and dignity for the South, if not as a nation in its own right, then at least as a culture, and to erase any sense of blame for the war in the name of national unity. It is not so well known, however, that the development of the plantation novel may have been a form of backlash against the growing popularity of the slave narrative.[14] Since black Americans were, despite post-war legislation, still not considered by many to be equal to their fellow white Americans, the slave narrative was their attempt 'to write themselves into being'[15] by describing their experiences under the oppressive system of slavery. Despite this, and despite the increasing popularity of black culture, there is still far from equal representation in the arts and in politics. Equality and liberty are primary characteristics in America's identification of itself, but they are not fully realised practically. Neither are they realised in Civil War films, where only a handful of narratives allow the black story to be told. The war, and consequently the nation, are imagined as white concerns and white domains, meaning that national identity is constructed as white.

Despite theorists of nation removing the emphasis of national identity away from a literal, geographical space, it seems that the land of America, the continent itself, is vitally important to a concept of American-ness. Frederick Jackson Turner's 'Frontier Thesis' of 1893 attempted to attribute the development of a national character to the uniqueness of the land.[16] Turner's viewpoint was that the American character owed its commitment to progression, advancement and expansion to the existence of its western frontier and the free, uncultivated land on the other side. Faced with the harshness of the frontier environment, the settlers were forced to adapt and deny their European standards of civilisation in order to survive. The further West the frontier moved, the less the settlers depended on Eastern culture and supplies. Once territories were settled and cultivated, the necessary adaptations in lifestyles had taken on a distinctly new, American, flavour. Although the frontier was declared closed before the end of the nineteenth century, i.e. the western coast had been reached and 'civilised', the spirit of the frontier lived on in twentieth-century politics and in the growth of American nationalism. The civilised space on the East of the frontier is described by another metaphor of the land, characteristic of nineteenth-century American views of the nation, as the 'Garden of the World'.[17] The cultivated areas within the frontier, once virgin land, were now gardens of civilisation, connoting ideas of growth, increase and fruitfulness. Despite the progress of industrialisation and urbanisation, this sense of America as a garden lives on.

The symbolic value of the frontier and of the garden are not lost in Civil War films, particularly those that can be found in the Western genre. Chapter 3 examines a number of Civil War Westerns, each of which employs the frontier as a device in the imagining of the nation. Through the various conflicts found at the frontier, the protagonists are faced with the need to consolidate their efforts despite their differences, and so uphold the American value of unity. Similarly, gardens, cattle-herding and respect for the land are representative of a surviving, unified nation with a productive future.

From the elements raised above (the home, the family, unity, liberty, equality, race, the land), the imagining of nation and national identity can be seen as a range of understandings and ideologies linked to notions of place, family and shared history. As I have noted, these ideologies can be investigated by turning to their material articulations, cultural products or symbolic forms, and one such form is film. In his study of American culture John Belton states the basic assumption of his work, that 'American cinema reveals, both directly and indirectly, something about American experience, identity, and culture'.[18] Although he admits that American cinema cannot be accepted as a cultural window or mirror, it does reveal perceptions of American identity. Anthony D. Smith similarly locates expressions of nation within cultural products that somehow bind the nation together.[19] Alongside such items as flags, uniforms, passports and ceremonies, he also lists popular heroes and fairy tales as part of a discourse of nation. This discourse helps to remind members of a nation of what they hold in common and encourages a sense of belonging. Films should also be added to this list. Civil War films quite clearly demonstrate a range of these national signifiers, including the flags, the uniforms and the heroes. These signifiers can be found to combine, co-operate with and even challenge the conventions of film genres, and from this relationship emerges certain constructions of American national identity.

The ideas of an American national identity that I have outlined own a distinctly mythical quality. The elements particularly of a frontier spirit, liberty, equality and so forth are more like aspirations than fully realised truths. Bhabha's study of nation picks up on this mythic-ness when he writes: 'Nations, like narratives, lose their origins in the myths of time and only fully realize their horizons in the mind's eye'.[20] This statement returns us to the Civil War and its representation in American cinema. Through narratives of the Civil War, origins of America are re-written in order to construct a particular myth, or imagination, of an American ancestry. An examination of that ancestry, by studying the narratives and fates of the central characters of the films, should help to reveal an ideology of national identity couched within a myth of origins. A number of studies of mythologies of the Civil War in popular culture and in written histories have been conducted, and Anderson's revelation of the ideological imperative to 'remember/forget' the war is perhaps the most important. This concept, when applied to Civil War films, exposes them as the imagining of a myth of origins, which in turn encourages an imagining of identity for the American viewer. Through analysing the myths reproduced by Civil War films, the ideologies upon which those myths are founded can be exposed.

It was noted earlier that much public knowledge of the American Civil War hails from the cinema. Film is just one of many cultural products, including other mass media such as television, that interpret and present to an audience certain versions of history and of reality. In each case, there is a goal or purpose behind that dissemination of information that goes further than mere commercial enterprise. It is important to identify what this goal may be, how it operates within the product and what social relations it attempts to reinforce. Although the idea of an ideological goal in a film implies an intention to manipulate the audience, it can equally be seen as a process that works unconsciously. Kevin Costner, for example, was accused of attempting a commercialised trite apology for decades of racism against Native Americans in his Western, *Dances With Wolves* (1990), an accusation that he flatly denied.[21] The film is, however, by its very difference from the majority of pre-revisionist Westerns of the classical Hollywood era, a challenge to a certain type of racist ideology that saw Native Americans as a homogeneous, savage race. Costner's denial, of course, does not make the film's message any less ideological.

John B. Thompson's definition of ideology is 'meaning in the service of power',[22] a term that is concerned equally with the content of the message and the systems it serves. If the meaning of a symbolic form or cultural product, such as a movie or a novel, can be found to be a means of establishing or sustaining relations of domination, then it is deemed to be ideological in nature. In other words, if the purpose of the dissemination of the product is one of self-promotion and self-preservation of a ruling body or system, it is therefore working in the service of power. The more power the ruling body owns, be it economic, spiritual, ethical, social, etc., the more profuse will be its symbolic forms and therefore even more worthy of critical attention since its effects are likely to be more widespread. Traditional studies infer a class-based agenda behind the ideology of cultural products, but agendas can be concerned equally with the promotion of racist or gender-based worldviews, amongst others. The task of ideological analysis, according to Thompson, is 'disclosing meaning in the service of power'[23] – to critically reflect on the cultural product in order to ascertain its ideological message and identify the relations of power, or the agenda, that it attempts to serve.

Adopting a similar approach for the cinema, popular film, according to Jim Collins, is 'allegedly the dominant or hegemonic ideology writ in celluloid',[24] particularly the Hollywood genre film. By this he means that popular cinema communicates and reiterates commonly held values, the values that help to maintain society's status quo, keeping those in economic, social and political power in their positions of authority. Collins writes that common opinion in film theory regards genre films as 'the purest manifestations of how the American public has been led to think about itself by a highly sophisticated capitalist system'.[25] Indeed, Hollywood is often referred to as a 'myth-making' industry, the products of which are constructed to reproduce and disguise (however thinly) white, middle-class, western values. However, Collins calls this point of view a 'monolithic conception of the State and its cultural production'.[26] It should be noted that Collins takes what could be called a post-Marxist position, seeing ideology in the service of various social, political and cultural relations, not simply class-relations. He also denies the existence of a dominant ideology in contemporary society. Instead he sees there being multiple, conflicting values identifiable through cultural goods. He understands the film industry to be engaged in '[a] competition between narrative discourses for an ever-shifting audience [...]',[27] hence the theory of a single, dominant voice emanating from Hollywood is, to Collins, mistaken. Taking the cue from Collins, then, there may not be one distinct and dominant ideology at play across the genres that depict the American Civil War. The ideologies present may be plural and conflicting, covering diverse issues such as race, politics and national identity, and may display differences across and within film genres.

In the 1970s, taking an alternative approach, Robin Wood suggested that looking at genres of the classical Hollywood era from an ideological viewpoint may help us to recognise their similarity – although genres have their own characteristics, each functions in a predictable manner as 'different strategies dealing with the same ideological tensions'.[28] Wood lists the tensions that he sees present within American capitalist ideology, the oppositions and contradictions that he believes are embodied across the genres in classical Hollywood cinema, for example the two concepts of nature as both agrarian paradise and wilderness so often found in the Western genre. What is predictable about genre, to Wood, is the treatment of these particular tensions for the purpose of upholding a dominant ideology. The question pertinent to this study, then, is whether the genres that depict the Civil War coalesce in a single, dominant ideological voice, or demonstrate a diversity of ideological projects, and whether such a trait belongs only to the classical era, or can be located across the breadth of Hollywood's history.

What now follows in Chapters 2 to 4 is a critical consideration of three key genres that deal with Civil War narratives: the domestic melodrama, the Western and the war film. Each genre is interrogated for its dominant traits and its underlying ideologies, then the films of the study are examined for their particular imagining of America's past and their themes in order to locate within them a common myth of origins. My enquiry uncovers the tendency of the Civil War narrative to bring changes to generic rule-systems and goes on to ask exactly why such changes might be necessary. From these discoveries a range of specific elements of American national identity will be proposed. The study begins with an examination of the most common type of Civil War film, the domestic melodrama.

NOTES

1   Renan, Ernest, 'What is a nation?' tr. Martin Thom, in H.K Bhabha (ed.). *Nation and Narration* (London, 1990). pp. 8–22.
2   Renan: 'What is a nation?'. p. 3.
3   Anderson, Benedict, *Imagined Communities*, 2nd edition (London, 1991). p. 6.
4   Anderson: *Imagined Communities*. p. 7.
5   Anderson: *Imagined Communities*. p. 143.
6   Smith, Anthony D., *National Identity* (London, 1991). p. 14.
7   Smith: *National Identity*. p. 76.
8   Reprinted in Hammond, H.E., (ed.) *We Hold These Truths... a Documentary History of the United States* (Bronxville, New York, 1964). p. 36.
9   Hammond: *We Hold These Truths*. p. 211.
10   Hammond: *We Hold These Truths*. p. 198.
11   Hammond: *We Hold These Truths*. p. 43.
12   Greenfeld, Liah, 'The Origins and Nature of American Nationalism in Comparative Perspective' in K. Krakau (ed.) *The American Nation – National Identity – Nationalism* (New Brunswick, 1997). p. 50.
13   Greenfeld: 'The Origins and Nature of American Nationalism'. p. 42.
14   Davis, C. and Gates Jr., H.L., (eds) *The Slave's Narrative* (New York, 1985). p. xvi.
15   Davis and Gates: *The Slave's Narrative*. p. xxiii.
16   Turner, Frederick Jackson, 'The Significance of the Frontier in American History' in G.R. Taylor (ed.) *The Turner Thesis: Concerning the Role of the Frontier in American History* (Lexington, Mass., [1893] 1972). pp. 3–28.
17   Smith, H.N., *Virgin Land: The American West as Symbol and Myth* (Cambridge, Mass., 1970). p. 123
18   Belton, John, *American Cinema /American Culture* (New York, 1994). p. xxi.

19   Smith: *National Identity*. p. 11.
20   Bhabha, Homi K., 'Narrating the Nation' in H.K. Bhabha (ed.) *Nation and Narration* (London, 1990). p. 1.
21   Costner, K., Blake, M. and Wilson, J., *Dances With Wolves: The Illustrated Story of the Epic Film* (New York, 1990). p. viii.
22   Thompson, John B., *Ideology and Modern Culture: Critical Social Theory in the Era of Mass Communication* (Polity Press, 1990). p. 7.
23   Thompson: *Ideology and Modern Culture*. p. 292.
24   Collins, Jim, *Uncommon Cultures: Popular Culture and Post-modernism* (London, 1989). p. 90.
25   Collins: *Uncommon Cultures*. p. 90.
26   Collins: *Uncommon Cultures*. p. 90.
27   Collins: *Uncommon Cultures*. p. 90.
28   Wood, Robin, 'Ideology, Genre, Auteur', *Film Comment*, vol. 13, no. 1 (January–February 1977). p. 47.

2

Civil War Melodramas: The Family and the Home

Some of the most well known of Civil War films hail from the generic category of melodrama. Most of the short films made by D.W. Griffith during the silent era for Biograph that represent the Civil War era were melodramas, as was one of the most popular films of Hollywood's history, *Gone With the Wind* (Victor Fleming, 1939). Directors as diverse as King Vidor (*So Red the Rose*, 1935), William Wyler (*Friendly Persuasion*, 1956) and Ang Lee (*Ride With the Devil*, 1999) chose to represent the Civil War in this form (each of these films will be considered below). Melodrama is possibly the most important of genres to deal with the war because there are elements of the melodramatic to be found in every Civil War film and, one could argue, across the breadth of the Hollywood film product. As a genre, however, melodrama seems to focus on its own particular themes and concerns that are not central to other genres. What is necessary to understand, then, is what melodrama is, how it treats the Civil War and, equally, what ideological statements can be discerned, before going on to consider some other genres.

MELODRAMA AS MODE – MELODRAMA AS GENRE

Since the early 1970s, melodrama has become the topic of several debates and, increasingly, its status as a film genre has been questioned. Understandably, these concerns are not necessarily shared by the historian or the Civil War enthusiast, but our understanding of the term 'melodrama' is of central importance if we wish to discover differences and similarities between categories of Civil War films. There are some convincing discussions that recognise the melodramatic as a dramatic *mode* rather than a genre; a method or style that can be present in a film that may not be labelled 'melodrama'.

Peter Brooks has been particularly active in the examination of stage and literary melodrama and its conventions. He writes that melodrama is 'a coherent mode of imagining and representing',[1] but goes on to treat it as a genre, rather than a mode. His clearest interrogation of the term 'melodramatic mode' is 'a certain imaginative complex and set of dramatic conventions [...]' that follows an 'aesthetic of excess'.[2] This makes melodrama, to Brooks, a set of narrative concerns and stylistic practices. This effectively treats melodrama as both genre and mode, and means that confusion arises. To avoid any confusion, melodrama as a mode can be understood as a certain *way of doing things*, a way in which a film, or part of a film, may be enacted and constructed, i.e. how the narrative is told. Cinema and theatre may also employ a comic mode, such as slapstick, which is a 'way of doing' comedy involving a certain brand of physical humour. These modes are therefore more usefully referred to as the melodrama*tic* or the com*ic*, emphasising the words' descriptive, adjectival functions. The means by which the melodramatic and the comic are identified are through signifying systems such as *mise-en-scène* (a term referring to that which is seen in the visual image of the theatre or screen, including set, lighting, colour, costume, etc.), and also through editing, music, sound effects and the performance of actors.

According to Brooks, melodrama's narratives contain emotion, moral extremism, exaggerated states of being and of expression, villainy, virtue and suspense.[3] They depict a Manichaeistic conflict between good and evil, in which these extremes are 'highly personalised' in the characters.[4] The stark characterisations of good and evil, according to Brooks, function to fulfil the task of the melodramatic mode: to identify and impose 'basic ethical and psychic truths' in the absence of a worldview rooted in faith and religion.[5] Brooks is situating the melodramatic historically in a western world whose religious and moral co-ordinates have waned in their effectiveness with the progress of reason and secular government, helping to affirm, in basic terms, what is right and wrong. In this view, the melodramatic is part of an ideological project that illustrates moral extremes, absolutes and solutions. Through the opposition of characters that represent conflicting values, that which is considered ideologically acceptable – and unacceptable – can be made plain. These moral absolutes are communicated through *mise-en-scène*, music and the performances of actors, allowing them to be 'embodied' or 'made real'. Brooks' closest articulation of this concept is the performance of the 'moral occult', the outward physical manifestation of hidden desires, values and morals through gesture, movement and expression.[6] The 'moral occult' in the melodramatic is the intangible, insubstantial emotion that exists within a character; it is that which cannot be seen or heard without the aid of material signs to make it manifest and readable. As part of the actor's performance it works alongside the other stylistic devices of cinema to make the moral co-ordinates and ideological messages of the narrative intelligible. Through a gesture, a red sunset or a mournful note on a violin, the unutterable emotion of a character and the dilemmas that he or she faces are made material, or 'melodramaticised', in the service of making plain certain ideological 'truths'.

A common understanding is that the melodramatic is a mode of 'excess', that it typically exaggerates each of its stylistic elements. Nowell-Smith writes that excess is expressed through the 'body' of the film text, principally the *mise-en-scène* and music, and is a means of articulating human emotions and dilemmas.[7] Brooks calls the actor's physical manifestation of these inner emotions 'bodily writing', in which pain, love or anger is inscribed across the face and body (a concept taken from Freudian analysis in the treatment of 'hysterical' patients, where the repressed emotion is expressed unconsciously on the body).[8] Other signs such as costume, hairstyle and vocal expression, can also be seen to contribute to this articulation of emotion.

Similarly, Roberta Pearson's work on the development of codes in early American cinema acting compares these external articulations of meaning to language, and defines two dominant styles, the histrionic code and the verisimilar code.[9] The histrionic code appeared to follow the rules of natural language, in that it was composed of isolated, meaningful gestures or signs.[10] The verisimilar code, one that seemed to develop during early cinema, was made up of a flow of smaller interlinking gestures, and so less resembled a language than an imitation of what the performers took for reality.[11] Whilst the histrionic code may be what many regard as melodramatic acting, and certainly seems to suggest an affinity with Brooks' idea of bodily writing, the verisimilar code can equally serve the emotional requirements of the melodramatic. In fact, the significance of particular moments, those in which emotion is the strongest, can be made more evident through a juxtaposition of both histrionic *and* verisimilar codes. A climactic scene gains much of its power through its difference from adjacent scenes composed in a more verisimilar style, according to what the filmmakers consider to be 'realistic'.

These ideas essentially summarise what is most commonly understood to be the melodramatic mode: the use of expressive colour, the significant employment of music at climactic or emotional points in the narrative and the actor's performance style, made up of facial expressions, gestures and other movements which communicate emotion tangibly. Each works to make material the emotional processes and ordeals of a character, in the service of a moral or ideological agenda.

There must be a way, however, that a melodrama can be identified as a genre film, in which certain dominant features are not accredited to another genre. Attention must turn to what Steve Neale calls the 'standard account' of melodrama in film scholarship. Neale lists conventions found in the nineteenth-century melodrama, including an inclination to be episodic, formulaic, action-packed, with a high frequency of coincidence,[12] and reminds us that these elements are present in a range of cinematic genres, such as thrillers and action films.[13] In fact, Neale reveals that until the 1970s, film industry output traditionally used 'melodrama' as a label to describe a thriller or action-adventure,[14] suggesting that what scholars may refer to as another genre was often initially marketed and received as a melodrama. Critical writing about certain films has effectively provided a different account to that of the industry, what Neale calls the 'standard account', in which melodrama is understood to be a genre about family, domesticity, gender and the female point-of-view and is considered to display an absence of realism.[15] It is a restricted understanding of the genre which connotes a film with a domestic setting and the presence of women and thus is expected to deal with the issues relevant to that environment and its key characters, such as emotions and relationships. This 'standard account' of the genre often typically refers to it as the 'woman's film'. Melodrama can in fact encompass a variety of films that could not be satisfactorily described as such. *Shenandoah* (Andrew V. McLaglen, 1965), for example, although it is usually referred to as a Western, can also be understood as a Civil War melodrama with its central male characters struggling to remain neutral in the war and coping with the survival of home and family against all odds.

Because the genre of melodrama encompasses films of such diversity, it has become necessary to make one's reference to generic labels overly emphatic: domestic melodrama, epic melodrama and of course Civil War melodrama. These are in fact sub-genres and are attempts by both the film industry and film critics to refine the broad category. The emphasis of sub-generic labels re-creates melodrama as a super genre at the top of a hierarchy of closely related film categories. For example, a Civil War melodrama can be seen as an example of domestic melodrama, itself a wide category, which in turn is part of the overarching super genre of melodrama. This would be a more broad understanding of the genre. What must be emphasised here, however, is that another hierarchy exists that is pertinent to the place of the melodramatic in cinema. This hierarchy sees the melodramatic mode as an overarching 'way of doing things', under which several genres can be found to exist, with melodrama at the top of the hierarchy as the archetypal genre conforming to this mode. Beneath it would be all genres that operate within the melodramatic mode.

Placing the genre of melodrama and the melodramatic mode side by side creates a useful starting point from which to move on and consider Civil War melodramas. Taking elements from the standard account of melodrama and placing them next to features of the mode, this category of films could thus be understood to be expressly concerned with the manifestation and resolution of moral conflict within the domestic or private sphere of relationships, during the American Civil War.

CIVIL WAR MELODRAMAS

The restricted understanding of melodrama could imply that a Civil War melodrama will be a woman's film, starring and appealing to women. This is not always the case but certain notable instances should be mentioned. *Gone With the Wind*, for example, could be understood as a woman's film, dealing with issues and themes affecting a central female character. *Barbara Frietchie*, a popular narrative produced several times in the silent era[16] illustrates the fate of a Southern belle, separated both physically and politically from her Northern lover by the war. However, many Civil War melodramas do not exclusively consider feminine issues or revolve around the fortune of women, so the category can instead be most comfortably described as domestic melodrama, since it principally concerns the threats brought to the home, the family members and relationships by the Civil War. The female character certainly holds a special place in this, but the films are not wholly concerned with her fate or what she may symbolise.

What links Civil War melodramas is firstly their location and secondly the threats facing the home and the family. In every case the main action of the film is located away from the primary battlefields of the Civil War, particularly on Northern farms and Southern plantations. Being situated in these areas, the characters found are farmers, workers, slaves, raiders, women and children. As Nowell-Smith writes, what is at stake in the melodrama is the 'survival of the family unit'.[17] Indeed, the matters that affect these individuals are to do with sustaining the land together, surviving loss, and protecting life and property when faced with the terrible threat of war. Regularly the characters are seen to choose to remain at home/on the farm/at the plantation, instead of enlisting in the army, and then struggling with the impulse to support the war effort after witnessing the destruction wreaked by the enemy, whether Union or Confederate.

Additionally, each person within the domestic situation has a role to play in the order of things, for example the father being the head of the family. In melodrama this status quo faces a crisis as the family and the home are placed under threat. The father may be required to enlist in the army, and in so doing is risking both his life and his role as the family's protector and provider. If he dies in service, or is absent from the home, the family is left to the mercy of enemy raiders or the encroaching regular army. The effect of the loss of the father, or of an older son, is that the role of women must necessarily change, making them protectors, providers and matriarchs. Father figure, mother figure and child are central to the films' construction of the family as metaphor of the nation. It must be remembered that the familial metaphor is central to an ideology of nation, meaning that the fate and identity of the family in these narratives can be used to draw parallels with the nation.

The presence of the slave force in narratives located in the South means that racial issues are difficult to ignore. In these films, playing one's role, or knowing one's place, is even more essential for the slave than it is for the family member. Drawing the parallel with nation would suggest that the slave's place in relation to the family, one of exclusion or marginalisation, is representative of his place outside of the national family. In this situation, the negative and harmful stereotypes dating back to the early years of cinema persist, depicting black characters as either faithful or rebellious, desexualised or ruled by passion, matronly or childish. These extreme characterisations endure in many Civil War domestic melodramas, even though the narrative rarely concerns itself consciously with slavery. The possibility of the good slave turning bad is a direct result of the progress of war – when Union troops draw near and when emancipation is declared, certain slaves respond by downing tools and seeking freedom (not to mention 'forty acres and a mule'). All that is left behind is a handful of faithful servants, dedicated to the family and prepared to lose life and limb in defence of their masters.

The war also frequently acts as the root cause of the development of romantic pairings, usually when war is declared and the enlisting man impulsively proposes to his sweetheart (in *Gone With the Wind* it is Scarlett who acts impulsively, not for romance but to spite Ashley for marrying someone else). One would also expect that the Civil War context would transpose the melodramatic convention of hero versus villain onto a stark conflict of North versus South. But whilst the heroic characters are carefully characterised and sometimes display a level of complexity not often expected of melodrama, the 'highly personalised' villain that Brooks speaks of has a problematic presence. The reasons for this tendency can be examined after a survey of some examples of Civil War melodramas.

THE SOUTHERN PLANTATION: THREATS AND LESSONS IN *SO RED THE ROSE*

So Red the Rose is based on the novel of the same name by Stark Young, published in 1934. Young was one of the writers of the Southern pro-agrarian manifesto of 1930, *I'll Take My Stand*, which was, as historians Grob and Billias put it, 'seeking to show the superiority of the agrarian South over the industrial North'.[18] Hugh Tulloch, similarly, claims that the writers 'postulated an imperishable Southern counter-culture rooted in soil, race and community'.[19] The era of its publication saw two key Civil War films set in the South, in agrarian environments, *Gone With the Wind* and *So Red the Rose*, and both have something of the spirit of the manifesto in their celebration of a Southern plantation community but without any overt political statement. *So Red the Rose* follows the wartime fortunes of the Bedford family and their plantation home, Portobello, described in a title as 'the proudest plantation in Mississippi'.

The *New York Times'* description of the film as a 'well-made sentimental drama'[20] indicates the central significance of emotion in its narrative. This aspect of the melodramatic mode is consistent throughout the film as it explores the emotional effects that the war has on the family (again, with similarities to *Gone With the Wind*). It is the topic of war that opens the film when mother Sally Bedford (Janet Beecher) worriedly discusses with her husband Malcolm (Walter Connolly) an ominous dream of her roses dripping with blood. It is the first instance in the film of Sally's clairvoyant gift, which brings her knowledge of impending disaster.

It is also the war that precipitates romance. When news arrives at Portobello that the Confederate army has fired on Fort Sumter, the son's university friend George (Robert Cummings) spontaneously asks to court Southern belle Valette Bedford (Margaret Sullavan) before leaving to enlist. The romance is short-lived and a letter soon arrives to tell of his death – news that impels son Edward (Harry Ellerbe) to join the Confederate army. The other candidate for romance is Valette's live-in cousin, Duncan (Randolph Scott), who refuses to enlist, declaring that Americans should not fight Americans; they have, he says, the 'same blood'. Thinking Duncan to be a coward, Valette treats her cousin with contempt. Eventually though, his love of the plantation, his compassionate care of the slaves (he removes a splinter from a slave child's foot) and his patriotic efforts to provide supplies for the South, win her over and they fall in love.

Sally's prophetic gift informs her that Edward is dying in a field in Shiloh, the site of a significant early defeat for the Confederacy, and her journey to the battlefield with Duncan is accompanied by aural flashbacks to her son's childhood voice, drawing the film viewer into the subjective pain and longing of the wartime mother. The finding of Edward's body is a turning point for Duncan, who decides to stay and join the Southern army. A tracking shot of Duncan walking towards the camera, rifle in hand, dissolves into a parallel image of him leading a troop of soldiers to attack. A similar transition from civilian to soldier occurs in *The Birth of a Race* (John W. Noble, 1918), the black response to *The Birth of a Nation*, which saw one white and one black farmhand dropping tools in the field and dissolving into Allied soldiers of the First World War. So, Duncan's pacifist worldview has been challenged and turned over by the death of his young cousin, wherein he adopts a new morality in taking up arms against an oppressor. These episodes of the film correspond to lessons that the principal characters must learn. Valette, for example, learns that a refusal to fight is not a sign of cowardice, but an admirable moral standpoint. Duncan, on the other hand, learns that there are certain circumstances in which one *must* fight, with an equally moral conviction.

Back in Portobello, the Union army draws near, signalled by shells exploding in the family's garden. It sparks off a revolt amongst the slaves, despite the faithful black servant, William, attempting to quell the violence (played by Daniel Haynes). In the midst of the uprising, the father, Malcolm, returns from a fatal attempt to fight for the South and lies on a couch, oblivious to the trouble outside. Valette marches to the barn where the slaves are declaring their freedom, slaps the face of one ringleader, and announces that all must work if they want to eat. The slaves redeem themselves *en masse*, demonstrating their understanding of the lesson of loyalty by returning to the house and singing spiritual (and perfectly harmonised) songs as their master dies. The episode seems rather pointless when Sally immediately emerges from the house and sets them all free. The lesson, however, should be clear: emancipation is a gift, not a right, according to this brand of the Southern myth.

Eventually, the war itself is brought to the home. A Yankee raiding party arrives and harasses the remaining family members, but when one young man is wounded by enemy fire, the women hide him in the home. This is reminiscent of D.W. Griffith's *The Fugitive* (1910), in which a Southern mother hides a Union soldier, hoping that a Northern mother would do the same for her own son, yet unaware that the young man is her son's murderer. At this moment in *So Red the Rose*, coincidentally, Duncan arrives and begins a search of the house for raiders. His harsh treatment of the hidden raider, once found, confirms that the experience of war has lost Duncan his former compassion. Yet he relents, or re-learns mercy, in the face of Valette's philanthropy.

Duncan is captured outside the house by Union guards (he spends most of the remaining film in a prisoner-of-war camp that is not shown) and the family is ordered to evacuate the home before it is burned. In a sentimental

3. *So Red the Rose* (King Vidor, 1935): The faithful servant attempts to quell the rebellious slaves.

gesture reminiscent of D.W. Griffith's *His Trust* (1911), William is permitted to keep his old master's chair (in Griffith's short film, the faithful slave is bequeathed his deceased master's sabre). Some time later the family are living in a small brick house, all helping to work the fields. The war has been over for six months. Valette seems to have inherited her mother's supernatural gift, although now it does not predict disaster. She says that she keeps hearing Duncan's voice calling for her. In a rather sudden resolution to the narrative, Valette runs through beams of sunlight, with Duncan's voice echoing amongst the trees, and they are reunited by a stream.

So Red the Rose is not only a romance narrative charting the obstacles and eventual union of two lovers; it is also a tribute to the old South. The metaphorical image of the rose dripping with blood symbolises the fatal wound sustained by the South through the Civil War. The war brings an end to a certain 'calm way of doing things' as Sally Bedford puts it; a particular lifestyle dies. It is a dominant component of the Southern myth, a nostalgic longing for an Edenic past, notably revisited a few years later in *Gone With the Wind*.

The melodramatic mode is clearly evident in the film's acting styles, its use of music at significant moments and in its *mise-en-scène*. In terms of acting, each character demonstrates a style of performance pertinent to his or her personality, either dominantly histrionic or verisimilar. Sally, for example, enacts the ominous warnings of her visions by use of a vocal monotone and a gaze off-screen, away from all other characters. It is a collection of signs used a number of times throughout the film to signify Sally 'seeing' disaster in the far distance. At other times, however, she performs in a more verisimilar style, allowing the ominous visions to own a greater significance. The performance of the black actors during the slave uprising is equally meaningful, composed of expressive gestures connoting rebellion: shaking fists in the air and stamping the feet. This complements the *mise-en-scène* in which actors fill the screen with frantic activity, jumping, running and gesticulating. It contrasts pointedly with shots of the slaves, once reformed and chastised, walking calmly in step with one another, singing spiritual songs and slowly waving their arms in the air. These signs create a distinction between the two conditions of rebellion and reformation.

Sullavan's acting style, as Valette, is more dominantly verisimilar. Her reaction to the burning of their home, for example, is understated and subtle as she gazes unbelieving at the destruction around her, in contrast to her aunt who is repeatedly shown in the film in nervous states of panic, waving her arms in the air. The use of contrast is also applied in the *mise-en-scène*, which creates a clear distinction between wartime and peacetime through its treatment of the plantation house: before and after the war the *mise-en-scène* is full of sunlight, bright porches and white dresses; during wartime the house is seen mostly in shadow and full darkness, with a lot of the scenes taking place at night.

Music is used predominantly to signify war. When news of Fort Sumter arrives, an enthusiastic medley of 'Dixie' and other military tunes accompanies the excitement of the Southern men rushing off to war. Later, when Duncan decides to enlist, a drum roll punctuates his march towards the camera, picking up speed and adding the power of brass instruments to signify bravery as he starts to run. Then a tune that is associated with the Civil War, 'When Johnny Comes Marching Home' (an old Irish song adapted for the Union army, but sung and played by both sections in the war), attends Malcolm's return to the plantation in a melancholy tone, predicting his imminent death. Music is only used in a handful of other scenes; to accompany romantic interactions between Duncan and Valette, Duncan's musing about the land he loves, Edward's departure for the army, the burning of the house and the final reunion between the lovers. In most cases the tonal quality of the orchestral music implies emotion, particularly sadness, linking most strongly to the loss of the family members and of the old South. The final reunion scene, conversely, uses melodramatic performances (Valette searching desperately through the trees for Duncan), *mise-en-scène* (soft-focused sunbeams with the possible connotation of otherworldliness) and music, which swells emotively as the pair are reunited.

Interestingly, there are several moments during the film where music is eschewed and instead there is silence, even though the narrative at those points is strongly sentimental. News of Valette's suitor's death receives no musical underlining. Instead, Valette registers shock, putting a hand to her cheek, and her brother Edward is seen nearby clutching the fabric of the curtains in his fists, clearly deciding that he must act somehow (he goes on to enlist). The moment is melodramatically expressed through the performance of the actors, but music does not intrude on the characters' highly significant responses. Similarly, music is only used at the *end* of the house-burning episode. For several minutes, the action is represented on screen as a horror and a travesty, only underlined by violins as the family leaves the house and looks back at the flames, highlighting their loss. It is an example of the sophisticated choices behind the production of the film, allowing appropriate climactic or emotional moments to be underscored with melodramatic devices, without flooding the entire narrative with overwhelming (and therefore less significant) musical and histrionic performances. Although melodrama as a genre, conducted in the melodramatic mode, uses music to such expressive effect, the choice here to incorporate silence is equally significant and contributes to the same result. In this context, silence encodes emotion as much as a surge of music.

If this film were to be a traditional melodrama it would represent its immoral forces through a 'highly personalised' villain,[21] an individual or group working consistently throughout the plot to discredit and/or threaten the heroes. Brooks writes: 'it is the rare melodrama that does not have a villain'.[22] *So Red the Rose* does not display this consistent and identifiable villainous character. During the threat from the slave revolt, there is one central ringleader, Cato (Clarence Muse), who sways the passions of his fellow slaves. The threat that he poses is very real – he can influence the group to loot the home and to desert the fields. However, the threat is overthrown by a slap in the face and the episode is swiftly concluded. The Union raiders also pose a threat to the safety of the family members, but just a handful of items are stolen from the home and the Bedfords are allowed to walk away unharmed. The most clearly characterised enemy, the man that is hidden by Valette, is at the mercy of the Bedford women. It is hardly a portrait of villainy. Even the soldiers that finally burn down Portobello are vaguely described characters despite their villainous actions. Why is it that the groups of people so evidently guilty of wrongdoing in the film are given such brief episodes and shallow characterisation? Is this treatment given to other Civil War melodramas? These are questions that can only be answered by looking further into this category of films.

THE LAND AND SURVIVAL OF THE FAMILY IN *GONE WITH THE WIND*

This most well known of Civil War films, adapted from Margaret Mitchell's 1936 novel of the same name is a hybrid of epic and domestic melodrama, like its infamous predecessor *The Birth of a Nation*, enacting the national story of the Civil War and Reconstruction through the personal trials of a family and its home. Although the film omits the staging of combat sequences and places its moral oppositions outside of any racial conflict, the two films are regularly compared on the basis of their epic characteristics (large-scale productions with a historical focus) and their technical achievements.

The narrative, beginning at the O'Hara plantation, Tara, revolves around daughter Scarlett (Vivien Leigh) and her efforts to either secure a relationship with another woman's sweetheart or, in the aftermath of war, to return herself to the antebellum riches that she and her family had initially enjoyed. The father, Gerald O'Hara (Thomas Mitchell), is from Irish stock and clings to notions of land and family traditionally associated with Irish culture. More practical and rational is his wife, Ellen (Barbara O'Neil), the Christian matriarch who has compassion for all. Despite Scarlett's spoilt selfishness, she inherits her father's passion for the land of Tara, and fulfils her mother's vocation as matriarch – although without her tender-heartedness and Southern gentility.

The principal characters and their relationships are established in the prologue, introducing Scarlett's love for Ashley Wilkes (Leslie Howard), his marriage to his homey, gentle cousin, Melanie (Olivia de Havilland), and Scarlett's torrid relationship with the womanising profiteer, Rhett Butler (Clark Gable). One of a handful of rare discussions on the political and national situation occurs in this part of the film, when the men discuss Southern rights – to keep slaves, to secede from the Union and to fight. The dichotomy between Ashley and Rhett is established here when Ashley, the honourable gentleman of the old South, declares that he will fight, but would prefer peace. Rhett on the other hand sets no store by the Southern cause, especially as they are technically and economically inferior to the industrialised North.

Titles occasionally link the episodes, announcing crucial stages in the conflict, such as the Battle of Gettysburg, 1863, often regarded as the turning point of the war in favour of the Union, which is poetically described as a time when 'a page of history waited for three days while two nations came to death grips on the farmlands of Pennsylvania'. The words reinforce one aspect of the Confederate philosophy: North and South – or United States and Confederate states – make up two separate nations. Like *So Red the Rose*, the film links the Confederate tune 'Dixie' to certain episodes, most notably the arrival of news that war has started – accompanied by cheering and men rushing in every direction – and in the Atlanta street scene, so often reproduced on the cover of books about American Civil War culture, when the camera cranes up from hundreds of wounded bodies to a battle-worn Confederate flag. The music here is comprised of a medley of Southern tunes, ending mournfully with the last notes of 'Dixie' (corresponding to the words 'Look away, Dixieland'). The shot emphatically, and melodramatically, states that the South is defeated. Here music, composition and camera movement combine to create an intensely emotional moment that laments the rout of the South.

The more typical use of music in melodrama, to highlight climactic or emotional moments, is strongly adopted in the film, particularly towards its end. From Scarlett's fall down the expansive staircase, and the consequent loss of her unborn child, music is practically constant until the film's conclusion, underscoring the final tragic events of Bonnie's death, the ruin of Scarlett and Rhett's marriage, and the death of Melanie. However, there are significant scenes in the film, as in *So Red the Rose*, that use no music at all. Possibly most significant is the amputation scene, which edits between shots of Scarlett's horrified and sickened response and the silhouettes of working surgeons. Without music, the scene gains a powerful sense of horror and authenticity, punctuated by the patient's screams of 'Don't cut!' Similarly, the women's journey back to Tara through the former battlefields of the South emphasises the terrible cost in human life through the *mise-en-scène* (countless dead, mutilated bodies, scattered across a shadowy wasteland) and by a lack of musical accompaniment. As in *So Red the Rose*, these scenes use the absence of music to accentuate the emotional impact of the image. In both films, silence highlights the effect of war on the South and its people.

One other dominant melodramatic aspect of *Gone With the Wind* is the acting style. Most of the actors employ expressions, movements and gestures loaded with easily understood meaning. Leslie Howard as Ashley, for example, enacts the trials and emotions of his character physically. After his return from the war he feels the South's defeat personally and is often cowed and with a lowered head. When he tells Scarlett about his wartime experiences he gazes off-screen as if he still sees his companions dying. His desperate attempts to withstand Scarlett's romantic advances regularly have him literally tearing himself away from her, shaking his head, as if to free himself from her spell, and delivering his lines in a monotone. These histrionic acting signs are thoroughly appropriate for the man torn between Scarlett and Melanie, and between hope and despair. Leigh's performance, with Scarlett being the primary focaliser (the point of identification for the viewer) of all but a handful of scenes, is also made up of overt and highly expressive signs – a lifted eyebrow, a pouting lip or a glance to one side as she constructs a lie. As with Ashley, it is usually clear what Scarlett is thinking, even when she is silent.

With each performer a distinct contrast of acting signs are used for peace and wartime, working alongside the *mise-en-scène*. During times of plenty and prosperity the characters walk tall and proud, but the war and its aftermath leave them bowed, pale and drawn. Thomas Mitchell's performance as Gerald O'Hara, for example, is composed of confident gestures and a strong vocal tone before the war. His costume is colourful and his face has a ruddy complexion. After the ravages of war and the loss of his wife, however, he dresses in dark tattered clothes, his face is drawn and pale, and his hair is wild. His former strides have become shuffles and his dialogue is delivered in a wavering tone. These external signs not only point to a man pushed beyond his inner emotional and psychological limits, but also reflect more widely on the devastation of the old South.

If the film is approached as having a two-part structure (Civil War and Reconstruction periods), a whole sequence of oppositions can be discovered between themes, values and characters across the two segments, i.e. war/post-war; loss of the old South/building of the new South and so on. Leger Grindon's work on *Gone With the Wind*, similarly, uses the Rhett/Ashley opposition to create a list of related dichotomies in the film, that can be seen to correspond to the two-part structure: new South/old South, future/past, commerce/plantation, realism/idealism.[23] Hernan Vera and Andrew Gordon's essay on Civil War films sees the series of dichotomies

4. *Gone With the Wind* (Victor Fleming, 1939): Scarlett travels home to Tara through the battle-torn South.

in *Gone With the Wind* headed up by old South versus new, represented by Melanie and Ashley (old) and Scarlett and Rhett (new).[24] The 'old' values and qualities are those of generosity, honour and monogamy and those which are 'new', as displayed by Scarlett and Rhett, are selfishness, dishonour and polygamy. Melanie, for example, marries only once and remains faithful to Ashley until her death. Scarlett, however, pragmatically marries three times for either financial gain or to spite another person.

The dichotomies are symbolised or described by many elements of the text. Rhett's sentiment about the upholders of the Southern lost cause is that they are 'living in the past', contrasting with Scarlett's final declaration that 'tomorrow is another day'. The commerce and plantation opposition is symbolised by the two products, timber and cotton. One is integral to the literal re-building of the South and it exploits the Union, the other is the lynchpin of the old Southern economy and it exploits the slaves (although the film certainly does not present this latter exploitation). Even aspects of the *mise-en-scène* contrast with one another, particularly colour. The former South is seen predominantly in green (vegetation, costumes, curtains) and the war-torn South in various hues of red (red skies, fire, at least two of Scarlett's outfits and the overwhelming reds of Scarlett and Rhett's Atlanta mansion). The *mise-en-scène* during peacetime is predominantly brightly lit, as in *So Red the Rose*, even down to Scarlett wearing a white dress on a sunny porch in the opening scene. The wartime *mise-en-scène* is strikingly dark, full of shadows, dark clothing and dilapidated property to signal the destruction of the Southern civilisation.

These oppositions form the kernel of much that is written about *Gone With the Wind* and are representative of the melodramatic nature of the film. What one would expect, therefore, is a carefully observed villain to counterpoint the heroes, in keeping with the convention of stage melodrama. The film does not, however, deliver such a person. Truly villainous characters – and even truly heroic characters – are problematic. Although the central protagonist is Scarlett, she has some distinctly villainous tendencies, as does Rhett. Perhaps, then, Scarlett and Rhett are some form of anti-hero, more common in post-classical Hollywood, owning undeniably positive characteristics such as strength of will, vitality and an ability to love. They cannot, however, be understood as villains.

If a distinct villain cannot be found amongst the central characters of *Gone With the Wind*, where else does threat hail from? The Union army is probably the most consistent villainous force, although it is not steadily characterised by one group or individual throughout the film. 'Yankees' are described as 'meddlin' rascals', but are only represented on screen by one raider, a few carpetbaggers and some post-war peacekeeping soldiers. General Sherman is never seen – known for the devastating attack on Atlanta – although the titles announce the force of his assault like a 'wind' blowing through Georgia, and a short montage of dissolves shows silhouetted Union troops marching through smoke and fire. The most distinct enemy of the film is Jonas Wilkerson (Victor Jory), Tara's former overseer who is dismissed for fathering the child of a poor white girl. Jonas is a harsh, unfeeling man, with no regard for others whether white, black, Southern or Northern. After the war he returns to Tara, a 'regular Yankee', having made profit from the South's defeat, and attempts to buy the heavily taxed estate from Scarlett for a meagre $300. Wilkerson is present only three times in the film, finally receiving a lump of earth in the face from Scarlett, and is not seen again. There are certain other Southerners who demonstrate villainous behaviour, but like the threats discernible in *So Red the Rose* they operate as forces of adversity, or trials that must be faced by the central characters and they are swiftly overcome, operating as single threats to the home and the family and as plot devices to spur new action.

Home is the driving force behind Scarlett, as it was for her father, who tells her that the land is: 'the only thing [...] worth fighting for, worth dying for, because it's the only thing that lasts'. In an early scene of father and daughter standing by a tree, looking down over Tara, he explains that to the Irish, 'the land they live on is like their mother'. It is effectively a family tableau underlined by emotive strains of music, in which the film makes a bold statement about the importance of the land and its owners. At the end of the film, following Scarlett's declaration that 'tomorrow is another day', the image cuts to a similar shot, with the same golden sky and green plantation, and Tara's theme playing triumphantly. Instead of father and daughter looking out over the land, however, only Scarlett stands there in silhouette next to the tree. It would be tempting to see this as a flashback to a previous time if it were not for the fact that she is now alone. It is not a flashback but a statement that Scarlett has returned to Tara, and that her father's words were correct in two respects: firstly, the land will always last (and therefore so will the spirit of the old South) and, secondly, that the land is the mother of the Irish, and of those viewers who identify themselves as Irish Americans. The shot is, in effect, of mother and daughter – Tara and Scarlett. Tara represents survival, not just of Scarlett but also of Irish American descendants and the sentiment that opens the film. The days of slavery and Southern cavaliers may be over, but a sense of hope ('tomorrow is another day') lives on through its remembrance. Melanie's death signifies the final nail in the coffin of the old South, but as much as Scarlett represents the new South, she is still intractably linked to that former civilisation, through her oneness with Tara.

NEW MORALITIES AND SELF CIVIL WARS IN *FRIENDLY PERSUASION*

When *Friendly Persuasion* was released in 1956, the *Variety* reviewer praised director William Wyler's time and effort spent on the film, predicting that the film 'will mean much to its viewers'.[25] It is a slightly puzzling comment, in that the narrative concerns a Northern Quaker family, the Birdwells, and their farm in Southern Indiana in 1862. According to their creed, the Quaker community (a subset of Puritanism) refuses to bear arms against its fellow man, so when a limping Union Major arrives at the Quaker meeting, early in the film, to encourage their men to enlist, he receives instead platitudes and verses of Scripture. How this film comes to 'mean much to its viewers' is a matter of the ideological, moral project found within the narrative, despite the protagonists' identity as staunchly pacifist Puritans.

True to the melodramatic mode, *Friendly Persuasion*'s structure is episodic, although many segments are dealt with through comedy, much of which revolves around what, to the viewer, is strange about the Quaker lifestyle. Their speech is liberally scattered with 'thee' and 'thy', their dark clothing is mistaken for mourning, and they prohibit certain 'innocent' pleasures such as music and dancing. The Birdwells, however, are an unconventional Quaker family. Jess, the father (Gary Cooper), shocks his community by striving to find a horse that will outrun his Methodist neighbour in a weekly buggy-race to their respective churches. Comic episodes show the youngest son, Little Jess (Richard Eyer), wanting to kill the family's pet goose; daughter Mattie (Phyllis Love) fantasising about and dancing with her Methodist soldier beau, Gard (Mark Richman); and eldest son Josh (Anthony Perkins) getting involved in a brawl. The mother, Eliza (Dorothy McGuire), being one of the Quaker preachers, tries desperately to keep her family under control at the County Fayre when each succumbs to temptations of the flesh: dancing, playing musical instruments, flirting and gambling. Even Eliza herself is seen tapping her foot to the music. So the comedy concerns itself with the family's morality, their purity from worldly pleasures and their struggles with conformity.

Also expected of the melodramatic mode is the expression of emotion – something that is discouraged by the characters' puritanical lifestyle. In contrast to the brightly coloured and musical Methodist service, the Quaker meeting's silence is broken only by occasional prayers. Little Jess's outburst of 'God is love!' is frowned upon by one stern church elder. When genuine emotion is expressed, then, such as sadness or joy, it is all the more significant, as the convention of melodrama to externalise emotion confronts the requirement of the characters' moral code of behaviour to deny themselves emotional displays. Eliza's goodbye to Josh when he leaves the farm to join the Home Guard (contrary to their pacifist teaching) is tearful and passionate, contrasting with her reserve and restraint up to this point. Then, when Josh finally shoots at Confederate soldiers, close-ups reveal his emotional pain at the taking of another's life (Perkins received an Academy Award nomination for Best Supporting Actor for his performance). Moments of crisis for these characters penetrate the outer veneer of self-control, allowing true feelings to emerge in the form of the 'bodily writing' that Brooks refers to, the physical expression of hidden emotions. It is as if the characters are at war within themselves, battling over the control of their feelings and passions. Through the externalisation of these inner workings, the characters' humanity is displayed, breaking through their disciplined Quaker exterior. The crises, however, are not internal in their cause; they come about directly because of the threat of the Civil War.

The war provides most of the action and suspense for *Friendly Persuasion*, although the first visible sign of a Confederate threat – smoke on the horizon – is more than one and a half hours into the film, and the first Confederate soldier seen is almost two hours in. Up to this point the narrative has concerned itself with a different conflict, that of the inner spiritual and emotional struggle of the Birdwells. Sacvan Bercovitch, writing about the traditions of seventeenth-century American Puritanism, explains that an inner conflict was recognised by the religion.[26] Each individual was called to live a blameless life, yet acknowledged an inevitable failure to do so, referred to as a 'Self Civil War', a perpetual inner battle. One part of the self is drawn towards sin; the other part that recognises sin resists or punishes the self in its urge to transgress. The struggle is selflessness versus selfishness; one is at war with oneself. It is on this Self Civil War that the first hour and a half of the film concentrates, providing a basis for the behaviour of the characters in the Civil War. The conflict is then, initially, not against any enemy character, it is against the temptations and threats of the world encroaching on the Quaker family.

At the film's beginning, Jess tells the Union Major that if the Confederate raiders come, it will be a 'test' for each individual: a test of will and a test of conscience. This is part of the Self Civil War that each character must fight. The requirement of melodrama to display a moral conflict is thus bracketed more within the individual than existing between distinctly good and evil personalities. So instead of the trials of the family representing the threats brought to the nation by the Civil War, it is the individual's trials that correspond to the national conflict. In a sense then the self comes to represent the nation.

The film employs an episodic structure to depict each person's test in turn and forms a series of Self Civil Wars. When her sweetheart leaves to join the Home Guard, Mattie overcomes her feigned propriety and disdain and runs to him barefoot, confessing her love for him. Her reward comes in the form of a marriage proposal. Eliza faces two tests. When Josh decides to fight, despite her disapproval, she allows him to follow his conscience and is overwhelmed by emotion at their goodbye. When the farm is raided by an untidy group of rebels whilst Jess and Josh are away, she tries to keep her usual control by offering food and supplies. However, when one raider tries to steal the pet goose, Eliza loses her self-control and beats him over the head with a broom. Although the episode is hidden from Jess, he eventually learns of it from his small son, and Eliza receives a reward of admiration

5. *Friendly Persuasion* (William Wyler, 1956): Josh fights with his conscience as he fires on the faceless enemy.

from her husband for her defence of their property – and her breaking of convention.

Josh's test operates more overtly as a rite of passage. Initially, Perkins' gangly, slender body, and nervous gestures depict Josh as a gauche and shy adolescent. On a trip to sell their produce, he reacts with terror to an all-female family and their aggressive sexuality (the three daughters shout 'Men!' and have to be restrained by their mother). When news arrives of the approaching Confederates, Josh obeys his own inherent sense of justice, saying that anyone who kills innocent people is his 'mortal enemy'. His reward – the transformation from boy to man – is received when, true to his word, he only fires on the Confederates once they have killed a fellow soldier. At the end of the film, Josh is seen with a wounded arm in a sling, calm, confident and manly.

Jess faces a threat of equal danger, and the test that he must pass is also deeply ethical. After Josh has left, Jess is seen bare-chested chopping wood by the farmhouse. A local Quaker man arrives and challenges Jess to take up arms against the raiders – this man had initially declared that nothing would ever convince him to fight, but his opinion is abruptly changed once his own farm has been raided. The challenge to Jess is in the form of a sleight on his masculinity and his duty to protect his family and home. He stays true to his conscience, however. His masculinity is not in question: it has already been affirmed by the display of his body as he chopped wood, and by the suggestions in the film of a healthy sexual relationship with his wife. So Jess passes this test and remains true to his morals.

However, Josh's horse soon arrives riderless (commonly used to signify to those left at home the wounding or death of a loved one at war), and Jess immediately collects his hunting rifle and leaves to find his son – the axe prominently stuck in a tree stump. After discovering his Methodist neighbour dying and horseless, Jess is grazed by a bullet from a stray Confederate horse-thief. He proves his courage by approaching the young man and pulling the rifle from his hands. Again, in accordance with his morality, Jess refuses to kill the soldier and lets him go. The Quaker's mercy reduces the soldier to tears and he numbly wanders away. The reward for Jess's moral victory is the swift location of Josh, lying wounded by his dead fellow soldier.

The only other test is for the youngest son, Little Jess, whose fascination for war and killing is quelled by the family's wartime experience, and is signalled by his ability to make friends with the pet goose. Every member of the family thus follows an individual journey in which their moral strength is tested and ultimately rewarded. In the final scene, as they leave for the church meeting, Jess says to his family, 'Well, c'mon, veterans,' indicating the victory that each has won in both the Self Civil War and the military conflict.

The ideological messages that the film delivers are made clear, as is required of melodrama. It is right to take up arms against an oppressor that slaughters the innocent; yet it is also right to show mercy. It does not harm one's faith to indulge in 'innocent pleasures' and to tend towards non-conformity as long as the resultant behaviour is within the boundaries of the mainstream, acceptable lifestyle. It is right to marry the one you love. It is also alright to have a free-man working on the farm, since he is not a slave. The Birdwells have a black farmhand who, he reveals, is a runaway slave and who also joins the Home Guard to fight. The home itself is also the locus of an ideology that sees the family and land existing in symbiosis, a kind of agrarian harmony that is underlined by the regular use of a theme-tune (of the same title as the film), hummed by a choir whenever the farm is seen in extreme long shot.

So *Friendly Persuasion* conforms to most of the expectations of the melodramatic mode (the manifestation of inner values and emotions, the identification of ethical 'truths', the presence of action and suspense, and so forth). Its narrative also revolves around the survival of the family and the home, typical of the genre of domestic melodrama. However, the villain, again, is missing. As previously noted, the Confederates are spoken of but not seen until almost two hours of screen time have passed. When they are presented it is only briefly. The Confederate troop that Josh and the Home Guard attack is only ever shown in long and extreme long shot, to contrast with the close-ups of Josh himself. None of the men are named or given any characterisation apart from 'Reb'. The raiders at the farm, although more clearly characterised as unruly and uncouth, appear only for that one episode, and even call out thanks to Eliza for the supplies. The horse-thief shown mercy by Jess is the most distinctly personified enemy, but his threat is easily overcome and he too is not seen after this episode. Each of these characters is less villain than tool for the tests that the family faces. They are instruments of the adversity that must be overcome, but none is consistently present in the way that the heroes of the film are. War itself could be understood as the true enemy and the true villain, being the source of adversity that the protagonists face and the means by which they are tested, but the question must again be considered as to why a consistently personalised villain is not present.

The answer lies in the concept of the Self Civil War. The characteristic melodramatic villain has no place in the Self Civil War, since the objects of the struggle are conceptual and ideological. It is as if aspects of the self become the villain. Since the moral standards then shift, certain villainous elements of the self lose their transgressive nature and become acceptable. There is a clear link here between the eventual acceptance of what was once considered to be sinful behaviour and the refusal to apportion guilt in Civil War films. As Bruce Chadwick explains of Civil War narratives dating back to the late-nineteenth century, neither side can be credited with blame.[27] Although the nation was in conflict against itself, the opposition was resolved at a political level and both sides were assimilated into one. It was then part of a post-war ideological project to represent that nation as whole in order to encourage a unified identity amongst Americans. In this ideology there can be no enemy, the war being instead a necessary evil in the creation of a permanently unified nation. Similarly, within the American individual, there cannot be a prevailing split. That which was a villainous tendency must be overcome or subsumed into a new moral outlook, so that the individual attains a mature identity without any inner conflict. In this sense then, the self in *Friendly Persuasion* acts as a metaphor for the nation, which sees the victory of a new morality over an old morality. What the film seems to say is that in certain circumstances it may be necessary for the purest of people to literally fight for what they hold dear, and as a result they are born to a new, more plausible, moral conscience. Correspondingly, the nation that this new morality stands for is a better nation than before the conflict began, older, wiser and confirmed in its unity.

The Birdwells may discover a new morality for themselves, but that morality, that ideology, is totally in keeping with sensibilities of the film's historical production context. There is in fact nothing 'new' at all about the Birdwells' revised morality. It operates as a confirmation of the mainstream American lifestyle. Through the trials of the Self Civil War, the Quaker Birdwells can be welcomed as members of American ancestry, having converted to mainstream American culture. It is for this reason that *Variety's* comment can be understood in a new light. Not only will the film 'mean much to its viewers' because the narrative concerns that most significant of conflicts, the American Civil War, but also because it uses an incontestably moral group of characters to affirm mainstream ideologies and lifestyles.

A NEW HOME AND A NEW FAMILY IN *RIDE WITH THE DEVIL*

In an interview shortly before the release of *Ride With the Devil*, Ang Lee described his film as a 'family drama',[28] going on to say that the characters in the film 'represent a larger kind of "family" – the warring factions of the Civil War and the division in the national character'.[29] He was highlighting a convention dating back to the earliest of Civil War films, in which the war is presented as a familial conflict of brother against brother. However, this film is a domestic melodrama with a difference. The principal characters have been forcibly wrenched from the domestic sphere because of the Civil War, and throughout the narrative they fight or search for a surrogate home.

Jake Roedel (Tobey Maguire) is a second-generation German immigrant living on the Missouri border with Kansas. His character comes from another long tradition in Hollywood cinema, that of the raider, represented by such colourful individuals as the James and Younger brothers, usually found in post-Civil War Westerns including *Jesse James* (Henry King, 1939), *Kansas Raiders* (Ray Enright, 1950), *Best of the Badmen* (William D. Russell, 1951) and *Frank and Jesse* (Robert Boris, 1994). During the war the raider was part of local guerrilla forces in areas where the regular army had not yet reached and where neighbouring communities supported opposing sides of the conflict. Possibly the most notorious of the Southern raiders, known as 'Bushwhackers', was William C. Quantrill, whose raid on the Northern-held town of Lawrence, Kansas, led to the deaths of around two hundred civilians.[30] Quantrill (John Ales) is the young, charismatic leader of a more historically accurate depiction of the travesty than found in other raider movies. During the raid on Lawrence, heroic strains of orchestral music are juxtaposed with the murder of soldiers and civilians alike. Musical codes for bravery clash with images of indiscriminate destruction, and so the film makes a display of the atrocities committed by the Bushwhackers. It is an interesting and deliberate conflict of values that the film seems to own, having central characters aligned to the Confederacy refusing to condone certain behaviour and philosophies, and so in the process exposing the myth of a noble South, whilst redeeming a generation who fought in its name.

One of these philosophies concerns a tradition, found in many Civil War films, of mourning the loss of the old Southern way of life, the passing away of a certain 'civilisation'. However, it is not dealt with in the longing manner of *So Red the Rose* and *Gone With the Wind*. Instead the film acknowledges the inferiority of this philosophy, despite its representation of most of the Southern characters in a sympathetic light. A farmer who offers supplies and a hiding-place to Jake and his three companions, Mr Evans (Zach Grenier), tells them about the town of Lawrence. Evans sadly explains that the Northerners constructed the schoolhouse before anything else. Education for all meant that anyone could learn to think freely, 'with no regard to station, custom, propriety', and so, he implies, will live and think like Northerners. The tragedy of this, to Evans, is that the Confederacy would therefore lose the war, because the South did not care about freedom and equality (the schoolhouse is seen in flames later in the film during the Lawrence raid). He concludes by saying that the Bushwhackers are fighting for everything the South has ever had but, in fact, they do not have it anymore. The sentiment is the opposite to that found in *Gone With the Wind*, which longs for former days that were better for the plantocracy, not dreading days to come that are – ideologically speaking – better for all.

Ride With the Devil has conflicts working on three levels: familial, factional and national. The familial conflict exists between Jake and his own father, who is a pro-Union immigrant. Mr Roedel (John Judd), who is seen only briefly at the film's beginning, wants his son to move to the safer town of St Louis, but Jake considers the Southern community to be his 'people', his real family, and refuses to 'huddle' with the other 'Lincoln-lovin' Germans'. Mr Roedel's warning is that Jake will always receive prejudice and suspicion for being a 'Dutchie'. Despite this conflict, Jake always carries with him the sense of honour instilled in him by his father, something that later causes him to question some of the Bushwhacker tactics. Some time after, Union supporters murder Mr Roedel because of his association with his son. His death is one link with home and family that is destroyed for Jake, causing a need in the young man to find an alternative domestic sphere.

The factional conflict within the Bushwhacker party that Jake joins is between those who see raiding as a political necessity and those who derive intense pleasure and satisfaction from killing. It is here that the film's one distinctly villainous character can be found in Pitt Mackeson (Jonathan Rhys Meyers), an arrogant and amoral man who poses the most serious threat of all to Jake. Mackeson gains an almost erotic gratification out of murdering civilians. His pride, arrogance and anger are captured by Rhys Meyers' histrionic performance: head tilted to one side, a staring, intimidating expression on his face and a repeated flick of the hand to dismiss concerns that are below him. Two important scenes depict this man's bloodlust. Near the beginning of the war, the Bushwhackers attack a store providing supplies to Union soldiers, and Mackeson not only kills the owner, but also sets the store alight, leaving the wife both widowed and destitute. Then later, when the group joins Quantrill's raid on Lawrence, Mackeson is representative of the men who killed civilians indiscriminately.

The factional conflict is personalised specifically by the rivalry between Jake and Mackeson. True to Mr Roedel's warning, the villain's hatred is initially sparked by Jake's ethnicity, and he mockingly refers to him as 'Dutchie'. Jake, however, is not alone in his enmity of Mackeson. When winter comes and the Bushwhackers disperse into hiding, Jake is joined by childhood friend Jack Bull Chiles (Skeet Ulrich), George Clyde (Simon Baker) and Clyde's ex-slave friend Holt (Jeffrey Wright). These four men form a kind of honourable, Southern group, each distrusting Mackeson. After the deaths of Jack Bull and Clyde, Jake and Holt become close companions, and during the Lawrence attack they are horrified by the behaviour of their colleagues. Instead of participating in the genocide, the two men eat breakfast at an inn. When Mackeson arrives and begins to harass the owners, Jake aims a pistol at him, less to protect the civilians than to make it clear to Mackeson that he considers him to be an enemy.

The other conflict is that between North and South, the national conflict. The individuals representing this are the Southern Bushwhackers and their Northern equivalent, the Jayhawkers or Red Legs. The film shows a small number of attacks by or skirmishes between the two groups, the first being the night-time Jayhawker attack on Jack Bull's home. His house is burned down and his father is killed – it is the event that spurs Jack Bull and Jake to join the Bushwhackers. The contrast in the *mise-en-scène* between the film's sunlit, relaxed beginning and this scene, with the farmhouse in flames in the night, is strongly reminiscent of the other films discussed in this chapter, particularly *So Red the Rose*. In other clashes Jake's small finger on his left hand is shot off and Jack Bull receives a mortal wound to the arm that eventually leads to gangrene and death. Thus, the group of men bear the loss caused by the national conflict.

Judging from these scenes of vivid and, at times, gruesomely authentic action, it would be quite acceptable to describe *Ride With the Devil* as an example of the war film genre (Neale in fact describes the film as a Western, which is equally acceptable, with its similarity to many Westerns and raider films such as *Kansas Raiders*).[31] The dirt, sweat and blood is certainly in keeping with the *mise-en-scène* of combat films such as *Glory* and *Gettysburg* (and these films also display much of the melodramatic mode). Acting styles throughout most of the film are verisimilarly coded according to conventional standards of 'realism' in late-twentieth-century Hollywood cinema. Climactic moments, however, employ more histrionic signs. The amputation of Jack Bull's arm, for example, is highly emotional with heavy breathing, screams and exclamations of emotional pain, whilst conveying a veracity that is absent from the amputation scene of *Gone With the Wind*, produced under the directives of the Production Code, Hollywood's self-imposed censorship of 1934–68. During violent clashes the Southern men scream out the 'Rebel Yell', which is both authentic for the period and is a melodramatic scream of anger and hatred.

Despite the climactic and spectacular nature of many of these scenes, the *factional* conflict is what is central to the narrative, particularly the rivalry between Jake and Mackeson. The very same scream that Jake aims at his Jayhawker enemies, he later directs towards Mackeson as an exclamation of hatred. The relationship between the two men is the central arena of conflict in the film and they represent opposite values, despite both following the same vocation as Bushwhackers. Jake repeatedly vows to return the South to its old ways and to heal the institutions of home, farming and family. Mackeson, on the other hand, destroys homes and slaughters families. He desires no return to the old South because the Bushwhacker's life is all that he values. In domestic melodrama it is the home and family that are the locus of meaning, the pivotal issue being their survival in the face of threat. The two characters of Jake and Mackeson represent the two aspects of this focal concern: Mackeson is the threat; Jake is the means of survival. So the moral ground on which these conflicting values sit concerns family and home, making the film more domestic melodrama than war film. It is the hope of home and the desire to return Southern life to the way it was, that drives Jake through the narrative. It is signalled by the recurring use of cultural musical codes, such as the banjo and harmonica – instruments connoting 'Southernness'. Interestingly, the film does not once use the theme of 'Dixie' on the soundtrack. It is likely that such a choice would imply a clichéd approval of the lost cause philosophy, but it also further removes the film from consideration as a war film.

6. *Ride With the Devil* (Ang Lee, 1999): Pitt Mackeson – a distasteful characteristic of American ancestry.

Jake's close colleagues also yearn for family and home. Holt hopes to find his mother who had been sold as a slave in Texas, and Jack Bull begins a relationship with a young widow, Sue Lee (singer and songwriter, Jewel). After a battle with Union soldiers, when both Holt and Jake are wounded, the two men return to the farm where Sue Lee now lives and find that she has a baby girl (it is Jack Bull's child). Although he is not the father and he considers marriage to be a 'peculiar institution' worse than slavery, Jake develops a gruff affection for the mother and child, and grudgingly marries Sue Lee. Jake's Self Civil War does not concern the temptation to fight, as it does for Josh in *So Red the Rose*. It is more concerned with a resistance to marriage and adult responsibility, despite an irresistible attraction to mother and child. On his first night as a married man, Sue Lee asks Jake if he is a virgin; he replies that he has killed fifteen men. He has clearly understood masculinity and maturity in terms of killing as opposed to sexual awareness. In the final section of the film, however, Jake is seen having his 'Bushwhacker curls' cut short, a symbol of his new maturity, and setting off to the West with his new family.

The trajectory of Jake's journey takes him from home and family, through the brotherhood of the Bushwhackers, to a new home and family and a new beginning. This journey stands in stark contrast to that of the villain, Mackeson, whose route travels from murder to murder, and eventually to suicide. He has no respect for marriage, race, age or creed – he is in effect a psychopathic killer. The final crisis of the film has Mackeson and his lackey, Turner (Matthew Faber), coming upon Jake and his new family camped in the woods. It is the climactic resolution towards which this conflict has been building, but it does not fulfil expectations. Mackeson says that he wants to return to his home, the Northern-held town of Newport, because he wants a drink, not, incidentally, to return to his family. Jake states that to do so would be suicide, yet aims a rifle at Mackeson to make it equally clear that he will die either way. Instead of a shoot-out, the expectation of both Western and war film, Mackeson chooses to die in his hometown, rather than at the hands of his real enemy, Jake, and he rides away.

The opposition between Jake and Mackeson is the focal point of what Lee described as 'the divisions in the national character'. Because both men are Southerners, one good and one bad, the danger of a villain representing the whole of the South is overcome. It is important to stress that this film, unlike the others described in this chapter, *does* have a consistent and carefully characterised villain in Mackeson, who represents something bad in the American psyche. He represents an element of the American character that craves war and conflict.

The reason why this film highlights such a dangerous element may be found in the words of Daniel Woodrell, the author of *Woe to Live On* (1987), the novel on which the film was based, and veteran of the Vietnam war. Woodrell felt distinct parallels between the motivation of young men in the 1860s and the 1960s. 'There was a war and I just thought I should go,' he says, but 'got a crash course in what was really going on.'[32] Woodrell saw his novel being 'as much about Vietnam and Bosnia as about Missouri and Kansas'.[33] Certainly, there are alarming similarities between the attack on Lawrence and the My-Lai massacre, despite more than a century separating the two events. The parallel with this more recent American war is unavoidable, subtly emphasised by the revelation at the end of the film that Jake is still only nineteen years old, often given as the average age of the American soldier in Vietnam. Lee's film thus seems to be saying that there is a disturbing, timeless facet to the American character that is drawn only towards prejudice and destruction. It is a narrative theme almost unthinkable to pre-Vietnam Civil War melodramas that strive instead to emphasise unity in the American national family. Here, the narrative consciously states that there are dangerous individuals who do not uphold the positive values of mainstream American ideology. However, like a number of films that I go on to examine, the narrative finds a way to expel or overcome this distasteful aspect of America. In keeping with the requirements of stage melodrama, the villain is punished for his unacceptable behaviour.

The film also overcomes any disconcerting connotations in Jake's identity as a Southern Bushwhacker through his thoroughly honourable philosophy and, very importantly, his relationship with the ex-slave, Holt. Both men are unusual Bushwhackers with one being black and the other German and each finds himself on the receiving end of prejudice for his ethnicity. Holt's story is particularly interesting. George Clyde had bought him out of slavery and the two became as close as brothers. Other acquaintances, however, are in the habit of referring to Holt as 'Clyde's Nigger', and once Clyde is killed Holt realises that only then is he truly free. The man he had come to think of as a brother was still, symbolically, his master. Paradoxically, the black man fighting on the Southern side finds his Northern enemy providing the means for his freedom by killing his best friend. The closeness that develops between Holt and Jake confirms their shared philosophy, which is more characteristic of perceptions of the North, believing in the freedom and equality of all. The two men, black and white, form a new brotherhood of the American family, so far ideologically from the new white family at the end of *The Birth of a Nation*. *Ride With the Devil* affirms, then, the positive values of freedom and equality on a political level, and home and family on a personal level.

THEMES AND MEANINGS IN CIVIL WAR MELODRAMAS

There are some striking similarities between the four films described above, despite their central characters taking different sides in the war. Two films represent Southern plantation families, one a Northern farming family and one an immigrant family divided in allegiance. Each film places the family and its fate firmly at the centre of the action, not only because domestic melodrama requires it, but also as a form of representative family of the American nation. The sectional loyalties of the family members, then, are less important than what they have to face because of the Civil War.

Trials, Tests and Rites of Passage

As recognised earlier, the core narrative concern of melodrama is moral opposition. In the domestic melodrama, moral oppositions directly affect the private sphere of family, relationships and the home. In Civil War melodramas, those oppositions gain an added significance by virtue of their historical situation. One would expect, then, that these films would effectively be about the manifestation and resolution of moral conflict in the home during the Civil War period. However, with the films examined so far in mind, it is less moral opposition than moral transformation that takes place within the family and home, and the opposition exists instead between old and new moralities. The result is that each film can be found to have three stages: old morality, transformation and new morality, echoing the conventional narrative structure of equilibrium, disruption, new equilibrium. The three stages are made manifest in the expressive devices of the melodramatic mode, specifically in the performance, *mise-en-scène* and music. The transformation stage, the dividing line between old and new, is the Civil War experience itself, acting as a crisis to bring about the birth of a new morality. The Civil War thus operates as a tool for the narrative structure, allowing the moral development of the central characters.

In *So Red the Rose*, both Duncan and Valette can be seen to follow a moral journey, made up of certain lessons, towards a new maturity. This moral rite of passage is represented by, firstly, the narrative structure (pre-war, war, post-war) and secondly, contrasting stylistic devices corresponding to each stage. The family members move from innocent immaturity, through threats and trials, to a wiser, more mature morality that embraces notions of respect, compassion and loyalty. *Gone With the Wind* similarly follows the three-stage structure to represent Scarlett's journey. Although calling Scarlett's personal story a 'moral journey' may seem difficult to substantiate given her consistent selfishness, the lesson that she learns is integral to the entire narrative: she and the land are indivisible and both will survive. It is something that she must learn to re-embrace on the occasion of the ruin of all else.

Friendly Persuasion's moral journeys are multiple, taking the form of separate tests for each family member. Every character faces and passes their test and in so doing adopts a new morality. *Ride With the Devil* sees Jake's rite of passage take him towards both a personal and a political maturity in which he accepts the role of husband and father as well as understanding the value of ideals such as freedom and equality. This film and *So Red the Rose* are the only films of the selection that concern themselves consciously with issues of race, *So Red the Rose* working to reinforce the racist myth of the old South, *Ride With the Devil* working to expose it.

These films are operating an ideological project within their narratives, reinforced by their employment of the melodramatic mode. Melodrama is using the Civil War as a means to fortify certain moralities through the personal changes experienced by the characters. Whether that be a morality that accepts fighting for a good cause or that reveres the American myth of the agrarian paradise, it is making use of the war as a device that structures the individual's transformation. Because the overt representation of villainy is (mostly) removed, the Civil War narrative is able to offer up a deification of the American ancestor.

The Missing Villain

In the first three films studied in this chapter, the consistent and coherent villain that Brooks identifies as crucial within melodrama is not present. Instead, a range of vague villainous types can be found who are seen only briefly and act primarily as temporary threats to spur the moral development of the heroes. The reason for the absent villain is rooted in the Civil War mythology that I refer to in the analysis of *Friendly Persuasion*. The family of this film are loath to understand the South as their enemy, since all Americans are, to them, their brothers. Duncan, in *So Red the Rose*, similarly, refuses to bear arms against the Union, because both North and South have the same blood in their veins. These characters eventually discover that they must bear arms against those who would threaten the innocent with violence, and as such are justified in their change of heart. This is in accord with the ideological project that Chadwick describes, to re-create and represent the Civil War as a means to achieve complete and permanent national unity,[34] as if the nation was a reunified family. It concurs with Benedict Anderson's description of Civil War histories and cultural products as a means to 'remember/forget' the past as a war between brothers, instead of nation states.[35] The vast complex history of the Civil War is distilled into a family story in which the real causes of the conflict are erased and replaced by tests of morality. War in these films is a stage in a process, one that is encoded as a moral journey towards a worldview that corresponds with specific, modern American ideologies. The Civil War, therefore, is operating as an essential rite of passage for the nation. Even when there is the troubling presence of an American villain, as found the post-classical Hollywood, post-Vietnam movie *Ride With the Devil*, it is conquered by the reassuring presence of the American hero. In essence, the ideological message is: that which is good will ultimately and always overcome the villainous tendencies in the American character.

What this means in terms of characterisation is that no one section (North or South) can be constructed as a collective villain. It is the dilemma and the irony of the war. To label one side of the conflict as villainous is to accuse oneself and is unacceptable ideologically to a united America. As a result, individuals may be constructed as antagonists, but they are not permitted to be representative of either North or South, only a set of 'evil' values. This is part of the 'forgetting' that Anderson describes. In the same way that *Friendly Persuasion* can be seen to map the Civil War onto a series of Self Civil Wars, these melodramas depict the American nation involved in its own Self Civil War, but its internal demons are faceless and nameless.

CONCLUSION

This representation of a transformed ideology through Civil War melodramas reiterates the central importance of the family in American national identity, no less significant in these films than in the speeches of Abraham Lincoln at the time of the Civil War. The lessons that the characters learn are the lessons for the nation, specifically the nation that watches the film. The transformed ideology is part of the viewer heritage: back in the 1860s my ancestors faced a trial that is the bedrock of my freedom/security/nationhood today, and the lessons they learned are part of my current worldview. What is created, therefore, is not only a sense of American family-hood, but also a historical American family-hood. Not only did the family survive the Civil War, but it has also stood the test of time. This is the lesson for the present-day viewer to learn, to 'remember/forget' the past in a learning of personal identity and a participation in the ideological project of the films. The ideology offers up a promise that no matter what enemy the American family may have to face, whether foreign or domestic, it will prevail. The identity of that enemy is not the primary concern; instead it is the hope that the family will survive, and the Civil War melodrama assures the nation that it always will.

NOTES

1   Brooks, Peter, *The Melodramatic Imagination: Balzac, Henry James, Melodrama and the Mode of Excess* (New York, 1995). p. vii.
2   Brooks: *The Melodramatic Imagination.* p. 202.
3   Brooks: *The Melodramatic Imagination.* pp. 11–12.
4   Brooks: *The Melodramatic Imagination.* pp. 12–13, 16.
5   Brooks: *The Melodramatic Imagination.* p. 15.
6   Brooks: *The Melodramatic Imagination.* p. 9.
7   Nowell-Smith, Geoffrey, 'Minnelli and Melodrama', *Screen*, vol. 18, no. 2 (1977). p. 117.
8   Brooks: *The Melodramatic Imagination.* p. xi.
9   Pearson, Roberta E., '"O'er Step Not the Modesty of Nature": A Semiotic Approach to Acting in the Griffith Biographs' in C. Zucker (ed.) *Making Visible the Invisible: An Anthology of Original Essays on Film Acting* (Metuchen, New Jersey, 1990). pp. 1–27.
10   Pearson: '"O'er Step Not the Modesty of Nature"'. p. 11.
11   Pearson: '"O'er Step Not the Modesty of Nature"'. p. 21.
12   Neale, Steve, *Genre and Hollywood* (London, 2000). p. 196.
13   Neale: *Genre and Hollywood.* p. 198.
14   Neale: *Genre and Hollywood.* p. 180.
15   Neale: *Genre and Hollywood.* p. 184.
16   Produced by Vitagraph in 1908, Champion in 1911, Metro Pictures in 1915, and by director Lambert Hillyer for Regal Pictures in 1924.
17   Nowell-Smith: 'Minnelli and Melodrama'. p. 116.
18   Grob, G.N. and Billias, G.A., (eds) *Interpretations of American History: Patterns and Perspectives, Volume I – to 1877*, 5th edition (New York, 1982). p. 397.

19   Tulloch, Hugh, *The Debate on the American Civil War Era* (Manchester and New York, 1999). p. 13.

20   *New York Times Reviews 'So Red the Rose'*, 28 November 1935.

21   Brooks: *The Melodramatic Imagination.* p. 16.

22   Brooks: *The Melodramatic Imagination.* p. 32.

23   Grindon, Leger, *Shadows on the Past: Studies in the Historical Fiction Film* (Philadelphia, 1994). p. 14.

24   Vera, Hernan and Gordon, Andrew, 'Sincere Fictions of the White Self in Cinema: The Divided White Self in Civil War Films' in D. Bernardi (ed.) *Classic Hollywood, Classic Whiteness* (Minneapolis, 2001). p. 272.

25   *Variety 'Friendly Persuasion'*, 26 September 1956.

26   Bercovitch, Sacvan, *The Puritan Origins of the American Self* (New Haven and London, 1975). p. 19.

27   Chadwick, Bruce, *The Reel Civil War: Mythmaking in American Film* (New York, 2002). p. 10.

28   Tibbetts, John C., 'The Hard Ride: Jayhawkers and Bushwhackers in the Kansas-Missouri Border Wars – *Ride With the Devil*', *Literature and Film Quarterly*, vol. 27, no. 3 (1999). p. 194.

29   Tibbetts: 'The Hard Ride'. p. 194.

30   Thomson, David, 'Riding With Ang Lee', *Film Comment*, vol. 35, no. 6 (November/December, 1999). p. 6.

31   Neale: *Genre and Hollywood.* p. 34.

32   Interviewed in Tibbetts: 'The Hard Ride'. p. 192.

33   Tibbetts: 'The Hard Ride'. p. 193.

34   Chadwick: *The Reel Civil War.* p. 10.

35   Anderson, Benedict, *Imagined Communities*, 2nd edition (London, 1991). p. 201.

3

War-Westerns: Shifting Lines of Conflict

In Chapter 2, the relationship between the American Civil War and the sub-genre of domestic melodrama was examined. What was found in this relationship was a distinct emotionalisation of the war according to the conventions of the melodramatic mode, as well as a focus on the fate of home and family in accord with the demands of the sub-genre. The war was seen to be modified to fit in with the requirements of melodrama, whilst certain adaptations had to be made to the genre's conventions, particularly through the absence of the villain, in order to conform to the Civil War mythology of a causeless, blameless conflict. Chapter 3 now goes on to analyse examples of Civil War Westerns, or War-Westerns as they shall be termed, to discover whether similar adaptations occur. Again, the goal is to ascertain what the genre seems to say about American national identity, with the narratives being set specifically during and/or shortly after the Civil War.

Beginning as a staple product of the early American cinema, the Western has gone through numerous permutations whilst retaining certain narrative and stylistic conventions in its films that make them immediately recognisable to the viewer as Westerns. A large proportion of Westerns follow conventions of the melodramatic mode, including expressive *mise-en-scène*, the underlining of emotion and action with music, and acting styles that externalise characters' inner feelings and conflicts. The films also tend to conform to the stark distinction between good and evil that is characteristic of melodrama, as well as providing the action, suspense and spectacle associated with the industry definition of the genre. It is no surprise then that some are described as 'outdoor melodrama'[1] or 'male melodrama'.[2]

Being a distinctly American cultural product, the Western has come to be regarded as the archetypal Hollywood film and has taken central position in genre studies, as if it somehow provides an inherent rule-system that can be used as a blueprint to analyse any genre. Steve Neale warns of the difficulties that arise with this approach, when the Western's conventions (such as its iconography and frontier mythology) are not typical or characteristic of other Hollywood genres.[3] As Neale notes, an analysis of the iconography of the musical or the comedy, which is widely varied, would reveal the inadequacy of such an approach. The sporadic release of Western films since the 'golden age' of classical Hollywood, Neale adds, is further proof that the genre cannot be used as a model for generic analysis.[4] The War-Western is not considered here to be the archetypal Civil War film, simply one important genre that is frequently seen to depict the war. This chapter surveys certain conventions that are often held to be characteristic of the Western, as well as the central oppositions that have been identified. It then suggests that some of these conventions and oppositions are forcibly adapted for the purpose of constructing a particular myth of the American ancestor.

THE SAVAGE WEST AND
THE CIVILISED EAST

Thematically, the Western returns repeatedly to three central issues: race, land and authority. Dramatic tensions rise in the three areas between opposing characters and the values that they represent. Racial tension, for example, is regularly found in the opposition of white American versus Native American. It is displaced from the reality of twentieth-century black/white racial conflicts, to the mythical past of the Wild West. Adjacent to the racial conflict is land, the ownership (or not) being the pivotal issue. As noted in the introductory chapter, the land is used metaphorically in American culture to identify the nation both as wilderness and garden, existing simultaneously on either side of a figurative frontier. A space known as the frontier did in fact exist or, more accurately, several spaces across the continent, which moved ever westwards as the white landowners, justified by the ethics of progress and, at times, God's will, increasingly cultivated and civilised the land that once was free. This continuing westward expansion is found in narratives of the Western genre, and originates in the mandates of authority, the third Western theme, whether that is a commercial directive to extend the reach of the railroad or a military and Christian duty to suppress the 'savages' of the West.[5] The ultimate authority of these directives is the Christian edict to 'subdue the land', the manifest destiny of the pioneers, a task that, if successful, justifies the colonisation of the continent. Interestingly, these three bedrock issues of the conflicts of the Western – race, land and authority – parallel the elements commonly held to be the causes of conflict in the American Civil War.

The generic expectations of the Western have been listed several times by film scholars. Robert Warshow, for example, saw the Western encapsulated in the elements of the gun, the land and the horse, coming together in the person of the 'Westerner'.[6] Other writers have seen the quintessential Western ingredient as the frontier, where the two worlds of West and East meet, generating lengthy lists of antinomies between wilderness and civilisation, nature and culture, and so on.[7] The antinomies listed by Jim Kitses in 1969 are made up of signifiers in the Western that represent a dialectic relationship between sets of values, associated with the dramatic conflicts of the narrative.[8] The opposition of East and West, for example, represents more than geographical spaces and differences. The East connotes a certain class-based society, closely related to European culture and refinement. It is often characterised by effete or corrupt individuals, bringing to mind the weak, 'feminised' dime novelist of *Unforgiven* (Clint Eastwood, 1992). The West, however, evokes ideas of agrarianism instead of industry, and brutality instead of civilised manners, captured in characters such as Aaron the homesteader (Walter Coy) and Ethan the wanderer with a suspicious past (John Wayne) in *The Searchers* (John Ford, 1956). These antinomies have operated as the structural and narrative conventions of the Western film genre, and despite the thematic and ideological changes evident in the Western over the twentieth century, examined for example by Will Wright,[9] they have persistently remained. They contribute towards creating and re-creating the mythical world of the Wild West with each Western produced.

The most likely reason for the endurance of the East/West dichotomy can be found in discourses about the western frontier. Frederick Jackson Turner's thesis, 'The Significance of the Frontier in American History', delivered at the Chicago World Fair in 1893, declared that because the western frontier no longer existed as a geographical space, the first period of American history was over.[10] Up to that point, he argued, the presence of a frontier was the primary influence on the development of an American national character; it was the place and experience that forced the pioneer to adapt or 'perish', and a space that itself was gradually transformed by civilisation. It thus becomes a space of birth and regeneration for the

American spirit. However, as John Saunders writes, '[w]hatever the validity of Turner's thesis, it represents what Americans would like to believe […]',[11] and so the consistent attention given to the frontier space in much of the Western genre is pertinent to an examination of the brand of national identity that is constructed.

Richard Slotkin's extensive study on the frontier further explains how it has been regarded as both a geographical space and an ideological concept.[12] The division of East/West marked by the frontier is not only a geographical marker, but is also an axis of dramatic opposition. As Hugh Tulloch writes of Turner's thesis, what he achieved was 'to turn the axis of historical debate latitudinally from North and South to a new dynamic longitudinal western frontier'.[13] If Kitses' antinomies were to be placed across that alternative axis, ideological differences could be seen between the two groups of characters that exist on either side. When the frontier becomes the line of conflict it will typically be characterised by the opposition of cowboys versus Indians. Slotkin writes that the frontier was the theatre in which a 'savage war' took place, which popular culture (such as the dime novel) represented as having been instigated by the Native Americans against the white Americans and characterised by violence.[14] With the Western being a form that is so distinctly American in significance and ownership, national identity is thus linked historically and mythically (through cultural products such as novels and films) to conflict along this line of the frontier.

The central figure in this arena is the frontier hero, who Slotkin calls 'the man who knows Indians',[15] the man who stands on the line between the worlds of East and West. He is called upon to mediate, interpret and, inevitably, to fight against the savagery of the West. This is the Westerner that Warshow describes, whose purpose in the Western is to be 'a killer of men'.[16] He is somehow complete, needing neither fruitful employment nor the love of a woman,[17] only his horse and his gun. In addition to this the Westerner needs an enemy on whom the violence is exacted: the savage living in the land beyond the frontier, a people group that I shall term 'Indians' or 'Red', since these pejorative terms are used within narratives typical of the genre. So the opposition of East and West is affiliated to a racial conflict of White and Red. Put in other terms, the Westerner and his Red enemy represent the clash of the two worlds of wilderness and civilisation; they signify the East/West line of conflict synonymous with the Western genre. Even in cases where the narrative constructs the Native American as the 'noble' savage, or the good Indian, such as the revisionist Western *Little Big Man* (Arthur Penn, 1970), he is consigned to a race that is vanishing, along with the shrinking Western wilderness, and therefore is relegated to the past.

However, it is not only the noble savage that is seen disappearing into a past age in Western films. The white Western hero, the cowboy or frontiersman, began to be represented as an anachronism in later films of the twentieth century, holding on to an old-fashioned lifestyle that was being taken over by technology, industrialisation and commercialism. Films such as *Ride the High Country* (Sam Peckinpah, 1962) showed the Westerner as an aging cowboy struggling at a different kind of frontier, between the old West and the new West. In this opposition, the conflict between white Easterners (feminine, civilised) and white Westerners (masculine, dangerous) is replaced by a conflict of old and new.

Although the conventions mentioned here work together to create a myth of the West, the Western genre itself does not ignore its mythical nature. Films such as *The Man Who Shot Liberty Valance* (John Ford, 1962) and *Unforgiven*, operate as self-reflective narratives that openly confess the genre's relationship between fact and legend. In these films, however, the blame for the dissemination of frontier mythology is placed with the journalists and dime novelists of the East who travel West for stories of heroism, villainy and violence, reinforcing again the opposition of East and West.

Douglas Pye credits the Western with constructing narratives that 'exist in a sense outside time', from a non-specific era that 'announces itself as the past' yet denies any truth or historical fact about that past.[18] Countless Western characters seem unaffected by real events, personalities or governmental issues that exist outside the world of the frontier. However, as Pye notes in his study of John Ford's cavalry Westerns, when an explicit date is introduced, such as the first year of peace after the Civil War, 1866, the lives and actions of the central characters are immediately historicised.[19] Because the individuals are placed into a specific historical moment with its own social and political conditions, the characters become historical figures. The American Civil War is one such historical moment. What this introduces to the Western is an appeal to historical authenticity, since the character on screen has now become an American ancestor.

THE CIVIL WAR AND LINES OF CONFLICT

The Civil War is often present in some form in the Western genre film, whether it is represented directly or referred to indirectly. Indirect references are often brief and may even go unnoticed in Westerns that ostensibly have nothing to do with the war. The death of a Southern sergeant, for example, in *She Wore a Yellow Ribbon* (John Ford, 1949), reminds the viewer that this man had fought for the Confederates, with a short burst of 'Dixie' on the soundtrack. Although the words of the tune are not sung, the sentiment 'I wish I was in Dixie' imply that this brave Southerner may have died in the West, but his soul is forever in the South. Musical signifiers of the war in Westerns may then be non-diegetic, 'soundtrack' music, suggesting a character's allegiance (other tunes include 'Battle Hymn of the Republic' and 'John Brown's Body'), or they may be diegetic, belonging to the dramatic world on the screen, sung or played as marching anthems or at public gatherings. Music with its source in the action of the film often becomes a site of conflict, for the purpose of externalising oppositions as is typical of the melodramatic mode. The outlaws of *The Long Riders* (Walter Hill, 1980), for example, force saloon musicians to play rebel tunes at gunpoint. Similarly, the Missouri ferry-operator of *The Outlaw Josey Wales* (Clint Eastwood, 1976) sings either Union or Confederate battle songs depending on his customers' political leanings. Accents and dialogue offer more direct evidence of a character's sympathies. Kenneth Branagh's twisted and crippled Confederate general in *Wild Wild West* (Barry Sonnenfeld, 1999) speaks in an absurdly exaggerated Southern accent as he promises to continue in the Southern cause, despite the surrender having taken place years before.

The *mise-en-scène* may also be scattered with signs of the war, such as tattered uniforms or wounds. A saloon bar may proudly display a Confederate flag on the wall, indicating the sympathies of the locals or the mayor, as in the corrupt town of Redemption in *The Quick and the Dead* (Sam Raimi, 1995). In this film, Gene Hackman's evil Herod is seen in flashback ripping down a Union flag whilst torturing the sheriff of the town, thus he is not only a sadistic criminal, but also anti-American (by dint of being anti-Union), as demonstrated by his treatment of the flag. Additionally, films might include an opening montage battle sequence, accompanied with military tunes, drumrolls and explosions. This device functions to situate the characters emphatically in a historical moment and to make plain their allegiances during the war for North or South. This can be seen in *The Outlaw Josey Wales*, which shows Wales (Clint Eastwood) fighting with a band of Southern guerrillas before their enforced surrender. In such a film as this, as the Civil War montage finishes, the historically authenticated plot then re-situates itself in the West where the main narrative begins – a tendency also noted by Thomas Cripps.[20] Edward Buscombe and

Roberta Pearson write that it is already commonly understood that the Western is not a reliable historical form, but history is still, nevertheless, 'at the heart of the genre'.[21] John Belton, however, emphasises the point that the West is 'a site for the telling of the story of American identity', citing the adage of 'print the legend' from *The Man Who Shot Liberty Valance*.[22] So the Western genre can be seen as both history and fiction, one at the same time.

There is nothing remarkable about the observation that with the introduction of the Civil War the Western narrative is more dramatically centred in a specific historical moment. The effect, however, is that the mythology inherent in the Western – of the frontier experience, of the threats and opportunities found at the frontier – is authenticated and justified by History with a capital H. The Civil War lends a stronger flavour of historical fact to the mythology of the genre. A sense is given of 'this really happened', whether or not it actually did. So the lines of conflict, such as the Red/White racial opposition, are given a historical resonance that is more deeply felt than one may find in other Westerns.

If one were to design a simple diagram to represent the line of conflict during the Civil War, it would be made up of two main groups, the Union and the Confederacy, plotted on either side of a horizontal axis between North and South, giving the diagram a quasi-geographical structure. The reality of the war of course was considerably more complex than such a crude diagram could ever demonstrate, since no 'front line' officially existed and individuals from the North or South did not necessarily fight for their geographical side of the conflict. The diagram would, however, serve as a representation of the opposition between the United and the Confederate states. It also serves to represent the basic dynamic of a film about the Civil War, to which could be added other strands, such as character names. It would act as a visual representation of the binary opposition that the conflict suggests of North/South.

If the North/South opposition can be represented across a horizontal axis, the East/West opposition at the western frontier must necessarily exist across a vertical axis. Therefore, when the Civil War becomes a narrative element in the Western, new dimensions are given to the antinomy of Union/Confederate, or North/South. The characters in Westerns that include the war in their narratives are relocated from where the war rages (mostly in the East) to the frontier (in the West). The civil conflict itself is unavoidably transformed, and the dichotomies of North versus South and East versus West are crucially affected. The possible lines of conflict include, first and foremost, East versus West, usually characterised by White versus Red, but also Good Red versus Bad Red, Good White versus Bad White and even White American versus Central American, most notably Mexican. Most of these oppositions are linked by association with the first of the dichotomies, that of East/West.

The separate factions are now character groups separated by a line that henceforward associates the geographical axis with an axis of dramatic opposition, hero versus villain. According to the conventions both of the melodramatic mode and the Western genre, one group of characters will be coded within the particular film as the 'heroes'. The viewer of the film will be expected to sympathise with that group, and this viewer sympathy can also be indicated on the diagram.

The analysis that follows makes use of this structural approach to the Western. Rather than raising issues of historical authenticity, I am examining how the addition of the Civil War to the Western affects generic conventions. I will focus on four films that sit firmly within the Western genre: *Escape from Fort Bravo* (John Sturges, 1953), *How the West Was Won* (Henry Hathaway, John Ford, George Marshall, 1962), *The Undefeated* (Andrew V. McLaglen, 1969) and *Dances With Wolves* (Kevin Costner, 1990). Like the melodramas examined in Chapter 2, the films star popular actors such as William Holden, James Stewart, Gregory Peck, John Wayne and Kevin Costner, and are regularly broadcast on television. The films offer direct references to and/ or representations of the Civil War, and demonstrate ways in which the basic North/South line of conflict is altered by an interaction with the Western genre. What emerges from the study is a particular and enduring ideology of national identity that requires the narratives to disrupt the Civil War's line of conflict in favour of other oppositions. Also identified within this process is the creation of an altogether different Westerner from the character described by Robert Warshow.

GOOD WHITE VERSUS BAD RED: *ESCAPE FROM FORT BRAVO*

Escape from Fort Bravo presents itself as a eulogy to frontier life, to the white man and his horse. It is set at the mid-point of the war, 1863, in and around a prisoner-of-war camp holding Confederate prisoners in Arizona. The opening song and titles place the war far away in the East and praise the special relationship between the lone rider and his horse, kindred spirits in the wilderness. Although the film's characters have been separated from the war by sheer distance, the dichotomy of North and South is clear. The Union protagonist, Captain Roper (William Holden) rides through the desert, not alone as his Western counterpart would be, but dragging an escaped prisoner by a rope. The battlefields may lie many miles away, but the war has been brought way out West. Geographically speaking, the Civil War drained the far West of its regular military presence and, as this film goes on to enact, the pacification of the aggressive Native American was an unwelcome distraction from the national conflict.[23]

Through the course of the film Roper demonstrates certain differences from the Western hero. He has the knowledge of the harsh environment essential for survival, a characteristic of the usual Westerner, yet he also loves the wilderness and desires to settle. He even tends a garden of roses behind his hut. He is the labourer creating a small portion of paradise in the wilderness, cultivating a miniature, civilised America within the camp. Then, when he falls in love with the Southern sympathiser, Carla (Eleanor Parker), he refers to the 'completeness' that he yearns for with the land and a woman, underlined in the melodramatic mode by the *mise-en-scène*. Shots of Roper and Carla together are frequently framed by the mountains and hardy vegetation of the wilderness, offering a kind of portrait of their oneness with the land and their endurability. The beauty of the locations, shot mostly in Death Valley and the New Mexico mountains, certainly lends a sense of greatness, awe and perfection to the romantic pairing of Northern man and Southern woman. Although Roper is not initially aware of Carla's Confederate sympathies, the romance between them is the first sign of the film's disruption of the North/South line of conflict.

The North/South dichotomy in *Escape from Fort Bravo* is tested to its limits when Carla helps a group of prisoners to escape. The prisoners themselves put the war and the Southern cause aside, in favour of returning home. They divest themselves of their Confederate uniforms and become distinctly 'cowboy' in appearance. When Roper finally catches up with them, the original conflict is further removed by the direct threat of a new enemy – the Mascalero Indians. The line of conflict has moved from North/South to East/West, the threat of the Civil War being transposed to the threat of the uncivilised West and the savage war. The only values demonstrated by these new enemies are those of aggression and intimidation of the whites. Union captain and Confederate escapees then fight side-by-side, using tactics learned from the war to mutual benefit, sharing weapons and saving each others' lives.

The geographical nature of the lines of conflict in this film mean that a diagrammatic representation can be constructed (see Fig. 1). The diagram may seem to impose a distinctly schematic means of representing the film, but the dramatic oppositions encourage such an approach. The first line of conflict, between Union and Confederate factions, deriving from the Civil War, is plotted on the right of the diagram, since the primary battles of the war are fought in the East. This is then replaced, when the two groups join at the frontier in the West, by a second line of conflict, this time between the united Good Whites and the Bad Reds. Viewer sympathy changes during the

7. *Escape from Fort Bravo* (John Sturges, 1953): Roper is the Westerner who fights the shared enemy of both North and South.

course of the narrative, beginning with the Union protagonists and ending with the integrated white band, and is indicated with bold boxes in the diagram. In constructing these particular groups as protagonists, the film makes it clear which sets of values are deemed to be ideologically acceptable.

Figure 1: *Escape from Fort Bravo*

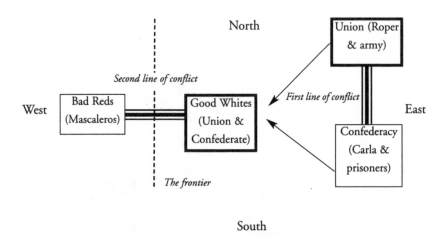

Note: The source of the first line of conflict is in the East between Union and Confederacy, who move westwards. The second line of conflict is in the West, between the Bad Reds and the Good Whites, across the line of the frontier. The bold boxes represent the groups in whom viewer sympathy is invested through point of view devices and structures.

The three concerns of the Western, of race, land and authority, are represented through the narrative in conventional ways. Race, clearly is a stark White/Red opposition that provides the impetus for the film's climax. Land is used as a device to separate the action from the war in the East and to frame the love affair of Roper and Carla. It is also essential to Roper's hopes to settle, signified by his rose garden. Authority is related to the dramatic action and message of the film. Roper is the keeper of the Confederate prisoners so his authority over them is linked to his status as a Northerner and is political in nature. This authority is laid down at the moment that North and South band together against their Red enemy.

Most of the reviews of *Fort Bravo* noted the narrative's progress away from concerns of war or romance towards the Indian conflict, or the East/West,

White/Red conflict. The *Monthly Film Bulletin*, for example, stated '[p]olitical and emotional conflicts are forgotten'.[24] The focus and appeal for most reviewers was the final battle and the remarkable tactics used by the Mascaleros in trapping the white band. So, despite the Civil War period setting, and despite the attention given to the romance, the ultimate line of conflict is racial, reaffirming the Western conventional conflict of Good White versus Bad Red. This foregrounds a hierarchical structure of conflicts, which changes over the course of the film. The new hierarchy is now headed by Good White versus Bad Red (to do with race), followed by Union versus Confederate (to do with authority). In the whites' winning of the ultimate conflict, with the arrival of a rescue party, the romantic tension and the North/South conflict are also fully resolved. It should be noted that the victory is partly down to Roper being a frontiersman as well as a soldier. He knows how to survive in the desert and how to fight his enemy as well as he knows how to command his new united troop. Both Civil War and Western conventions work together within him as a protagonist. Not only this, but he is also reunited with Carla, meaning that he is now free to indulge in the completeness with the land and the woman that he yearned for at the beginning of the narrative. As such, Roper seems to be very different from the Westerner described by Warshow, who required neither a useful occupation nor a woman.

AN INTERRUPTION IN THE WINNING OF THE WEST: *HOW THE WEST WAS WON*

How the West Was Won was hailed as a spectacular epic by *Variety* on its newsworthy release in 1962. The author described it as 'the blockbuster supreme, a magnificent and exciting spectacle'.[25] Whilst *Sight and Sound* called it 'a big, boisterous, fully stereophonic spectacle', the magazine's reviewer John Gillett went on to speculate that it was an example of 'the ultimate in Hollywood elephantiasis'.[26] Similarly, Bosley Crowther of the *New York Times* wondered if its title ought to have been changed to 'How the West Was Done – to Death'.[27] These reviewers reflect the fact that the film's fundamental appeal to audiences was less in its clichéd narrative than in its status as the first feature to be produced and exhibited using the three-strip Cinerama process.[28] The Cinerama camera was comprised of three cameras in one, each separated from the other by a forty-eight degree angle, the resultant filmstock being projected on a vast curved screen. Each of the three images came to form one truly widescreen image, with three vanishing points and often two vertical lines visibly dissecting the screen. Compositions of scenes were dictated by the need to disguise these lines. Sheldon Hall calls the film a 'Western of attractions',[29] aligning it to Tom Gunning's theory of early cinema as a 'cinema of attractions',[30] in which spectacle offers the dominant appeal over any consideration of narrative or characterisation. The Cinerama process was itself the attraction for audiences and this film was its showcase, not simply because of the star-billing, the spectacle of the Western *mise-en-scène* and the amazing stunts, but also because of the technology used in its production and exhibition.

The film was thus produced and received as an epic spectacle, but it was also made to be a definitive example of the Western. Reviewers admired and despised it in fairly equal measure with its reiteration of countless Western themes and elements. *Motion Picture Herald* praised its treatment of Western conventions, which made 'other tellings fade away',[31] and would, apparently, inspire all viewers to thoroughly appreciate the role played by the pioneers in 'building a great nation'. Crowther, on the other hand, stated: 'Don't look for any enlightenment as to the conquest of the American frontier', since the film only amounts to 'a mammoth patchwork of Western fiction clichés'.[32] Mark Shivas, in *Movie*, reminded film enthusiasts of the essential problem with the film: the contradiction at the heart of the myth of the winning of the West. He wrote, 'it celebrates an American contradiction – a longing for the simple life, idealizing the man of the soil, and at the same time the headlong rush of Progress'.[33] Somehow, the mythology of manifest destiny is used to justify the destruction and losses incurred by the steady march of civilisation and the establishment of the railroads. The contradiction is typical of the pre-revisionist Western, so it seems inevitable that a film on the scale of *How the West Was Won* is going to magnify this shortfall.

The film is made up of five separate acts or episodes following consecutive strands of the narrative, credited to three different directors: Henry Hathaway ('The Rivers', 'The Plains' and 'The Outlaws' episodes), John Ford ('The Civil War' episode) and George Marshall ('The Railroads' episode). The narrative follows the fortunes and misfortunes of the Prescott family across three generations, beginning in 1839 in the East as pioneers seeking a new life, and ending in the West with the crossing of the continent by railroad and the establishment of law and order in 1889. Throughout the time span of the narrative, the frontier is seen to move steadily westwards with each episode of the film. In noting this, the principal theme of the film can be clearly seen to concern land – one of the central issues concerning the Western genre.

Hall sees the episodic structure of the film as owing much to Turner's frontier thesis, which described westward expansion across the land as a series of phases in which those at the frontier regressed from a civilised state in order to survive, but were renewed and strengthened by the experience.[34] With each new phase, Hall explains, the characters face a new environment and a new narrative situation. Indeed, in the terms of my particular approach, the characters are facing new lines of conflict at each new phase. Instead of the starting point of the film being the Civil War and the North/South line of conflict, the film begins twenty-two years before the outbreak of war and the dichotomy starts out as East versus West (see Fig. 2).

Figure 2: *How the West Was Won* – episodes 1 & 2

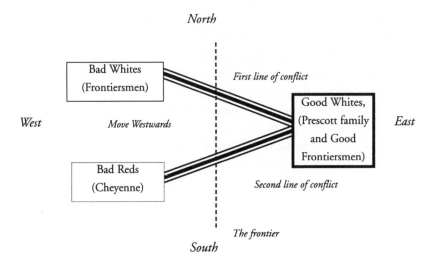

Note: The first line of conflict at the beginning of the film is between the Good Whites and Bad Whites, once the Prescotts have crossed the frontier from East to West. The second line of conflict follows in the film's second episode between the Good Whites and Bad Reds. Again, the bold box indicates the group that demands viewer sympathy.

It is a Western that is interrupted by the Civil War, and the North/South dichotomy does not emerge until the third act of the film. Up until then the family faces the harshness of frontier life, losing both parents to a raging river and meeting frontier traders, both good and bad. The family represents the American characteristic of progress and development through the experience of life at the frontier. Taking place before the war, this part of the film lays within the boundaries of expectation of the Western, except for its attention to the fate of a single family instead of an individual protagonist, a band of men or a small-town community. In this respect, *How the West Was Won* could be said to merge with the domestic melodrama, placing the fortunes of the family at the centre of the narrative events. In other respects however, Western conventions are fully expressed: the search for gold, the frontier town, the bad Indians (Cheyenne) and so on.

The Civil War comes as an interruption to the Prescotts' move westward (Fig. 3). Again, the frontier brings North and South together, but by a different means. Zeb (George Peppard), from the third generation of the Prescott family, joins up as a Union soldier. His initial experiences of war at Shiloh, the 'Western front' of the Civil War, are frightening and disorientating and he befriends a Confederate soldier, referred to only as 'Reb' (Russ Tamblyn), the primary link between the two men being their identity as Westerners (not to mention the similarity of their names helping to suggest that they are somehow akin to each other). In this sense, and in their mutual confusion in the face of war, the frontier has brought North and South together. Reb remarks to Zeb: 'This fool war started in the East, what's us Westerners doing in it?' and the young men plan to desert together. The issue of race does not emerge at all in this interaction of the two men. Racial concerns are restricted to White/Red oppositions in this film, not to any debate over slavery, despite the inclusion of a Civil War episode.

Figure 3: *How the West Was Won* – the Civil War episode

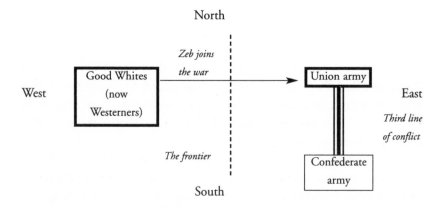

Note: Zeb travels back from the frontier to the East where the war is fought, being the film's third line of conflict, between North and South.

What Zeb and Reb share is an acute awareness of the East/West divide and they are temporarily blind to the North/South divide (as well as a permanent blindness to the black/white divide). However, the Westerners witness a discussion between two Union leaders – the only actual historical figures represented in the film – General William T. Sherman (John Wayne) and General Ulysses S. Grant (Harry Morgan). Reb plans to shoot them, but is killed by Zeb, taking a life for the first time in the name of the Union. A Westerner thus prevents the deaths of two future Union victors, one who will eventually become a president of the United States of America.

Several reviewers of the film remarked that the only episode that was imbued with a sense of believability and conscious regret was this section directed by John Ford. It does not carry with it the same sense of triumphalism as the other episodes. According to the *Monthly Film Bulletin*, 'the whole screen bursts with life and movement,' showing a kind of horrific beauty of warfare.[35] Gillett saw the success of the Civil War episode as due to Ford's skills in composition and imagery, stating 'immediately one feels that the giant screen has been conquered'.[36] Ford

8. *How the West Was Won* (Henry Hathaway, John Ford, George Marshall, 1962): The Westerner Zeb faces the brutality of war.

combines scenes of emotion and intimacy as young Zeb leaves for the war, with dark views of violence, despair and filth in the aftermath of one of the bloodiest battles of the conflict. Gillett even wondered if the Cinerama process might have met its full potential had Ford directed the whole film.

The episode gives a dark, authentic impression of war (despite the sentimentality of the scenes at Zeb's home), with the moans and cries of wounded men and the loss of faith in the aims of war. In a sense it seems dislocated from the rest of the film, thematically and visually, held in place only by the presence of Zeb. But by its inclusion in the film it reasserts the positive ideological message of progress. The Civil War is an interruption in the film's narrative, and is thus an interruption, an abhorrence, in the narrative of westward progress. After the episode, concentration can be re-located again to the principal narrative.

As the film progresses, the frontier continues to move westwards (Fig. 4). Zeb returns West to fight Indians and protect the frontier. Sobered by his experiences, he is now not only the man who knows Indians, but also the man who knows war. Although an earlier part of the film had placed White and Red firmly on opposing lines, the penultimate act of the film returns to the East/West dichotomy by introducing a conflict of Good Whites and Reds versus Bad Whites, with a battle between the railroads, claiming and destroying the free land of the Good Reds, the Arapahos. Zeb's mature war veteran has acquired certain values that reject corruption, commercialism and greed.

By the film's final 'Outlaw' episode, Zeb has settled, married and started a family. The line of conflict shifts once more in this episode, in which Zeb, now a US Marshal, fights and kills outlaw Charlie Gant (Eli Wallach), a Mexican bandit. One of the bedrock issues of the Western, that of authority, can now be explored. The dichotomy concerning authority is explored in terms of lawful/lawless, but Gant's ethnicity cannot go unnoticed. The line of conflict, although it concerns law and order, has been mapped onto race, and is represented as American/ Mexican. Authority and race have been inextricably woven together, by identifying the law-breaker as not American, almost as if Zeb's duty as a US Marshal is to keep America safely white. In the light of the Civil War episode, in which the tragedy of white disunity is explored, this movie works to reinforce a white national identity.

Figure 4: *How the West Was Won* – episodes 4 & 5

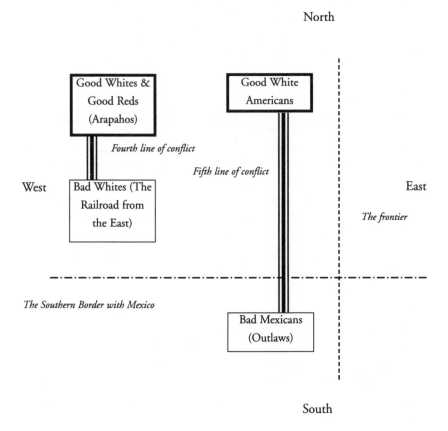

Note: *The film's fourth line of conflict is between Good Westerners, both White and Red, against Bad Whites from the East. The final conflict of the film is between American and Mexican, another racial clash.*

THE INTERRACIAL NATIONAL FAMILY IN
THE UNDEFEATED

The Undefeated begins as the Civil War ends in 1865. The opening scene presents a battle that takes place needlessly before news of the Confederate surrender has arrived. The 'undefeated' of the title are the Southern troops who refuse to lay down their cause, even remaining in uniform to express their steadfast faithfulness. So the conflict of North and South is in place as the film begins, but the two groups go on to be paralleled and mirrored within the ensuing narrative. A Union troop on the road home passes a Confederate troop marching in the opposite direction, each singing the battle song relevant to their particular sympathies. The two tunes battle for space on the soundtrack, but no fighting occurs, signifying that the armies have retained their allegiances, whilst turning away from armed combat.

Whereas *Escape from Fort Bravo* operates as a eulogy to man, horse and frontier life, *The Undefeated* grounds its sympathies with the community of Americans who love their country and identity, whose purposes – particularly for the Northerners – extend little further than beginning a new life after having seen the horrors of war. The main threats to this priority are the demands of the East and authority, requiring that the men play their part in the official Reconstruction of the nation. The Northerners of the narrative are expected to sell their herd of horses to the new United States; the Southerners are expected to remain in their home state, pay their debts and submit to official authority. The Western theme of authority is indirectly addressed in this way, for the purpose of spurring geographical movement of the central characters towards a new line of conflict. Additionally, with both groups in opposition to the Eastern government, an equal identification with North and South is required of the viewer.

The new community of North and South is represented by two groups of ex-soldiers, the Union troop led by Colonel Thomas (John Wayne) and the Confederate troop and families led by Colonel Langdon (Rock Hudson). The theme of authority is explored principally through these men, both protagonists, who are mirrored as community leaders. Both men care deeply for those in their charge, as father figures, and are respected and obeyed without question. Both are accomplished military men who have lost loved ones at the same battles. Both are stubborn, yet highly moral and honourable. Their poses and gestures are often mirrored in consecutive shots, such as Langdon lifting his sabre to attack a French soldier, immediately followed by Thomas brandishing his rifle. A shot towards the end of the film shows the two men riding side by side, left hand holding the horse's reins, right hand on hip. These twin images serve to create a link that creates a visual association between them, despite the difference of their political positions. It presents them as brothers, or equal father figures of the two small American communities.

The East/West dichotomy of the Western genre is displaced when it becomes clear that White and Red are working together to tame wild horses and defeat bandits. Northerner Thomas has an adopted Indian son, Blue Boy

(Roman Gabriel), who fought in Thomas's troop in the war and who later becomes the romantic partner of Langdon's Southern daughter. The North/South dichotomy is further displaced by the presence of enemies at the Southern border in the form of Mexicans. So, North, South *and* West are brought together because the war is over and because of the introduction of a new conflict. The Civil War is replaced by the Mexican revolution, 'somebody else's war' as Thomas remarks. In a sacrifice that characterises the new unity of North and South, Thomas surrenders his herd of horses in exchange for the lives of the Confederates, held by the revolutionaries (see Fig. 5), the new savages. The Mexican revolutionaries represent a dishonourable rebelliousness, unlike the highly moral and honourable Confederate community. They are seen to be deceitful and unethical in the waging of their war, interested only in how to promote their own cause. The Union men and Confederate community, however, are prepared to lay their differing causes aside to protect or save one another, thus creating a distinct racial opposition between Americans and Mexicans.

Noel Carroll's study of the professional Western is helpful here. The professional Western is a sub-strand of the genre, in which its central characters are paid, professional gunfighters working in a team 'South of the border'. An example would be Sam Peckinpah's *The Wild Bunch* (1969), released in the same year as *The Undefeated.* Carroll proposes that when the narrative moves into Mexico a national boundary has been crossed, and so an ideological viewpoint is taken by the narrative concerning international relations.[37] This is helpful in looking at the dichotomy of American versus Mexican and the values mapped onto it. The Americans are the central, white protagonists who are prepared to unite in the face of threat. The Mexicans are 'not-white', and are coded as deceitful, bloodthirsty guerrillas. Like the 'Outlaw' episode of *How the West Was Won*, race and land are inextricably linked to create a racial ideology of American national identity, forcing the viewer to identify with the Good Americans.

Once reunited and on their way home, North and South go on to exchange partners – for example, Thomas pairs off with a Southern widow – and a new all-American community is created, with echoes of the nation/family metaphor of the Civil War melodramas of Chapter 2. What has been at stake is the lesson of how to live together and let go of the previous conflict. What the ex-soldiers are able to do by the end of the film is forge a union without the aid of political or economic Reconstruction, by the laying aside of their previous conflict and aligning their values. This union is signalled at the end of the film by the new romantic pairings and the

Figure 5: *The Undefeated*

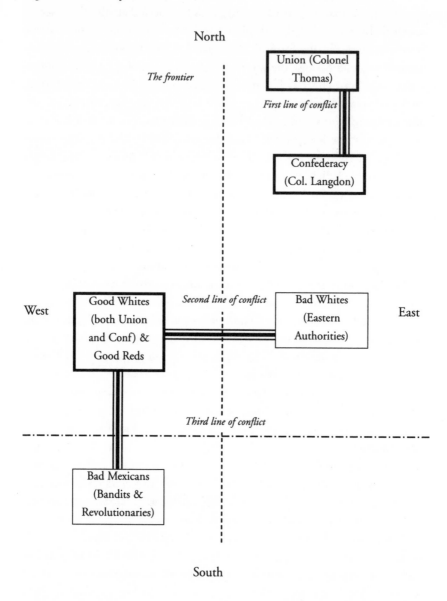

North

The frontier

Union (Colonel
Thomas)

First line of conflict

Confederacy
(Col. Langdon)

West

Good Whites
(both Union
and Conf) &
Good Reds

Second line of conflict

Bad Whites
(Eastern
Authorities)

East

Third line of conflict

Bad Mexicans
(Bandits &
Revolutionaries)

South

Note: The film's first line of conflict is between North and South, both of whom require equal audience identification. Beyond the frontier they join with the Good Reds in conflict with the Bad Whites from the East, and finally face a third line of conflict South of the border.

9. *The Undefeated* (Andrew V. McLaglen, 1969): The Southern women stop the brawl on 4th July, endorsed by the Confederate flag.

playing of 'Yankee Doodle' on a mouth organ, shunning any renditions of 'Glory Hallelujah' or 'Dixie'.

A strong current of comedy runs through much of *The Undefeated*, particularly in the comic tensions created between Northerners and Southerners. When the two bands of people meet in Arizona, the Southerners invite Thomas and his men to a July 4th celebration. At this impromptu party a wrestling challenge escalates into a brawl, North versus South, involving all but the women and children. The impression of the North/South conflict here is one of good, healthy fun and the war itself is trivialised in its transformation into comic form. The *Monthly Film Bulletin* recorded, 'There's no difficulty that can't be ironed out by a good fight and plenty of liquor'.[38] The result is that the only real tension of the film exists in the American/Mexican conflict in the melodramatic mode. This is one more way in which the film removes the line of conflict from North/South to another focus – in this case, American/Mexican. The one American character who has *not* fought in the war, Mudlow (played by Big John Hamilton), because of the fear of being 'shot at', is branded a coward by North and South alike. Because he did not participate honourably for his 'nation' he has lost the right to be accepted within the new reunited America. The fact that this character is a Southerner indicates subtle but material evidence for the pro-North leaning of the film.

One glance at my diagram for this film (Fig. 5) shows that both North and South (the Good Whites) and Indians (the Good Reds) are crossing another frontier, in the form of the Southern border, which is where they become involved in the Mexican revolution. The racial conflict of Red and White, therefore, has been displaced to another expression of racism. Instead of engaging in warfare, however, they do whatever is necessary to survive and to return to the United States and begin their new American community. As with the vast majority of War-Westerns, black faces are hardly seen. Any kind of black/white dichotomy is ignored, despite this film being produced well into the course of the Civil Rights Movement in the USA. The opening scenes of the film show glimpses of freed slaves leaving the plantations of the South, but this is all, apart from Roman Gabriel as Blue Boy. Gabriel was at that time one of the nation's favourite American footballers for the LA Rams and was from a Filipino immigrant family. The choice of a national sporting hero is an interesting one, made even more intriguing in that he is not white. Cripps mentions that the new post-second World War racial sensibilities allowed for this casting of non-white American heroes.[39] Blue Boy is a device in *The Undefeated* to demonstrate acceptance of Native Americans as American citizens. The choice has been made in the narrative to ignore the black/white issues of the day, and another choice has been made (in the casting) to represent a Native American by a second-generation immigrant. But both African American and Native American actors are denied central roles. So the magnanimous inclusion of Native Americans in the new united community at the film's conclusion disguises a continuing covert racism.

In the narrative, the first stage of Blue Boy's adoption is his participation in the Civil War as part of the Union troop led by Thomas. It is more firmly emphasised when his own 'uncivilised' Indian culture is deemed unacceptable in the new community, and he is finally seen riding by his Southern sweetheart with his hair cut short – civilised. Since the bonds of nationhood are made manifest in (amongst other things) its customs,[40] Blue Boy's acceptance of the male white American custom of wearing short hair signifies his full adoption into the national family.

THE RE-BORN WAR-WESTERNER: *DANCES WITH WOLVES*

The increasing visual complexity that can be observed in the diagrams so far reflects the introduction of new, diverse conflicts within the narratives and the flow of viewer identification as the protagonists encounter new enemies. In each case, the divisions of North and South are being marginalised or resolved for the sake of the survival of the protagonists and their identity as members of a new united American community. The tendency is repeated in many other War-Westerns, including *The Last Outpost* (Lewis R. Foster,

1951) and *Major Dundee* (Sam Peckinpah, 1965) in which Union and Confederate forces team together against a 'non-American' enemy either at the western frontier or the Southern border. Numerous post-Civil War Westerns follow a similar vein, such as John Ford's cavalry Westerns that placed veterans from both sides of the war side-by-side against the savage Indians. Despite the presences of Bad Whites, these films demonstrate a distinct ideology, one that upholds the expansion and nationalism of a predominantly white United States of America. This ideology is threatened directly in *Dances With Wolves*.

Dances With Wolves operates as a kind of movie-apologetic, trying to set the story straight about the injustices of westward expansion in the nineteenth century, particularly the systematic destruction of Native American communities and culture. It is compared, quite rightly, to films such as *Little Big Man* (Arthur Penn, 1970) by Margo Kasdan and Susan Tavernetti (1998), in its story of a white man who reinscribes himself as Native American, leaving behind his former identity, constructing what they describe as an 'initiation archetype'.[41] Great efforts were made in *Dances With Wolves* to produce an authentic and historically accurate version of frontier life and the treatment of the Indian nations. The film, like the original novel by Michael Blake, is occasionally given a documentary feel with the inclusion of excerpts from the central character's journal. It allies the film with the documentary series broadcast in the United States in the same year, Ken Burns' *The Civil War*, which was predominantly composed of photographs and voice-overs of letters and diaries. The decision to include a voice-over in *Dances With Wolves*, offering extracts of a fictional diary, thus adds a suggestion of truthfulness to the narrative, as if 'this really happened'.

The Civil War is only seen for a fraction of the film's running time but it has vital importance as a starting point for the narrative and influence over the central protagonist. Beginning in 1863, mid-war, Union Lieutenant John J. Dunbar (Kevin Costner) is seen on the surgeon's table in a bloody and dirty field hospital. Escaping the prospect of amputation of his leg and in suicidal despair, he rides up and down in front of the Confederate line, arms spread in a Christ-like pose, asking God to forgive him, suggesting 'overtones of resurrection'.[42] War is being represented as something to do with pain, blood and madness, a far cry from the light-hearted brawl of *The Undefeated*.

When Dunbar receives his posting to the frontier, at his own request, the Union officer he meets also seems to be suffering from a kind of madness. Major Fambrough (Maury Chaykin) has lost respect for military authority; he has forgotten decorum and even urinates on himself. As Dunbar leaves the

10. *Dances With Wolves* (Kevin Costner, 1990): Dunbar's suicide ride ends with admiration from the General.

fort, Fambrough commits suicide. This is an important point of the film. It is doubtful that the war has been the cause of this officer's madness. It is more likely that his proximity to the frontier has affected him to such an extent that he has lost any hold on civilised life and mental stability. Indeed, Blake's novel confirms that Fambrough's isolation has caused him to become 'delusional and quietly deranged'.[43] Whether war or frontier though, this suicide has a structural and a genre-specific significance. All that has occurred up to this point has concerned the Civil War and the conflict of North and South. From this point onwards, generically, the film becomes a Western, and for Dunbar the war is over. Despite this shift, however, the war remains a vital factor in Dunbar's choices as he travels to the isolated Fort Sedgwick.

The film is revisionist in that it rejects classical Western paradigms of White hero and Red villain and it tries to present itself as the Western 're-born', just as Dunbar is 're-born' after his suicide attempt. The revisionist form, however, is nothing new to the genre. Many reviews and articles have pointed to notable precursors offering a sympathetic approach to the Indian and his way of life: *Broken Arrow* (Delmer Daves, 1950), *Devil's Doorway* (Anthony Mann, 1950), *Little Big Man* and *A Man Called Horse* (Elliot Silverstein, 1971) amongst others.[44] But what is interesting about the opening scenes of the film is that Dunbar faces the beginning of a new life, whilst Fambrough faces only death, and both are brought about by the presence of the frontier.

Dunbar has a number of similarities to the other protagonists studied. He demonstrates a certain oneness with nature, with his horse, and with the wolf he befriends, despite a dangerous naïvety. But his desire is to *be there*. His wish is to see the frontier before it is gone (the frontier was not to be declared officially closed for another thirty years). Thus the theme of land is vital to the dramatic oppositions of the film. It is not only used to create a 'frontier-ness' in keeping with the Western genre, but it is also central to the Eastern treatment of the Indian nations and the film's particular inflection of the East/West dichotomy.

Dunbar's Sioux counterpart, Kicking Bird (Graham Greene) shares his love of the land and of nature, and this link between them is signalled by the parallel movements by each character, brushing their fingers over the tips of grass. Both men belong at the frontier, unlike the previous inhabitants of Dunbar's deserted post at Fort Sedgwick. The reason for their departure was cut from the released film, but replaced by the ABC television network broadcast of the film in 1993 and in subsequent special edition DVDs. The men were isolated and forgotten at this most remote of frontier outposts, subjected to Sioux raids of their supplies and horses. Michael Walker's article about the film suggests 'like the American soldiers in Vietnam, they simply do not belong there'[45] – an example of the parallel of the frontier experience to the war in Vietnam.

Dunbar leaves behind the North/South conflict and at the frontier must learn to survive the threats of environment and of Indians. He is successful in both respects and the East/West divide is crossed by his initiation into the Sioux tribe, the Good Indians. As their ally, the Sioux' enemies become his enemies and he becomes involved in the line of intra-racial conflict between Good Red and Bad Red (Pawnee) (see Fig. 6). Dunbar's war experience contributes towards his support of the Sioux, even donating Union weapons for the battle against the Pawnee. So, Dunbar has travelled through and beyond a number of lines of conflict. North and South have been forgotten; East and West have been overcome by his adoption into the Sioux and his marriage to Stands With a Fist (Mary McDonnell) and he has become part of the Good Red/Bad Red line of conflict.

However, the East/West divide is only resolved between Dunbar and the Sioux; it still exists on a national scale. The issue of authority over Dunbar is raised by the arrival of the Union army at his deserted post, bringing a reminder of Dunbar's duty as a Union soldier with it, the irony being that his original fellow soldiers have become his enemies. The protagonist has swapped allegiances, not from North to South, but from East to West, and goes on to fight against his own kind. This is how *Dances With Wolves* serves to disrupt the ideology of westward expansion and progress. Dunbar no longer submits to the authority of his occupation (as a soldier), and hence rejects the authority of his race. The veteran who fought almost to the death to defend the Union now fights for survival against that Union. If this transferral of loyalties in Dunbar is viewed on a national scale, his choice can be understood as a direct challenge to the Union's purpose in the war, to make a nation. He is, in effect, denying the part that the West plays in that making, wanting to keep the wilderness unsullied by the new emergent nation in the East. Alternatively, given the film's overall plea to understand Native American races *as* truly American, Dunbar's choices could reflect a desire to exclude the violence of the war and the frontier fort from an ideal America. Seen in this way, the true American nation is the West.

Figure 6: *Dances With Wolves*

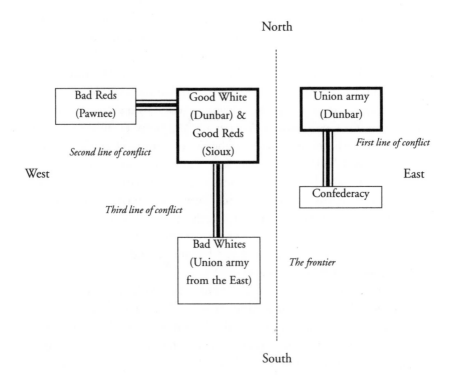

Note: The first line of conflict is, again, in the East during the Civil War. Dunbar moves westwards and joins with the Good Reds against the Bad Reds. The final line of conflict is against Dunbar's Eastern compatriots.

The construction of the war hero as a man who 'goes Indian' raises important issues of identity. Dunbar turns his back on the war, he travels to the frontier and through certain experiences rejects his previous identity. He gradually sheds the signifiers of his past life, mostly through changes of costume, only to add to his person signifiers of the new life, indicating the process that is happening within. This happens at stages in *Dances With Wolves* – Dunbar continues to wear his uniform and display the Union flag when he is at the frontier as a declaration of his particular form of American-ness: white, Eastern, military. He gradually loses these accoutrements in exchange for Sioux accessories and costume, together with his acquisition of the tribe's language. His telescope loses its purpose as a means to survey an enemy, and is put to use instead during the tribe's buffalo hunt. By the time the transformation is over he is no longer John J. Dunbar, Union officer, but – as Chief Ten Bears (Floyd Red Crow Westerman) tells him – he is a Sioux tribesman called Dances With Wolves.

The film is as much about discovering one's identity as it is about the effects of westward expansion on the Indian nations. Recalling John Belton's comment, that the West is 'a site for the telling of the *story* of American identity',[46] *Dances With Wolves* tells the story of how one man discovers his true American self, or even the true American self, and this has been his quest since surviving the Civil War – the finding of the authentic American national identity. The Native American is given the admirable qualities that in so many Westerns belonged to the white man: a sense of justice, the closeness of the community, intelligence and wit. Dunbar even compares the tribe's collective movement during the buffalo hunt to that of an army, with its swiftness and organisational prowess. Each of these qualities are positive attributes for the American to admire within himself, as if they represent some kind of American-ness. For Dunbar, the realisation of these qualities in himself is made possible because of the Civil War and is aided *by* the Civil War. Dunbar's miraculous 'resurrection' on the battlefield paves the way for this physical and spiritual journey of discovery. The war opens the door for the telling of the story.

Dances With Wolves demonstrates a shift in the casting strategies and attitudes of Hollywood if compared to *The Undefeated*. Indian roles are exclusively played by Native Americans, including the central character Kicking Bird, but Dunbar's romantic partner, Stands With a Fist, is a white woman (played by white actress Mary McDonnell) adopted from childhood into the tribe. She has made the complete change of identity to Sioux woman, yet in her liaisons with Dunbar she re-embraces aspects of her past by remembering the English language and eventually marrying the white man. Miscegenation is avoided, making the film less revisionist than, for example, *Little Big Man*, twenty years earlier, which paired its central protagonist with an Indian woman in the narrative. And whereas *The Undefeated* presented a national family as White and (civilised) Red, *Dances With Wolves* keeps the two races separate despite its desire to recast the true American as the Indian.

Dances With Wolves can perhaps be contrasted most clearly to *How the West Was Won*, which overtly celebrates the winning of the West, whilst blatantly silencing the voices of those who lost it.[47] *How the West Was Won* incorporates a partial apology in the railroad episode of the film, but the Native American point of view itself is neglected. Both films use the westward movement of the frontier as an impetus for the narrative, although one sees it as progress, the other sees it as the loss of a vanishing West. Both also keep the racial divide clear between white and not-white, although *Dances With Wolves* is undoubtedly a celebration of a morally acceptable Native American culture.

THEMES AND MEANINGS IN CIVIL WAR WESTERNS

Despite the obvious ideological shift, *Dances With Wolves* conforms to other traits discovered in the films of this study. The Civil War soldier inhabits the frontier region, he desires to be there, he respects and/or understands the environment and the Native American, and at the frontier he finds the woman who makes his life complete. In the process, he is relocated from the North/South line of conflict to one or more other lines of conflict, linked conceptually to the East/West dichotomy. As with the other films mentioned here, *Dances With Wolves* reveals the two main changes that the Civil War brings to the Western: a displacement of the line of conflict explored by the narrative, and the presence of a different kind of Western hero from the lone cowboy or gunman that the genre tends to idolise.

No North, No South

The two dichotomies of East/West and White/Red exist in the Western genre almost universally. The close relationship between the two (one to do with geography or land, the other with race) is due to the narrative requirement to embody oppositions between characters and is manifested through opposing values and behaviours. However, especially with the emergence of the revisionist Western from the 1950s onwards, other lines of conflict apart from White/Red become increasingly evident. As has been observed above, the Indian tribes are not seen as a homogeneous, villainous mass, but are divided into Good Red and Bad Red. The value conflict inherent in this dichotomy is sometimes along the lines of pacifism versus single-minded aggression. White characters meeting this kind of conflict are expected to side with and help the Good Indians, and play their part in resisting and defeating the Bad Indians, as does Dunbar in *Dances With Wolves*. Additionally, the white antagonist – maybe an Eastern soldier or capitalist – will often oppose all Indian forces, whether good or bad, as with the powerful railroad manager, King (Richard Widmark) in *How the West Was Won*.

As can be found in the Westerns studied in this chapter, when this basic narrative structure includes the Civil War, the protagonist will be seen to leave the Civil War behind, only to find himself involved in somebody else's 'Civil War', usually a land or an interracial disagreement. The East/West divide is still present in the Good White/Bad White scenario, but the values associated with the two sections have swapped sides. It is a common reversal associated with the revisionist Western. Finally, the line of conflict faced by the War-Westerner may move southwards to the border with Mexico, which although not strictly the western frontier, has still been the focus of a certain sub-strand of the genre. The war hero, whether Union or Confederate, finds himself again mixed up in somebody else's war – possibly becoming caught up in the revolution against Emperor Maximillian, as in *The Undefeated*. Additionally, allegiances amongst the protagonists may be challenged to the point of being rejected – as in the putting aside of the North/South conflict in the face of other priorities and other enemies. Basinger's description of this narrative shift is summarised as '[i]nstead of us against us, it was us against them [...]'.[48] The war must be put aside in order for the Westerner to become engaged in the 'savage war'. Despite the character's change of values, viewer sympathy continues to be drawn towards him, with those values reflecting ideologies of American honour, unity and supremacy. As in the Civil War melodramas of Chapter 2, a relationship is thus created between the American historical character, with his transformed ideology, and the viewer.

There is, however, another significant reason for the shifting lines of conflict found in the War-Western, and again it relates closely to discoveries made in the last chapter about the domestic melodrama. The missing villain was found to be an essential component of the ideology of unity. In order for the American film viewer to identify with the ancestors portrayed in the films, the characters had to be blameless. In that way the protagonist, whether Northern or Southern, could be considered part of the historical American family. In the War-Western the same is true. The North/South line of conflict cannot be seen to endure because in the new united nation there can be no North or South, only America. Thus the film viewer is not presented with Warshow's Westerner, but instead with a predecessor who represents a real, historical American figure, in the form of the 'War-Westerner'.

The War-Westerner

As mentioned above, the Western hero at the frontier is faced with a harsh environment and an enemy – one who may be either White or Red. So what is at stake, first and foremost, is his survival. His mettle will be proven by the test of the environment and the enemy. However, when this Western convention interacts with the Civil War there is more at stake than bravery and resourcefulness. The hero is also required to defend his own, distinctly military, values. His reason for being at the frontier will be directly related to his duty as a soldier or to his experience of the war. He may, for example, be in charge of a prison camp surrounded by miles of wilderness and desert, as in *Escape from Fort Bravo* or *Two Flags West* (Robert Wise, 1950). Alternatively he may be trying somehow to leave the war behind to begin a new life, as in *Dances With Wolves*.

What seems to be true of most of the protagonists in this type of film is that he wants to be there, he has a deep-seated desire to live in the West. The frontier is his home. Like the classic Western protagonist, he displays evidence of a oneness with nature and a respect for the environment. He has a healthy but wary respect for the Native American; he is the 'man who knows Indians'. He is also the man who knows war, and the lessons of mortality learned through warfare inspire a desire, perhaps unconsciously held, to find a woman and start a family. Unlike Warshow's Westerner, the War-Westerner *does* need the love of a woman, and he may even actively pursue it. In keeping with the ideology of national unity, his partner is often his political enemy, and their union further represents the displacement of the North/South line of conflict. With their joining by the end of the narrative, they become the parents who will birth the new nation. It is a powerful illustration of the need for an alignment of values at a national level, and may suggest that the production of Civil War Westerns plays a part in encouraging American nationalism in the face of exterior threats, such as socialism, communism and so-called 'non-democratic' powers.

CONCLUSION

What runs through each of the differences that I have outlined between the Western and the War-Western is the central fact that because of the frontier the Civil War has to be put aside in order to preserve national unity. Yet, no matter how much the original conflict is marginalised, its effects remain evident. The four films studied in this chapter each demonstrate this vital effect. If the West is the site for telling the story of American identity, the Civil War is a means of opening the door to that story, it informs the story. It breathes historical specificity into the Western narrative, lending it a higher degree of authenticity. More importantly, however, the Civil War brings with it messages about American national identity. Returning to Shelby Foote's comment cited in the introductory chapter, the Civil War both defined Americans and opened them up to a new future. The line of conflict between North and South was officially dissolved and unification began. Despite all the complexities of opposing war aims and reasons for the conflict, what emerged was a politically unified nation – albeit perhaps the myth of a politically unified nation. Civil War films shape the conflict as the start of this process, the moment of the birth of the nation. The identity of this new nation, however, in the War-Western, has one dominant characteristic – it is almost always white. Thomas Cripps sees the common device of the Civil War introduction at the beginning of so many Westerns as a means to 'portray the sectional disunity out of the ashes of which eventual national unity must arise'.[49] The community that represents this new birth is the united white group. As Cripps describes it, the union of Northern and Southern sections out West gives rise to 'an intersectional, white lovefeast' in which troublesome issues of race and racism against the black race can be ignored.[50]

The 'intersectional, white lovefeast' that Cripps identifies is an ideological means of further strengthening the bond of ancestry between character and film viewer. Its purpose, however, does not stop there; it is also a pragmatic choice on behalf of the filmmaker. Depending on the production context of the narrative, either the White/Red or the American/Mexican line of conflict is acceptable to its audience in the formulation of American identity. The line of conflict cannot be coded as White/Black. Such an opposition could be detrimental to the popularity of the film for one important reason. Cripps notes that following the furore at the release of *The Birth of a Nation* (D.W. Griffith, 1915) Hollywood learned an important lesson: 'never again to lecture its audience on historical racial politics'.[51] Occasionally race is a focal narrative theme, in films such as *Buffalo Soldiers* (Charles Haid, 1997), but this is a post-war Western, charting the trials of black Civil War veterans in the West. Instead of carefully avoiding a White/Black opposition for ethical reasons then, the absence of the black race from the War-Western is a conscious tactic to discourage controversy.

An enemy, however, is part of what the Western genre demands of its narratives, and since the making of national unity requires the resolution of the North/South conflict, the enemy must be found elsewhere. In order to emphasise the sense of self or identity, there must be an 'other', the enemy, against which the self can be defined, hence the establishment of new lines of conflict in the films. The consequence is that the enemies at the frontier are constructed as opposites in racial qualities and/or moral values, in other words anti-Americans. What is achieved by this process is the assurance that through unity, the nation can resist all external threat.

In each case, the individual is defined by the Civil War, as Foote's comment suggests, and he is redefined by the Western. The definition of the American is transformed with his relocation to the frontier, by describing what he is, as well as what he is not. In this sense then, the story of American identity, which is the task of the Western genre, is made even more overt and self-conscious by the addition of the Civil War. It could then be said that the Civil War Western succeeds in the telling of this story to an even greater degree, making it perhaps the most Western of Westerns. The story becomes a lesson about the making of a historical American family, with the War-Westerner as the film viewer's ancestor.

Finally, it seems that twenty-first-century sensibilities are asking too much of the Western to expect the representation of a holistic, multi-ethnic American national identity. From a historical perspective, this may not even be a realistic hope, since the America of the late-nineteenth century was indeed a white nation in terms of social and political power. The colour of American national identity was, for the most part, white, despite the presence of countless ethnic populations across the nation. But the Western genre goes further to practically ignore the black story; examples of Westerns that do pay it attention are still extremely rare. So, the genre that has consistently been regarded as characteristic of American cinema has created an image of national identity that excludes a significant portion of the population. The addition of the Civil War to the genre, despite being the event that placed racial injustices centre stage, does little if anything to challenge this tendency in the Western. This is a clear example of genre and ideology working hand in hand to reflect back to the nation an acceptable image of itself. It requires steps into another genre, the combat film, to see the relationship between white and black being explored, but even then, the picture that is painted is too often predisposed to a white American national identity.

NOTES

1   Review of *Escape from Fort Bravo* (John Sturges, 1953) *Kinematograph Weekly* 'Fort Bravo', vol. 444, no. 2436, 4 March 1954, p. 23.
2   Douglas Pye's description of Anthony Mann's Westerns: Pye, Douglas, 'Genre and History: *Fort Apache* and *The Man Who Shot Liberty Valance*' in I. Cameron and D. Pye (eds) *The Movie Book of the Western* (London, 1996). p. 173.
3   Neale, Steve, *Genre and Hollywood* (London, 2000). pp. 133–4.
4   Neale: *Genre and Hollywood*. p. 142.
5   Explored in Neale: *Genre and Hollywood*.
6   Warshow, Robert, (1954) 'Movie Chronicle: The Westerner' in J. Kitses and G. Rickman (eds) *The Western Reader* (New York, 1998). p. 37.
7   For example, see Kitses, Jim, *Horizons West* (London, 1969); Belton, John, *American Cinema/American Culture* (New York, 1994).
8   Kitses: *Horizons West*. p. 11.
9   Wright, Will, *Sixguns and Society: A Structural Study of the Western* (Berkeley and Los Angeles, 1977).
10   Turner, Frederick Jackson, (1893) 'The Significance of the Frontier in American History' in G.R. Taylor (ed.) *The Turner Thesis: Concerning the Role of the Frontier in American History* (Lexington, Mass, 1972). p. 28.
11   Saunders, John, *The Western Genre: From Lordsburg to Big Whiskey* (London, 2001). p. 6.
12   Slotkin, Richard, *Gunfighter Nation: The Myth of the Frontier in Twentieth-Century America* (New York, 1992). p. 4.
13   Tulloch, Hugh, *The Debate on the American Civil War Era* (Manchester and New York, 1999). p. 118.
14   Slotkin: *Gunfighter Nation*. p. 11.
15   Slotkin: *Gunfighter Nation*. p. 16.
16   Warshow: 'Movie Chronicle: The Westerner'. p. 39.
17   Warshow: 'Movie Chronicle: The Westerner'. pp. 36–7.
18   Pye: 'Genre and History'. p. 111.
19   Pye: 'Genre and History'. pp. 111–12.

20   Cripps, Thomas, 'The Absent Presence in American Civil War Films', *Historical Journal of Film, Radio and Television*, vol. 14, no. 4 (1994). p. 369.

21   Buscombe, Edward and Pearson, Roberta, (eds) *Back in the Saddle Again: New Essays on the Western* (London, 1998). p. 6.

22   Belton: *American Cinema/American Culture*. p. 208.

23   Cook, Robert, *Civil War America: Making a Nation, 1848–1877* (Harlow, 2003). pp. 281–2.

24   *Monthly Film Bulletin* 'Escape from Fort Bravo', vol. 21, no. 243 (April, 1954). p. 52.

25   *Variety* 'How the West Was Won' (7 November 1962).

26   Gillett, John, 'How the West Was Won', *Sight and Sound*, vol. 32, no. 1 (Winter 1962/1963). p. 41.

27   Crowther, Bosley, 'How the West Was Won', *New York Times* (1 April 1963). p. 54.

28   Hall, Sheldon, 'How the West Was Won: History, Spectacle and the American Mountains' in I. Cameron and D. Pye (eds) *The Movie Book of the Western* (London, 1996). p. 257.

29   Hall: 'How the West Was Won'. p. 258.

30   Gunning, Tom, (1989) 'The Cinema of Attractions: Early Film, its Spectator and the Avant Garde' in T. Elsaesser and A. Barker (eds) *Early Cinema: Space, Frame, Narrative* (London, 1990). pp. 56–62.

31   *Motion Picture Herald* 'How the West Was Won', vol. 228, no. 11 (28 November 1962). p. 700.

32   Crowther: 'How the West Was Won'. p. 54.

33   Shivas, Mark, 'How the West Was Won', *Movie*, no. 6 (January, 1963). p. 28.

34   Hall: 'How the West Was Won'. p. 259; Turner: 'The Significance of the Frontier in American History'. p. 4.

35   *Monthly Film Bulletin* 'How the West Was Won', vol. 29, no. 347 (December, 1962). p. 167.

36   Gillett: 'How the West Was Won'. p. 41.

37   Carroll, Noel, 'The Professional Western: South of the Border' in E. Buscombe and R. Pearson (eds) *Back in the Saddle Again* (London, 1998). p. 60.

38   *Monthly Film Bulletin* 'The Undefeated', vol. 36, no. 430 (November, 1969) p. 237.

39   Cripps: 'The Absent Presence in American Civil War Films'. pp. 372–3.

40   Smith, Anthony D., *National Identity* (London, 1991). p. 76.

41   Kasdan, Margo and Tavernetti, Susan, 'Native Americans in a Revisionist Western: *Little Big Man* (1970)' in P.C. Rollins and J.E. O'Connor *Hollywood's Indian: The Portrayal of the Native American in Film* (Lexington, Kentucky, 1998). p. 126.

42   Walker, Michael, 'Dances With Wolves' in I. Cameron and D. Pye (eds) *The Movie Book of the Western* (London, 1996). p. 286.

43   Blake cited in Costner, Kevin, Blake, Michael and Wilson, Jim, *Dances With Wolves: The Illustrated Story of the Epic Film* (New York, 1990). pp. 10–12.

44   See Prats, Armando José, 'The Image of the Other and the Other *Dances With Wolves*: The Refigured Indian and the Textual Supplement', *Journal of Film and Video*, vol. 50, no. 1 (1998). pp. 3–19; Georgakas, Dan, '*Dances With Wolves*', *Cineaste*, vol. 18, no. 2 (1991). pp. 51–3; Ostwalt, Conrad, '*Dances With Wolves*: An American *Heart of Darkness*', *Literature Film Quarterly*, vol. 24, no. 2 (1996). pp. 209–16; Baird, Robert, '"Going Indian" Through *Dances With Wolves*', *Film and History*, vol. 23, nos 1–4 (1993). pp. 91–102.

45   Walker: '*Dances With Wolves*'. p. 285.

46   Belton: *American Cinema/American Culture*. p. 208.

47   A point also made by Hall: '*How the West Was Won*'. p. 260.

48   Basinger, Jeanine, *The World War II Combat Film: Anatomy of a Genre* (Middletown, 2003). p. 239.

49   Cripps: 'The Absent Presence in American Civil War Films'. p. 369.

50   Cripps: 'The Absent Presence in American Civil War Films'. p. 372.

51   Cripps: 'The Absent Presence in American Civil War Films'. p. 373.

4

Civil War Combat Films: Masculine American Ancestry

Chapters 2 and 3 looked at the ideological imperatives and meanings of two genres that are the most common forms of Civil War film, the domestic melodrama and the Western. Both genres display similar ideologies of American national identity revolving around an imagined relationship between film viewer and characters. In the case of the domestic melodramas, this relationship places the viewer as part of an imagined historical American family tree that reaches back to the time of the war. What is at stake for that family is its survival and its blamelessness, made evident by the family's metaphorical association with the nation itself during and after the war. In this relationship between past and present, creating an ancestral link across time, there can be no one section (North or South) identifiable as villain, since an enemy can only possibly be construed as an enemy within the nation, which is detrimental to Civil War mythology.

Similarly, the War-Western constructs its protagonists as American ancestors, the united (mostly) white group that takes its strength from its solidarity against a common enemy. The white group's metaphorical association is, like the family in the domestic melodrama, with the nation, empowered by the joining together of previous enemies. The united group faces new lines of conflict that, unlike the Civil War melodramas, demand the presence of an enemy, who is necessarily external to the heroic group. Even if American in origin, this enemy is not only marginalised but also excluded from American ancestry. The united group then looks forward to a bountiful, productive future by virtue of the protagonist's romantic pairing with a woman in the West. So both genres display the ideological mission to re-present to the American viewer a blameless, brave and invincible American ancestor.

The third most common film genre in which the Civil War can be found is the war film, or to be more specific, the combat film. Despite Jeanine Basinger's claim that '[t]he combat of the Civil War is actually seldom depicted on the sound screen',[1] a comment that literally speaking is true, there are several very significant films in this category, and more continue to be made. It makes sense now to question how Civil War battles themselves have been represented in film, as well as the individuals who fight those battles. As with the other two genres, the combat film needs to be examined in terms of its broad ideological project, and how it is affected by an interaction with the Civil War. It should also be asked whether the relationship between the combat film and the Civil War displays similar ideological tendencies to the genres previously discussed.

As with most film genres, the war genre is difficult to define conclusively, having typically blurred boundaries that cross over with several other genres. Many war films are, to a greater or lesser extent, hybrids with one or more other modes or genres, such as melodrama, biopic and comedy. Definitions range from the broadly inclusive to the exclusive. Belton's description encompasses all representations of war 'from the points of view of those whose lives it touches', including all narratives with war-related conflicts, irrespective of the amount of film footage devoted to combat.[2] Basinger, on the other hand, identifies the different genres that might represent wartime, writing: 'If you fight it, you have a combat film; if you sit home and worry about it, you have a family or domestic film; if you sit in board rooms and plan it, you have a historical biography or a political film of some sort.'[3] Neale's account concentrates on combat films that depict the wars of the twentieth century, although he does note that in early Hollywood cinema the term 'war film', i.e. combat film, usually referred to a Civil War or Indian wars narrative.[4]

Civil War films cause the confusion to increase. Since no single Civil War genre can be said to exist, how does a Civil War film fit into the above definitions? In the most inclusive definition, all Civil War films would be seen as part of the war genre since they are all set during a time of war. This is unacceptable, as so many of these films are clearly part of another genre, such as melodrama. A clue may lie in Belton's definition, which, although it does not raise any questions about the Civil War in particular, acknowledges that the amount of combat represented on screen varies across films in the war genre. In the combat film, a sub-genre in Belton's definition, a much higher percentage of film time is given to conflict on the battlefield, comparing films like *Bataan* (Tay Garnett, 1943), a Second World War film that devotes much of its running time to combat, to others like *Dances With Wolves*, that assign only a few short scenes to battle. It is the amount of screen time given to the showing of combat that is relevant here and it seems that it corresponds to differences across the whole generic landscape. A domestic melodrama may be set during the Civil War era (take any of the cinema versions of *Little Women* for example),[5] but it will not be found to represent any combat, even though in this example the family's father is away fighting for the Union army in the war. Similarly, *Red River* (Howard Hawks, 1948), a Western, skips the war years and picks up the narrative after 1865. At the other end of the scale can be found *Gettysburg* (Ronald F. Maxwell, 1993), which attends exclusively to the three-day battle of the same name. This film shows a large degree of combat, and thus is unquestionably a Civil War *combat* film, as opposed to a Civil War melodrama or a War-Western.

It seems logical, then, to ascribe a Civil War film to the combat sub-genre if it has a high percentage of on-screen combat. This does of course exclude Civil War spy narratives with a minimum of combat scenes, such as *Alvarez Kelly* (Edward Dmytryk, 1966) and *Springfield Rifle* (André de Toth, 1952), as well as many raiders narratives, like *Kansas Raiders* (Ray Enright, 1950) which depict raids and scuffles amongst characters and in locations that are more characteristic of the Western. Most of these films do have very strong Western and/or melodramatic overtones. For the purpose of this study, I will restrict my definition of the war genre to the combat film in order to retain a sufficient distance from the other genres I have examined that represent the Civil War. Clearly, this approach is an exclusive one, concentrating attention on films with a relatively stable identity, but this is employed in order to extricate the dominant themes and meanings to be found in the relationship between Civil War and combat sub-genre.

Before considering the films themselves it is necessary to make an overview of the nature of the combat sub-genre, since it would be wrong to assume that its only dominant characteristic is the presence of a certain measure of combat. One of the earlier explorations of this film category comes from Robert B. Ray.[6] Although Ray restricts his study to the Second World War combat film, the characteristics that he identifies are broadly applicable to films of other wars. He lists five motifs that seem to be universal in the films, beginning with 'the isolated male group involved in a life-and-death task', which operates as a means of personalising the war.[7]

Secondly, this group is comprised of a number of 'types', and its survival depends on both the men operating as a team and on individual heroism, according to the dictum that 'you can't do it alone'. The third motif requires both bravery and professionalism amongst the group members, although the films often recognise the possibility that even the bravest man may experience fear.[8] And the fourth and fifth motifs show an outsider, or a 'malcontent' within the group, threatening the mission's success, before eventually being accepted by virtue of a shift in his values.[9] Each of these characteristics combine to achieve what Ray considers to be the goal of the combat film, to 'reconcile the individual-group conflict' and thus to resolve any opposition of values raised by the narrative.[10]

This task of the combat film is remarkably similar to the one I have identified as the ideological project of War-Westerns: the erasure of the North/South line of conflict in order to create a united American group. In both cases, the reconciliation of individuals and their values is essential to ensure survival against an outside enemy. Where the combat film differs, however, is in its united American group being all-male, warfare being a traditionally masculine sphere, whereas the Western tends to incorporate communities, together with wives, sweethearts and even children. Ray concedes that women are occasionally present in the combat film, but they tend to be encoded as 'outsiders' who threaten the all-male group's mission by their feminine and emotional appeal.[11] Additionally, as far as the Civil War combat film is concerned, the action tends to take place in the principal theatre of the war, which was the East, whereas the Western locates its action at the frontier. It must also be borne in mind, however, that Ray's analysis is particularly concerned with films from the eras of classical and 'new' Hollywood between 1930 and 1980. He does not consider combat films produced in the pre-sound age of cinema, because the tendency towards an ideology of reconciliation that he highlights is characteristic of the classical period. What Ray's list of motifs provides, however, is a generalised structure by which the relationship between the Civil War and the combat film can be assessed.

John Belton's study of American cinema also provides an overview of the war film, broadly describing it as 'a representation of war from the points of view of those whose lives it touches', and he locates the combat film at the core of this definition, concentrating its narratives principally on 'men in war'.[12] Belton lists a range of characteristics and narrative themes, not the least important of which is the spectacle of on-screen violence and death.[13] He also notes that, although in war conventional ethics, such as the immorality of murder, are suspended, war films do demonstrate 'relative moral distinctions' in the behaviour of the protagonists and antagonists.[14] Belton remarks on the genre's requirement that individuals lay aside their own needs and motivations in order to align themselves with the military group, like Ray's 'reconciliation of the individual-group conflict'. Belton also, like Ray, acknowledges the threat of emotional distraction that the woman poses in the war film.[15] What Belton adds to the list, and which is particularly important to this study as it seeks to discover themes of American national identity, is the male soldier's repression of emotion and his transformation into a 'ruthless, unemotional, fighting machine'. Belton explains that the primary hazard faced by the soldier is a crisis of masculinity, a necessity to overcome all within him that is vulnerable or feminine, or else risk his life and the lives of his group.

A more recent investigation into Hollywood's combat films, from Michael Hammond, turns its attention to the Vietnam war film and the modifications this war has brought to the genre.[16] Apart from the increased authentic portrayal of armed combat, one legacy of the Vietnam war film is the foregrounding of the soldier's emotional trauma to explain character motivation.[17] This trauma is something that the Vietnam veteran is seen to carry with him after the war, adding to the sense of 'futility, duty and sacrifice' that Hammond locates in the films.[18] However, is Hammond correct in assuming that ideas of trauma and futility originate in the Vietnam war film, or can they be found in combat films before the 1970s that explore different wars? Similarly, is the 'scene of atrocity' in the Vietnam war film, which is a response to the male group's fear of a 'terrifying unseen enemy', apparent in other types of combat film?[19] Lastly, is the Vietnam war film alone responsible for the de-emphasis of blame on the enemy, as Hammond seems to suggest?[20] These questions are all pertinent to an examination of Civil War combat films.

The following analyses locate within a range of films the characteristics highlighted by Ray, Belton and Hammond, yet identify ways in which the conventions are challenged by the Civil War narrative. Thomas Ince's *The Drummer of the 8th* (1913) is chosen principally as an example of the many silent short films devoted to a Civil War theme. Other choices could have included *The Battle* (D.W. Griffith, 1911) or *Days of '61* (Kalem, no director credited, 1908), but like the films of Chapters 2 and 3, *The Drummer of the 8th* is now more readily available and more frequently consumed, and it acts as a reminder that D.W. Griffith was not the only director approaching the topic of the Civil War in this era. *The Red Badge of Courage* (John Huston, 1951) is of particular interest, being a film that continues today to receive critical consideration, and the value of *The Horse Soldiers* (John Ford, 1959) lies in it being one of the rare Ford films that deals with the Civil War itself, rather than its aftermath. Finally, *Glory* is chosen as a more recent, post-Vietnam combat film.

FIGHTING TO BE A MAN:
THE DRUMMER OF THE 8TH

Thomas Harper Ince (1882–1924), although not as prolific as his contemporary, D.W. Griffith, directed and produced over one hundred films during American cinema's silent era. He is known for his innovative contributions to the development of the studio system during the 1910s, particularly at his Californian studio 'Inceville', founded in 1912. Ince's main output was the action film or the Western, but he is credited with the production and direction of several Civil War films, beginning with *The Drummer of the 8th* and followed by others including *The Battle of Gettysburg* (1913), *The Sharpshooter* (1913), *The Coward* (Reginald H. Barker, 1915) and *The Sinews of War* (1913). *The Drummer of the 8th* could be described as a hybrid of melodrama and the combat film, dividing its screen time between warfare and a family's responses to the war. More attention, however, is given to the world of battle (with sets representing two battlefields, a Confederate officer's tent, a prisoner-of-war camp and an army hospital) than to the family home. The narrative follows the fate of a child, Billy (Cyril Gardner), who moves between these two worlds, as he follows his desire to fight in the Union army. Most of that which takes place in the home concerns Billy's fate on the front, so the focus is very much on war itself.

Billy is the younger son of a Northern family, whose older brother, Jack (actor's name not credited), joins the Union army in 1861. Billy's family lives next-door to two sisters, both of whom are linked romantically to the two boys. After Jack leaves for war, Billy escapes at night and joins up as a drummer. Immediately, one of the expectations of the combat films is disrupted. The all-male, all-adult arena of warfare has been breached by a child, not a child accidentally caught up in the midst of conflict, but one who desires to fight. In his first battle Billy retrieves the gun of a fallen soldier and begins to shoot at the Confederate enemy. Shortly afterwards he is captured and taken to a prisoner-of-war camp. Despite his family's efforts to locate him, Billy is not found, and he eventually escapes from the camp, only to overhear

Confederate battle plans. On his way back to the Union army he is seriously wounded, but at a hospital passes on the intelligence he has learned. The Confederate plans are changed when they discover that they may have been overheard and the Union regiment is massacred. Shortly before dying in the hospital Billy sends his mother word that he will soon return home. The film ends with the arrival of Billy's coffin at the family's house.

It is interesting to note that only a few years after the release of this film, Ince co-directed *Civilization* (1916), a pacifist film about a fictional war in which Christ himself converts a warring king to peace.[21] *The Drummer of the 8th*, similarly, does not seek to glorify war. Instead it points towards loss and death, ending as it does with the image of Billy's coffin. Although Billy is a Northerner, nothing is communicated about the reasons why these men fight. Some brief shots show a public speaker rallying support for the Northern cause, but no intertitle describes his discourse. Slavery, race and even the unity of the country remain unmentioned and invisible – Billy and his brother seem to want to fight simply because that is what men do. The loss seems all the more poignant, then, since Billy dies simply because he wanted to be a man.

Billy's 'crisis of masculinity', as Belton might put it, revolves around his desire to participate in the male world of war, which is in tension with his family's desire to keep him in the safe, feminine space of the home. Adapting Ray's idea of the individual-group conflict, Billy's family is concerned for his individual safety, whereas he wants only to be a part of the male group. Billy successfully achieves his goal firstly by running away, and secondly by attaining solidarity with the men of war when he picks up the rifle of a dead man and begins to fire. In this way he becomes the equal of his fellow soldiers. One memorable shot in the prisoner-of-war camp has Billy sitting by an elderly soldier, both deep in thought of 'visions of home'. They sit together as brothers, equals, as if both have experienced the same horrors. Billy has, in a sense, aged beyond his years and the old soldier by his side reflects his new maturity.

Despite Billy's equality with the other fighting men, the fact remains that he is still a child. It is the story of a boy becoming a man, but he dies, physically, a minor. In the prisoner-of-war camp a guard begins to bully another boy, offering a distraction for Billy to escape. Then, after his escape, Billy is shot by a Confederate scout; no mercy is shown because of his age. Children are thus seen as being attacked and abused in a manner equal to the wartime treatment of adults yet, to our sensibilities, thoroughly inappropriately for children. The sphere of war is being recognised by Ince as not only a masculine space, but also an adult space that mistreats the young, making the loss of Billy an emphatically moral statement against war.

Ince's depiction of battle itself is most interesting. The two battle scenes are edited chaotically, with barely any sign, except in the costuming, to suggest which army is in shot. The one hundred and eighty degree rule, still in its infancy in 1912, is virtually ignored (although adhered to in other non-combat scenes) adding to a sense of chaos. After the Union massacre, 'The Aftermath', Ince composes a smoky *mise-en-scène* in which a horse paws at a dead body and officers wander aimlessly through the field. There is an impression of senseless loss and pointless sacrifice, particularly as the film has given no concrete explanation for the conflict.

Considering that this film was released five years before American involvement in the First World War (and two years before the war had even begun in Europe), its markedly pacifist tone cannot be linked to some isolationist standpoint at a political level. Ince's film recognises war as a form of masculine test, one that Billy passes despite his youth, but it concludes that the result is loss and death. The young soldier is certainly granted glory by his death, yet the film's message of futility is startling, being produced

11. *Drummer of the 8th* (Thomas H. Ince, 1913): Maturity beyond his youth – Billy sits with an elderly soldier in a prison camp.

more than half a century before the Hollywood cycle of Vietnam war films. It is a theme that seems to repeat itself in many Civil War films of the combat sub-genre.

A STORY OF COWARDICE AND A STORY OF COURAGE: *THE RED BADGE OF COURAGE*

The Red Badge of Courage is an adaptation of the classic nineteenth-century American novel of the same name by Stephen Crane, published in 1895 when the author was still in his early twenties – too young to have seen the Civil War for himself. Crane's own description of the novel was as 'a psychological portrayal of fear', and its style corresponds to this suggestion, being a naturalistic internal drama of a 'Youth' facing battle for the first time.[22] Huston's film follows the novel closely, although the released film contains extended battle footage and has lost some of the non-combat scenes,[23] whilst gaining a voice-over and a musical score.[24] Arguably these changes made by the studio led to it becoming regarded as, in Basinger's words 'that notorious flop'.[25] Regardless of its commercial success, however, *Red Badge* adroitly uses the camera, editing and sound in ways that mimic the interiorised nature of the story of Henry Fleming (Audie Murphy) as he struggles with the fear and experience of cowardice and dishonesty.

The film's messages of scepticism about war, despite its exultant ending, seem in keeping with what historians Grob and Billias call a more 'hostile' approach towards the Civil War and the nation's failure to 'realise any of the ideals for which it was fought', which was an attitude that found favour with the development of the critical, anti-war culture of 1960s America.[26] However, this attitude was clearly not sufficiently widespread in 1951 when the film was released, and it failed commercially. The idea of an American hero showing signs of cowardice and running from the front line of battle was simply not acceptable. 'Americans did not do that,' as Bruce Chadwick notes.[27] Guerric DeBona, on the other hand, writes that audiences simply did not want to see an anti-war film at a time when the nation was involved in the Korean war, and the changes made by the studio to construct a more positive, triumphant ending were a direct consequence of audience indifference to the film.[28]

The film is structured into two main parts, which could be called a story of cowardice followed by a story of courage. The story of cowardice begins with Fleming's regiment endlessly drilling, a task that they have repeated for several months. When news of a forthcoming battle arrives Fleming is seen in a medium shot walking away from the group of men with a look of stunned horror on his face. This is the first of many close-ups and medium shots of Murphy, often hemmed in tight to the camera, conveying his fear not only of battle, but also of proving himself to be a coward. These shots are frequently accompanied by the voice-over of a narrator (James Whitmore) who speaks on Henry's behalf, often directly quoting dialogue and description from Crane's novel. Unwanted by Huston, the voice-over narration was added by MGM to impress upon audiences the importance of the narrative, it being adapted from an American classic novel.[29] The narration even explains that the writing of the novel made its author, Crane, into a 'man', just as war turns the Youth into a man. The insistence of the studio to make such changes to Huston's original film implies a certain ideological understanding of the Civil War, that it was not only about the making of a nation, but also the making of men. As DeBona puts it, the released film is a story of 'a conventional initiation into manhood, guaranteed by the canonical author himself'.[30] It conforms to Belton's suggestion that the combat film is concerned with the masculine crisis of proving one's manhood.

Through the device of the voice-over and the frequency of the close shots, *Red Badge* is constructed as one young man's personal story. But in the first part of the film, the story of cowardice, Henry is the opposite of the heroic protagonist of most wartime combat films. According to the narrator, Henry feels like a 'mental outcast' who has no place in the army. He conforms to Ray's idea of the combat film's 'outsider', whose motivation conflicts with and threatens the mission of the male group. Shots often show Henry isolated from the soldiers in his regiment, excluded from their discussions. Where his fear is made explicit through the voice-over, the thoughts of the other soldiers are spoken aloud, with expressions of bravado and impatience for battle, such as 'We're gonna lick 'em good'.

When battle is first visualised on screen, the Confederates are barely seen except as silhouettes in the smoke that emit the chilling Rebel Yell. Throughout the combat sequences the film edits back and forth between extreme long shots of the field and extreme close-ups of the Union men's faces, sweating and trembling in fear. All that can be clearly distinguished in the field at this stage is the Confederate flag as it is held high by the enemy. This ignoring of the Confederate personality, as it were, allows the narrative to concentrate on Henry's subjective experiences. The political conflict of North and South becomes subsidiary. It also proves that the Vietnam war film is not alone in diverting attention away from the enemy, as Hammond suggests. With the accent on Henry's subjectivity, the Confederate soldier's part in the conflict is played down.

Henry's worst fear is realised when he is overcome by terror and runs from the field. In this action, he can be seen to have failed in the repression of his emotions. But it must be noted at this point that he is not the only figure to flee; several other men can be spotted in the shot running away from the line, revealing that Henry's abandonment of the male group's mission is nothing unusual. The rest of the story of cowardice shows Henry witnessing the death of the 'Tall Soldier', his friend and father figure Jim Conklin (John Dierkes). Henry receives an accidental wound to the head from another deserting soldier but is eventually reunited with his regiment. DeBona sees this wound as a 'psychological scar', the result of Henry's 'existential encounter with himself' and his cowardice.[31] It can just as easily be described as a melodramatic externalisation of the conflict that is taking place within the Youth. Once returned, Henry lies about his wound, or 'red badge', saying that a bullet caught his head in combat. His deceit is hidden from his friend Tom (Bill Mauldin), who

12. *The Red Badge of Courage* (John Huston, 1951): The viewer is party to Fleming's cowardice in a probing close-up.

stands to the rear of the shot, but it is exposed to the viewer in another probing close-up.

The story of courage shows Henry overcome his fear, realign himself with the male group's task and prove himself to be brave in two more skirmishes with the enemy. In the final battle he even carries the Union flag to urge his fellow soldiers onwards and gently takes the Confederate colours from their dying flag-bearer. This is the first moment that an enemy is clearly seen, at the moment of his death, giving a human face to the source of Henry's terror. Once the battle is over, the defeated soldiers usurp Henry's place in the close-ups of the first part of the film. One Southern man wishes that he were dead rather than captured. So, it appears that Henry has completed a journey from youth to man, overcome his masculine crisis and proven his courage.

This understanding of the narrative, however, is unsatisfactory. As Henry is praised by his fellows, he walks aside and confesses to Tom that he ran at the first battle, but he tempers the truth by saying that he felt so ashamed he joined another regiment and continued fighting. In relief, Tom confesses that he ran too. Moments later, the men move on, admiring the sunlight and the birdsong, and the narrator concludes that Henry has become a man. Henry never in fact tells the whole truth, his deceit remains hidden, his 'red badge' still a lie. So the man that he has become, as brave as he has proved himself to be, is dishonest. There seems to be a contradiction, then, between the voice-over narration, taken from the novel, and the action of the central character. One claims Henry to be a hero whose soul has changed; the other exposes his lack of purity and a guilty conscience. The two messages clash, and hence the ultimate meaning of the film is questionable. This tension is neatly underlined in the final minute of the film, when a group of tattered but lively Union soldiers walks past. They claim to Henry and his regiment that the 'real battle' is over the hill – as if somehow what has been relayed in the film is a mere disagreement, rather than proper combat. But based on what we now know of Henry, are these claims truth or are they mere bravado? Have these men been involved in something even more horrific, or is this another deceit? The film does not answer these questions, and they give the triumphalistic narration a hollow ring.

The tension found here can be traced to the difference of opinion between the studio and the director. As DeBona's article makes clear, Huston's desire was to 'demythologise the American soldier' and to challenge the conventional Hollywood 'warrior myth' that saw the fighting man as a consistently brave and honourable ancestor.[32] The studio, on the other hand, chose to melodramaticise the American soldier, adding the voice-over as well as a sentimental musical score in order to externalise the Youth's journey from boy to man.[33] As DeBona suggests, this restoration of the 'warrior myth' means that the Civil War operates in this film as a confirmation that wars make warriors of American youths, and the author himself, Stephen Crane, can be regarded as a 'patron saint of masculinity'.[34]

Whatever the intended meaning of the film, Huston's original focus remains on the emotional impact of war amongst those who fight. Like *The Drummer of the 8th*, at no point do the characters discuss political issues concerning state rights or slavery. The drama is that which occurs within Henry. The only reason given for fighting, according to the narration, is to earn the symbol of courage – the wound. It is a sign of the passage from childhood to manhood. The film therefore, as Belton's description of the war genre highlights, is about a crisis of masculinity, the drive to prove one's right to be accepted as a man.[35] Henry has passed that test, although the new man that he has become has a distasteful secret that is never brought to light.

It should be added that the version of masculinity that is presented here, as well as being morally questionable, is white. Such a comment may seem rather obvious, but its very obviousness is the source of its invisibility. Not a single black face is seen on the screen; every soldier without exception is white. Richard Dyer's examination of the representation of whiteness in cinema explains that 'white' is not considered to be a race. Whiteness is not 'racially seen' by white people and hence is taken for granted to be a 'human norm'.[36] The injustice of the ideology of white supremacy ensures that white people speak for all humans, whereas people who are racially seen 'can only speak for their race'.[37] Henry's story, therefore, speaks for all men in war – his story is one of many that say the same thing. When this idea is placed alongside the opening narration of the film, it reveals its ideological message concerning national identity. The story, says the voice-over, is of many 'frightened boys' who came out of the war a 'nation of united, strong men'. What emerges from the crucible of war is a united nation. If the characters of the film are representative of that united nation, then it is a nation of white men.

THE HUMAN COST OF WAR IN *THE HORSE SOLDIERS*

As Tag Gallagher's analysis of John Ford's career recognises, Ford's Civil War and post-Civil War narratives usually sided with the Union army.[38] *The Horse Soldiers* is no exception, and Ford's treatment of the Confederacy, through the handful of Southern characters in this film, is ambiguous, fluctuating between respectful mythmaking and disparagement. The narrative is loosely based on an actual event, the sixteen-day raid by Union Colonel Benjamin Grierson in 1863, deep into Confederate territory. John Wayne plays Colonel John Marlowe, a former railway engineer, leading his regiment into the South to destroy a railway station. Marlowe is a tough, bitter man, who blames the medical profession for the death of his wife during an unnecessary operation. His bitterness is the root of a rivalry between himself and Major Hank Kendall (William Holden), the surgeon commissioned to the regiment. On their journey they pick up a white Southern widow, Hannah Hunter (Constance Towers), and her black maid (Althea Gibson), who Kendall has caught spying on their plans. As Gallagher remarks, the events of the film are largely incidental and episodic,[39] culminating in Marlowe's recognition of his love for Hannah, before attacking the station and returning northwards via the 'underground railway', the route used to smuggle runaway slaves from the South.

Gallagher explores the ambiguous treatment of the South in this film, focusing particularly on the relationship between racial imagery and characters. During the march southwards the regiment passes by a black shanty area, where Kendall's conscience forces him to aid a woman in childbirth against Marlowe's orders. The black people in the scene are mostly youths and children – all slaves – who are dressed in rags and seem poverty-stricken. It is a clear image of the destitution caused by slavery. Ford, however, does not follow through this image at an ethical level within the narrative, since 'the Southerners are virtually never depicted as slavers or racists'.[40] Indeed, slavery seems here to exist independently of the war and its causes. It is recognised as abhorrent, yet never traced to a source or to any kind of blame, and as such it becomes marginalised in this re-writing of the Civil War. This corresponds to a complaint made by black historian, Nathan I. Huggins, who writes that the national narrative – the story of American history – marginalises the true story of slavery.[41] The white man's history of the Civil War thus tells the story of a white conflict fought over white issues. Just as in this white national narrative, the focus of Ford's film is not race. The purpose of including the scene at the black shanty area is to contribute to the tension between Marlowe and Kendall and the opposing expressions of masculinity and femininity that they represent.

Hannah presents herself as the mannered, cultured Southern belle on the regiment's arrival at her plantation, but her home lacks the wealth and grandeur of the antebellum Tara in *Gone With the Wind*. She has but one maid. She is in fact a Southern spy (and is thus the outsider threat that Ray discusses in relation to combat films) and it is to her great distress that she finds herself falling for her enemy, Marlowe. She further redeems herself by aiding Kendall's surgery, in effect aligning her values to those of the male group, so her ambiguity is resolved. The Southern woman proves her honour by helping the just cause of the North and by cleaving to a Northern man – North and South united together through the heterosexual couple.

One of the more disturbing representations of the South is the military cadet school that attacks the Union regiment. In this episode, the Southern enemy is represented by children, and is treated in a comic mode – one boy is dragged home by his mother, another is given a spanking over a Union soldier's knee, all to a light, jaunty tune on the soundtrack. It is, however, rather uncomfortable. Boys did go into battle during the Civil War, and many died in the process. Gallagher notices an echo of Ince's *Drummer of the 8th* when one child escapes his mother to join his fellow cadets in battle.[42] This may be a comic interlude in *The Horse Soldiers*, but children are being used to delay Union progress until reinforcements arrive. It relates to the film's treatment of masculinity that threads throughout the narrative. War is emphatically a pursuit/space for men, and not for children. It is as if the possibility of children in war is too painful to contemplate, and thus must be delivered in a comic mode. But this only makes the prospect seem all the more immoral, and that immorality is attributed to the Confederate army.

Having said this, the locus of tension in the film is less that between North and South, than it is between the two male central characters, Marlowe and Kendall. One is an engineer, the other a doctor. Marlowe represents a tough, disciplined masculinity, but when Hannah joins Kendall in dispensing care to the wounded, it reinforces the surgeon's craft as feminine. Kendall and Hannah alike are not permitted to participate in combat; that is the responsibility of men like Marlowe. The rules of the combat film appear to state that the battlefield is no place for feminised characters such as women and medics, it being reserved as a thoroughly masculine space. In *Red Badge* and *Drummer* those who fight for, and are representative of, the nation are white male adults. Women, children and people who are racially seen must be excluded from combat, or will face the fatal consequences, as in the case of Billy the drummer-boy. In *The Horse Soldiers* it is also those men who demonstrate feminine characteristics who must be marginalised. It is not Kendall (the doctor) that develops a romance with Hannah, but Marlowe (the soldier). The future of a united America is made possible in the pairing of the thoroughly masculine male and the woman. The ideological implication of this in terms of national identity is that American paternity is white and emphatically masculine.

The presence of femininity in a combat film, which is itself also a masculine space, causes a disturbance in the treatment of masculinity, as both Ray and Belton suggest. However, although Hannah is seen to align her values with the male group, and so is accepted amongst them, Marlowe himself also undergoes a transformation. Through Hannah, Marlowe is able to lay his wife's memory to rest and learn to love again. Through Kendall and his consistent faithfulness to his Hippocratic oath, Marlowe is also able to forgive the medical profession for his wife's untimely death. Marlowe thus goes through a process that overcomes or heals his masculine crisis, not only because of the extreme circumstances of war and death, but also because of the presence of a woman.

In keeping with the film's ambiguity, though, masculinity is not as secure as this resolution for Marlowe suggests, and the insecurity revolves around death. One review recorded that *The Horse Soldiers* 'puts the emphasis on the human cost',[43] identifying the repeating theme of unnecessary death. Marlowe's wife, before the narrative begins, has died on the surgeon's table despite having no illness. A Union soldier dies of gangrene because he refuses to observe Kendall's directions to care for his wounded leg. The fear of a slow death in the Confederate prisoner-of-war camp at Andersonville looms over the regiment. The film then, despite its typical Fordian humour (Hannah repeatedly doused with water after fainting or misbehaving; the

13. *The Horse Soldiers* (John Ford, 1959): A Southern military cadet is punished for involving himself in a man's war.

spanking of the cadet), is part of a noticeable tendency in the films examined that sees this genre decrying the human waste of war. Again, Hammond's claim that the Vietnam war film is responsible for a sense of futility in war films of the late twentieth century can be challenged. Death's effect is not glory, since in each case the death was needless. Glory, a reward for the passing of a masculine test, has no place in these deaths. The glory is reserved for Marlowe, Kendall and Hannah, who survive against the odds, having learned to love and respect one another.

MAKING BLACK AND WHITE VISIBLE: *GLORY*

Glory is a central component of this next film, one that combines both historical figures and fictional characters in its narrative. Like the other films of this study, *Glory* situates its story in a Northern regiment and very little is explored of the Southern experience during the war. The film is partly based on the letters of Robert Gould Shaw, an actual historical figure and the white officer of one of the first all-black regiments of the Union army, the 54th Massachusetts.[44] His words, written to his parents, are related through Matthew Broderick's voice-over and act as a means of understanding Shaw's political and emotional feelings. Much contained in the letters does not make it into the film, which incorporates a dominant fictional element. In fact, the purpose of the film is not specifically to examine the Civil War, but to create a space in which a black voice can be heard, a voice that is conspicuous by its absence in most Civil War films. *Glory* is one of very few films to deal with the Union's use of black soldiers, and it is to be commended for that. Rather like *Dances With Wolves*, it operates as an apologetic for Hollywood's historically inaccurate portrayals of racially seen people, as well as exposing the presence of white racism during the Civil War era. There are significant problems with its means of communicating the story, the principal difficulty being the use of point-of-view, but its ideological message is one of racial equality, in praise of American idealism.

In the opening scene, Shaw's voice is heard relaying a letter written to his parents. To him, the purpose of the war is to make it possible for all people to 'speak', and for America to be a 'whole country'. As a poetry lover, Shaw believes that his motivation to fight is these people, 'whose poetry is not yet written'. Herein lies the central problem of the film. Although it is Shaw's desire that the black people of America may have the opportunity to speak on their own behalf – and it is the filmmakers' hope to allow the 'whiteness' of history to be redressed – the voice that tells the story is that of a white man. Despite the inclusion of scenes amongst the black soldiers themselves, scenes in which Shaw has no part, it is in fact Shaw's story, beginning with his first experience of battle, at Antietam Creek, 1862, showing in horrific detail the trauma of Civil War combat. It is in keeping with Shaw's response to the battle in his letters, where he writes: 'It seems almost as if nothing could justify a battle like that of the 17 [September 1962], and the horrors inseparable from it'.[45] A number of reviewers saw in this scene from *Glory* links to Ford's Civil War episode in *How the West Was Won*.[46] Shaw's regiment panics and tries to flee from cannon-fire, despite his order of 'For God's sake, come on!' There is chaos and terror. An officer's head explodes. Shaw himself is lightly wounded and falls to the ground, shielding his ears from the noise of explosions, and the experience leaves him emotionally traumatised. At a party in his parents' Boston home he becomes detached from the social gathering. Through point-of-view shots, the replacement of realistic sound with the voices of a boys' choir and slow motion, Shaw's subjective perception is foregrounded and the viewer is drawn into a closer identification with him.

There is one point worth making about this traumatic scene in the Shaw family home. The subjective devices that are used to externalise Shaw's state of mind are fundamentally melodramatic. This may be a combat film, but it uses the melodramatic mode to allow the personal experience of war to be evident. In this case, camera placement, sound and film speed all contribute to a vivid expression of Shaw's mental state. The important message of the scene is that war is harmful mentally as well as physically, conforming to Hammond's suggestion that war films of the late-twentieth century owe a foregrounding of the soldier's trauma to the Vietnam film cycle.

Shaw's point-of-view remains dominant throughout most of the film, although the experience of the black soldiers is dealt with thoroughly. The means of achieving this is by focusing on a group of four black soldiers, Rawlins (Morgan Freeman), Trip (Denzel Washington), Sharts (Jihmi Kennedy) and Searles (Andre Braugher). Herein lies the second problem with the film. As mentioned above, although *Glory* is based on actual historical documents, the four black characters are each fictional, despite the presence of at least one historically significant black soldier, Lewis Douglass, son of the abolitionist Frederick, in the real 54th Massachusetts. Each of the characters is a social type verging on stereotype, forming a microcosm of the black soldiers of the war. Although they do not conform strictly to the black stereotypes listed by Black Cinema historian, Donald Bogle, there are echoes of the Tom, Coon and Buck amongst the characters.[47] Rawlins is an older escaped slave who becomes a firm but fair father figure to the group, who teaches the others to respect the authority of their white officer, rather like a free version of the faithful Tom. Sharts is an illiterate country boy with a stutter, who has amazing skill with a rifle, but whose gaucheness relates to the simple, naïve Coon. Trip is a young escaped slave, who has experienced the harsh, cruel life of slavery and who carries great bitterness and resentment to all, both black and white. He demonstrates certain traits of the Brutal Black Buck of Bogle's list, being the most disrespectful and physically powerful of the group. Searles is a wealthy privileged Northerner, who has grown up with Shaw in Boston, and is thus a figure rarely represented in Civil War culture or the plantation myth, although, as one of my undergraduate students once pointed out, his consistent approval and support for the white officer, Shaw, effectively makes him an Uncle Tom figure.

Each of these central characters, including Shaw, goes through a personal process that leads to their solidarity with the all-male group, having a common purpose together. As one reviewer wrote, the purpose of the film was not to focus on the individual, but on 'the fused, spiritually indestructible regiment' in the light of the emancipation of the slaves before America came to terms with the realities of ensuring racial equality.[48] Zwick's subject is the all-male group, conventionally central to the war genre, but here it is the all-black all-male group. Remembering Dyer's comment that a 'racially seen' person can only speak for his race, this therefore can also be seen as a film about race. Since a white man also commands the group, these views together reveal *Glory* to be a discourse on both white and black masculinity.

Shaw's 'masculine journey' begins with his experience at Antietam. He is seen to be subject to fear and trauma, which, because of their connotations of vulnerability, might be viewed as conventionally feminine characteristics. He then goes through a tough, controlled period during the training of the black regiment, and finally softens as he acquires a new 'emotional intensity'[49] from his men – a kind of revelation of his spiritual equality with them, signalled by his choice in the final battle to attack Fort Wagner side-by-side with them on foot. What he demonstrates is the reverse of the repression of emotion that Belton locates in the combat film; here Shaw's emotional side is renewed instead of denied, and as a result his solidarity with the black group is reinforced.

The initial stark opposition set up between Shaw and his men (officer/recruits, white man/black men), is moderated by the contrast of Shaw with other white men in the army, amongst whom racial prejudice is painfully clear. The Quartermaster (Richard Riehle) who denies the regiment boots, and Colonel Montgomery (Cliff De Young) who gives another black regiment free rein to loot and burn the Southern town of Darien, are both there to demonstrate the shortfall in Northern ideology towards race during the Civil War. They are, in fact, the real enemies of the film, since – like *Red Badge* – there is scant attention given to the Confederate army in the narrative. These 'bad whites,' like the bad whites of the Western, help to provide the tensions and challenges against which the 54th must fight at a moral and ideological level, making the film, according to Neale, 'new revisionist', in its exposure of white racism.[50] The horrified response of Shaw and his regiment to the travesty in Darien clearly situates *Glory* as an examination of race and masculinity. The Darien scene, whilst it reconstructs an actual historical event described by Shaw himself as a 'dirty piece of business' and a 'barbarous sort of warfare',[51] creates a form of dialogue with Griffith's *The Birth of a Nation*, acting as a rectification of the Piedmont looting scene, in which a black regiment led by a white officer loots and, effectively, rapes the town. In *Glory* the presence of 'good' blacks disrupts Griffith's perception in *Birth*, leaving the 'bad' white man with the greater portion of the blame.

By these means *Glory* is making 'white' visible. Like the uncomfortable resolution of *Red Badge*, which questions Henry Fleming's honesty, *Glory* seeks to acknowledge a lack of moral purity in the white American, conventionally implied by Hollywood cinema's construction of the Civil War. The Darien episode in *Glory*, however, carefully avoids blaming this 'scene of atrocity' on the protagonists of the film, as Hammond sees occurring in the Vietnam war film. The perpetrators are clearly encoded as the Brutal Black Buck stereotype, controlled by an immoral white man. Both black and white masculinity, then, are being reviewed and found to be wanting.

The personal journey of the group of four black men is one from unruly disorder and ignorance towards devoted service and committed sacrifice. Their purpose is to fight as free men, just as white men have fought, in order to secure the ongoing abolition of slavery. What they must learn in order to achieve this falls into two stages. Firstly they must learn the skills of the soldier and secondly they must acquire respect for their officer, following the conventional requirement of the combat film to show its male group becoming proficient soldiers. Each of these lessons raises a challenge to their masculinity, but eventually leads to a state of equality between white masculinity and black masculinity.

The newly recruited regiment is placed under the control of Irish drill sergeant, Mulcahy (John Finn). He is the stereotypical foul-mouthed, harsh sergeant of the war film genre identified, for example, by Belton, whose purpose it is to bully the regiment with repeated drilling and offensive insinuations about the men's masculinity.[52] In forcing the men to learn how to march, he barks at Trip: 'You half-wit black bastard – is it true they cut your balls off at birth?' The training period is a masculine test which the men must pass in order to face battle as professional soldiers, and to fulfil the conventional requirement of the recruit to prove his masculinity. So, as Burgoyne points out, whilst Shaw achieves a sort of emotional growth by the end of the film, the black troop gains instead the masculine characteristics of 'rigor and discipline'.[53]

The second test that the group faces concerns the dynamics of their relationship with Shaw. This is specifically located in the tension between Shaw and Trip, the angry young black man, and progresses in stages. Trip is a vivid example of the male group's outsider that Ray describes, who must align his values with the other men for the sake of their survival and their mission. At the mid-point of the film, Trip is caught as a deserter, and Shaw orders that he be flogged. Trip's back is already heavily scarred from whippings during his days of slavery. It is a highly melodramatic scene, with emotive music underscoring the use of slow zooms to close-ups of Trip, holding eye contact with Shaw, eventually unable to prevent himself from weeping. After the episode, Shaw learns that Trip was not deserting, he was in fact out looking for boots, items that are, according to Basinger, signifiers of the embracing (or in a few cases, the rejection) of combat.[54] This helps to reinforce the injustice of the event, that Trip should be punished for attempting to acquire something that makes himself and his fellow soldiers ready for combat. Robert Burgoyne refers to the comments of Nathan I. Huggins in his analysis of this scene, and his insistence that 'there can be no white history or black history', since 'white and black [...] are joined at the hip'.[55] The flogging is a re-enactment of the relationship between white and black under slavery. For Shaw, a Northern abolitionist, and for the film viewer, Trip's scars and composure are an education in the realities of slavery.[56] Indeed, the onlookers, both black and white, are shocked at this brutal treatment. Shaw is noticeably distressed, but insists that the example must be made in order that the regiment respects his authority. The scene helps to make Huggins' comments on history clear: Trip's experiences of slavery are embedded within a past that is both black *and* white history, and so Shaw is educated in a past that belongs to both himself and the black soldiers.

The Trip/Shaw relationship moves into a phase in which Shaw's respect for Trip develops, whereas Trip's anger and hatred of the white man refuses to break. Shaw stands with Trip as he tears up his payslip when they are informed that the black soldiers will receive lower pay than their white counterparts.

Trip also refuses the honour of carrying the regiment's colours during battle, a reward for his bravery in their first skirmish. Trip's turning point comes when Rawlins, the older father figure of the group, challenges him for being so full of hatred that he wants to fight everyone. On the night before the attack on Fort Wagner, Trip confesses before the other men at a spiritual gathering that they are the only family he has. This family is extended to Shaw the next day, when Trip sees his officer die and picks up the colours he had previously rejected and dies under enemy fire.

Shaw and Trip are the only central characters of the regiment that are seen to die on screen – the others are seen in a brief shot facing enemy cannon, before the film cuts to the next day. The bodies of Shaw and Trip then slide into a mass grave, in slow motion, and fall into a death embrace. This is another direct challenge to Griffith's *The Birth of a Nation*, which saw two white friends die in each other's arms.[57] In this case it is not friends who are forced to be enemies, but enemies who learn to be brothers, equal in their death. This is the reason that the deaths of these two men are seen and the others are not. Shaw and Trip, and their death embrace, somehow represent the twentieth-century climax of the ideological struggle against racism in the USA, the Civil Rights Movement. The rest of the regiment, instead, represent the involvement of black men in the Civil War, and their image is effectively, although not literally, frozen on screen as a kind of memorial to the 54th Massachusetts.

John Belton writes that the all-male group of the war genre is a kind of reinforcement of the melting-pot ideal, a conglomeration of social types who both win the war and 'demonstrate that the idea of America really works'.[58] The relationship of Trip and Shaw, and their equality in death, demonstrates a certain mutual respect between black and white, demonstrating – or urging us to recognise – that the American ideal of equality also really works. Paul Gilroy comments that the experience of battle forges 'a mystic nationhood' between its participants,[59] and adds that combat allows the nation to remember 'what truly "turned it on"'.[60] In the case of *Glory* the 'turn on' is equality.

THEMES AND MEANINGS IN THE CIVIL WAR COMBAT FILM

A number of common traits emerge from the films in the combat category that should be considered in more depth. Firstly, there is a strong similarity between the films and the domestic melodramas analysed in Chapter 2 in that the presence of a personalised villain is problematic. The films keep their attention firmly on the experience of life and death as a Civil War soldier, without scrutinising his enemy. The second trait, that of the authentic representation of the Civil War period, principally through the *mise-en-scène*, is observed as an attempt to reinforce the truthfulness of the films' depiction of history. Interestingly, the verisimilitude of the films, their realism and authenticity, operate within the melodramatic mode, externalising the subjective experience of the soldiers in order to construct a fuller, truer depiction of the Civil War. What these traits work towards is a certain construction of the historical figure of the Civil War soldier, one who undergoes a test to allow his entry into a masculine American ancestry.

Pro-Northism

It cannot fail but be noticed amongst the four films of this chapter that each of the narratives makes the Northern experience dominant. The central

14. *The Birth of a Nation* (D.W. Griffith, 1915): The 'death embrace' of the two chums – North and South as a family again.

15. *Glory* (Edward Zwick, 1989): The 'death embrace' of Trip and Shaw – black and white made equal in their sacrifice.

protagonist of each film is a Union soldier: Billy of *Drummer of the 8th*, Henry of *Red Badge*, Marlowe of *The Horse Soldiers*, and the regiment of *Glory*. Individuals from the Confederacy, or characters from the South, are sometimes represented, but their place is secondary to the Northerners. This is due in some part, inevitably, to the films chosen for the analysis. However, a pro-North strain is evident in other combat films, including those that appear to be a 'fair' depiction of both North and South, or even those that take a Confederate point of view.

Gettysburg, for example, is an epic-combat hybrid that seems to allow a fair distribution of film time to North and South, yet there is a subtle bias towards the stories and footage given to the Union army. Ronald Maxwell's second Civil War film, *Gods and Generals* (2003, see Chapter 6) concentrates its narrative on the story of the Confederate General 'Stonewall' Jackson, and yet it instils within its central protagonist several distinctly Unionist sensibilities, such as a desire for the freedom of the slaves. The South of the Civil War combat film, as in the other genres of this study, is either 'Unionised', re-written as similar in its mission to the Union, or it is absent altogether. Alternatively, the South is seen through the distortion of plantation mythology, which lends itself more to melodrama than to the war film, for example in *Gettysburg*. Martin Sheen's performance as General Lee is made up of romantic references to Old Virginia and the prevailing of God's will. The Southern experience is predominantly left to be explored in other genres, such as the domestic melodrama, or sub-sets of the war film genre, some raider and spy narratives, such as *Kansas Raiders*, and films about the James and Younger brothers, which are frequently hybrids with the Western and domestic melodrama.

Consequently, what is missing from these combat films is a considered exploration of the political motivations behind the Civil War. In each film, *Glory* being a glaring exception, the characters enter war without any clear exposition concerning their reason to fight. Politics are sidestepped, making the war more a matter of personal conflicts and crises. Thoughts on the blame for the Civil War are rarely entertained. This is a long way from *The Birth of a Nation*, in which slaves themselves, and the abolitionists who sought to secure their freedom, were given the full portion of blame for the conflict. These combat films, as one reviewer wrote about *Gettysburg*, are 'equally absurd', since they blame no one.[61] The Confederates are referred to in dialogue as 'the enemy', but they are either ignored by the narrative action, or they are revealed to be honest, good men fighting for some ethereal 'lost cause' that is not explored by the film text.

This sounds remarkably similar to the propensity of the domestic melodrama to avoid the characterisation of an enemy or villain in depth. Since the war raged within America, between Americans, it cannot be perceived as a First or Second World War in which the enemy was 'out there' and represented some kind of anti-democratic ideology. Those who fought for the Confederacy, in effect the 'losing side', were absorbed back into the nation. The Union's adversary became part of the 'us' of the modern USA, so it is tantamount to treason to call them the enemy. As a result, the South of these films loses enemy status.[62] Instead, the two armies of the Civil War must be seen to fight a war that somehow just happened, like an uncontrollable and unavoidable force. In the absence of a Nazi or Communist enemy, an enemy from the outside, the adversary must be dehumanised to become some other abstract concept (fear, cowardice, death, corruption, racism). On occasion these concepts are represented by individuals, but these few are routinely found within the Union army, bad Northerners who wish to take advantage of the war to exploit others for their own gain – the racist officer Montgomery in *Glory* being an example. Like the Civil War melodrama, they are given only brief episodes in which to offer a threat to the heroic group. What this allows the Civil War combat film to do is to turn its attention to the worthy individuals involved in the conflict. Without having to deal with thorny political issues the film can concentrate on the 'sterling qualities which, by implication, helped forge the American character'.[63]

A second consequence of the sidestepping of political concerns is the marginalisation of slavery and race in the films. Again, *Glory* aside, the films' central characters are, without exception, white, and they demonstrate little if no concern with the politics of abolitionism. The films correspond to the master narrative of American history criticised by Nathan I. Huggins – the 'conspiracy of myth, history, and chauvinism' to exclude race and slavery.[64] In this, the mainstream version of American history, slavery is perceived as an abnormality or an accident. It does not live up to the values of American ideology, particularly that of equality, so it must therefore be excised from the war film genre. As Cullen states, '[h]eroic or otherwise, in no major Civil War movie since World War II has race played any major role, with the exception of *Glory*'.[65] Only *Glory*, which seeks to give a voice to those who have been marginalised, comes close to Huggins' plea for a 'revised Master Narrative', one which acknowledges that 'there can be no white history or black history' – only 'history'.[66]

Authenticity

Throughout the combat films of this chapter, a growing impression of authenticity can be identified. In each case, the effort made to re-present the details of combat rises to ever-greater heights. In *Glory*, Shaw's own candlesticks were used in shots and the inside of Matthew Broderick's cap was dyed with exactly the correct colour, even though it is never seen on screen.[67] The historical mode, of course, demands a degree of accuracy in sets, costumes and props – even facial hair – but this drive for authentic detail seems to reach almost fetishistic proportions.

The sheer scale of the production of battles, a spectacle in itself, gives weight to the theme of loss, particularly in after-battle shots of dead bodies strewn across the *mise-en-scène*. A number of the films, notably *Glory*, used hundreds of Civil War re-enactors as the extras for these scenes. Stephen Crane, in the creation of *The Red Badge of Courage*, closely examined the work of Civil War photographer Mathew Brady. John Huston, similarly, based many of his compositions on Brady's photographs in his adaptation of the novel, as had a number of directors reaching back to Griffith and Ince. The viewer is thus able to see certain proxemic relations between actants on the battlefield that are indisputably accurate. Photography can also aid historical authenticity in its depiction of real figures from the war. *Gettysburg*, for example, begins and ends with photographs of the actors and their historical counterparts, as if the filmmakers are appealing to the viewer to acknowledge that these were real men. These visual referents are a calling card for the film's verisimilitude, functioning with visual authenticity to underline and strengthen the ideological effects of the films and their celebration of the brave ancestors of the American nation.

Another common tool that appeals to authenticity is the voice-over, used in *Red Badge* and *Glory*, and also in other Civil War combat films such as *Class of '61* (Gregory Hoblit, 1993) and *Gettysburg*. Even though in many cases the source of this monologue is not documentary (i.e. actual letters and diaries written during the war), it gives the impression of a subjective truth. At times this is employed in tandem with manipulations of the film speed or the soundtrack, as in *Red Badge* when the voices of other soldiers fade away to be replaced by the voice-over. Whatever the means, the resultant impression is of the individual's personal experience of war. The Civil War is personalised, and thus the melodramatic impact is brought to the fore. This may seem strange, in that what seems to be the most masculine of genres, emotions such as fear are of such importance. However, it must be remembered that the melodramatic mode is a means of outwardly expressing that which is usually hidden. By foregrounding the subjectivity of Civil War soldiers, the total experience is thus made more, not less, real.

The climax of this subjective experience is the battle itself. Common elements are the extreme long shot, rapid editing and histrionic music, often orchestral or choral, and frequently underlined with a military drumbeat. The atmosphere created is tremendously emotive, the voices of the actors often giving way to the musical soundtrack and significant visual moments frequently slowed down, such as the deaths of central characters. For the American film viewer, for whom the Civil War narrative is so significant, these moments constructed in the melodramatic mode act as cues for an emotional involvement in the film.

Each of these elements of authenticity – the input of re-enactors, the use of documentary evidence, voice-overs, and other subjective devices – work together to reconstruct the Civil War world with the central message of: 'this is what it was really like'. It helps to invest the relationship between viewer and film text with a truthfulness that infuses the narrative. In a sense, if the viewer accepts the authenticity of the reconstruction and finds pleasure in it, then he or she may be more inclined to accept the veracity of the narrative and whatever ideology it may serve.

The Masculine American Ancestor

The narrative in each of the films revolves around the central ideological issue of the combat film: the masculine crisis and the affirmation of a particular brand of masculinity. Questions of masculinity are common to many genres, but in a film that concerns the Civil War, the particular masculinity that is being explored is a masculinity of origins, or an original masculinity. As with the Western when it represents the Civil War soldier, a certain type of American male is depicted – in that case, the War-Westerner. In the Civil War combat film, because of the battlefield setting and the significance of the period, what is represented is emphatically to do with a kind of original American masculine character. The crisis takes the form of a test of courage and is faced by the problematic male: the coward, the youth, the bitter man, the rookie. His masculinity is tested through the preparation for war (the insults of the drill sergeant, the separation from home and family) and in battle, where he must work together with his regiment against the threat of injury and death. Some survive and some die, but all pass the test because of their bravery and honour. The result is glory and the resolving of the masculine problem: the coward proves his courage, the youth grows up, the bitter man learns to forgive and the rookie gains experience.

He has in one sense been re-born, a metaphor that could be applied to most, if not all, Civil War films across the genres. John Dunbar's attempted suicide on the battlefield in *Dances With Wolves* is a passage from his old life into the new. Henry Fleming's taking of the Confederate flag in *Red Badge* has been described as a 're-birth' as the enemy soldier dies.[68] Placing this metaphor next to the idea of the masculine test, it could be said that the Civil War soldier traverses the gap between one life and another, from civilian to soldier, from teacher or engineer to trained killer, from physical safety to the threat of death – effectively from boy to man. As Cullen writes concerning *Glory*, the pride and dignity promised to the 54th Massachusetts is delivered in the form of a 'reaffirmed sense of manhood'.[69] The soldiers go from being called boys repeatedly by the drill sergeant and mocking white troops, to declaring their own identity as men at their spiritual gathering on the eve of battle, having passed through the hardships of training and survived their first skirmish.

The individuals must pass this test for one very important reason that joins the combat film together with the Western and the domestic melodrama: these characters are the forefathers of the American viewer. As Anthony Smith explains, an understanding of the metaphor of family and paternity is essential to a study of national identity.[70] Commitment to 'ancestral homelands and to the generations of one's forefathers' is, according to Smith, a powerful nationalistic tool.[71] So the opening voice-over of *Class of '61*, which says that this is the story of his great-great-great grandfather, constructs a link of paternity from the beginning of the film. An emotional relationship between the American viewer and Civil War films is created, since the actants are encoded as his or her ancestors. In the case of those that survive the battle, these men are 'our fathers'; those that die in combat are 'our sons'.

The glaring problem with this identity of origins, simply put, is that most of these fathers and sons are white. Only when *Glory* was produced was some measure of restitution attempted. Until then, according to the Civil War combat film, slavery and race are peripheral to the conflict, and hence peripheral to American paternity. They are not given the place of importance that they certainly had during the era of the Civil War, not in the representation of characters nor in the discourse on the war itself.

CONCLUSION

The films of this chapter each, to a certain extent, condemn the human waste of war, telling stories of American sons lost to the civil conflict. Since the reason that these men fought is not fully explored (except the securing of emancipation by the black soldiers in *Glory*) their deaths seem like unfortunate, avoidable sacrifices. Even the deaths of the soldiers of the 54th Massachusetts, in the service of a higher moral goal, are a great loss, as the Fort remained in Confederate hands. There is a tangible impression across the films that the Civil War was a tragic undertaking for all involved.

However, in tension with this impression is an evident sense of glory that is the reward of these men who have passed their masculine test. The covert message is that these men are fighting and dying for a cause, whether the 'just' cause or the 'lost' cause, and they deserve immortalisation within the filmic form. The Civil War becomes a necessary evil, playing a part in forging the American character that devotes itself to the protection of all that is right and good, albeit not expressed in any detail as an ideology to be defended. Characters like Billy, Henry and Marlowe are fighting for what is right, whatever the viewer believes that to be. So, despite an acceptance that the Civil War was catastrophic on a national scale, these films teach the present-day viewer that it is part of the American nature to die for what is right, for the good of the nation.

Glory, despite its poignant images of loss and death at the end of the film, is a reminder that the Civil War achieved one thing: the beginning of emancipation. Something was actually fought for and it was won, and those that stood to benefit most from that achievement were able to participate in the struggle. The war in this sense is necessary and meaningful. A number of reviewers commented that *Glory* somehow re-routed the war genre back beyond the Vietnam film and its messages of the senselessness of war. The enemy, slavery, was vanquished – a truly just cause was fought for and won. John Pym's statement is typical: 'it vaults clean over the shame of Vietnam, to reaffirm the almost prehistoric notion of the value of gallantry in a just cause'.[72] There is, then, a contradiction at the heart of the Civil War combat film category. War is being hailed as both necessary and unnecessary at the same time: necessary in the ending of slavery, unnecessary in the extensive and protracted loss of life over four years of conflict.

The other single most significant film to foreground black participation in the war was one produced almost seventy-five years earlier, Griffith's *The Birth of a Nation*. As mentioned above, *Glory* overtly parallels elements of *Birth*, creating a dialogue between the two that works towards exposing the ideological assumptions behind Griffith's project. It is now necessary, therefore, to examine Griffith's controversial film of 1915, to interrogate its generic components, its narrative and its particular construction of the American ancestor. Chapter 5 reviews the production of *Birth* and its initial reception, before asking how relevant it is that Griffith should choose the Civil War itself to tell the story of the birth of the United States.

NOTES

1   Basinger, Jeanine, *The World War II Combat Film: Anatomy of a Genre* (Middletown, 2003). p. 74.
2   Belton, John, *American Cinema/American Culture* (New York, 1994). p. 172.
3   Basinger: *The World War II Combat Film*. p. 9.
4   Neale, Steve, *Genre and Hollywood* (London, 2000). p. 125.
5   George Cukor, 1933; Mervyn Le Roy, 1949; Gillian Armstrong, 1994.
6   Ray, Robert B., *A Certain Tendency of the Hollywood Cinema, 1930–1980* (Princeton, New Jersey, 1985).
7   Ray: *A Certain Tendency*. p. 115.
8   Ray: *A Certain Tendency*. pp. 116–17.
9   Ray: *A Certain Tendency*. pp. 117–18.
10   Ray: *A Certain Tendency*. p. 120.

11   Ray: *A Certain Tendency*. pp. 117–18.

12   Belton: *American Cinema/American Culture*. p. 172.

13   Belton: *American Cinema/American Culture*. p. 164.

14   Belton: *American Cinema/American Culture*. p. 165.

15   Belton: *American Cinema/American Culture*. p. 168.

16   Hammond, Michael, 'Some Smothering Dreams: The Combat Film in Contemporary Hollywood' in S. Neale (ed.) *Genre and Contemporary Hollywood* (London, 2002). pp. 62–76.

17   Hammond: 'Some Smothering Dreams'. p. 63.

18   Hammond: 'Some Smothering Dreams'. p. 65.

19   Hammond: 'Some Smothering Dreams'. p. 66.

20   Hammond: 'Some Smothering Dreams'. p. 70.

21   Thompson, Kristin and Bordwell, David, *Film History: An Introduction* (New York, 1994). p. 74.

22   Bassan, M., (ed.) *Stephen Crane: A Collection of Critical Essays* (Englewood Cliffs, New Jersey, 1967). p. 4.

23   Lambert, G., '*The Red Badge of Courage*', *Sight and Sound*, vol. 21, no. 3 (January–March 1952). p. 124.

24   DeBona, Guerric, 'Masculinity on the Front: John Huston's *The Red Badge of Courage* (1951) Revisited', *Cinema Journal*, vol. 42, no. 2 (2003). p. 66.

25   Basinger: *The World War II Combat Film*. p. 75.

26   Grob, G.N. and Billias, G.A., (eds) *Interpretations of American History: Patterns and Perspectives, Volume I – to 1877*, 5th edition (New York, 1982). pp. 402–3.

27   Chadwick, Bruce, *The Reel Civil War: Mythmaking in American Film* (New York, 2002). p. 257.

28   DeBona: 'Masculinity on the Front'. p. 58.

29   See Ross, Lillian, *Picture* (New York, 1952) and DeBona: 'Masculinity on the Front'. pp. 58–9.

30   DeBona: 'Masculinity on the Front'. p. 59.

31   DeBona: 'Masculinity on the Front'. p. 75.

32   DeBona: 'Masculinity on the Front'. p. 60.

33   DeBona: 'Masculinity on the Front'. p. 66.

34   DeBona: 'Masculinity on the Front'. p. 67.

35   Belton: *American Cinema/American Culture*. p. 168.

36   Dyer, Richard, *White* (London, 1997). p. 1.

37   Dyer: *White*. p. 2.

38   Gallagher, Tag, *John Ford: The Man and His Films* (Berkeley and Los Angeles, 1986). p. 373.

39   Gallagher: *John Ford*. p. 369.

40   Gallagher: *John Ford*. p. 370.

41   Huggins, Nathan I., 'The Deforming Mirror of Truth: Slavery and the Master Narrative of American History', *Radical History Review* (Winter, 1991). pp. 24–47.

42   Gallagher: *John Ford*. p. 371.

43   *Monthly Film Bulletin 'The Horse Soldiers'*, vol. 26, no. 311 (December, 1959). p. 155.

44   A collection of Shaw's letters can be read in Duncan, R., (ed.) *Blue-Eyed Child of Fortune: The Civil War Letters of Colonel Robert Gould Shaw* (Athens, Georgia, 1992).

45   Duncan: *Blue-Eyed Child of Fortune.* p. 242.

46   See *Variety 'Glory'* (13 December 1989); Doherty, T., '*Glory*', *Cineaste*, vol. 17, no. 4 (1990). pp. 40–1.

47   Bogle, Donald, *Toms, Coons, Mulattoes, Mammies and Bucks: An Interpretive History of Blacks in American Films*, 3rd edition (Oxford, 1994). pp. 4–15.

48   Pym, J., 'For the Union Dead: *Glory*', *Sight and Sound*, vol. 59, no. 2 (Spring, 1990). p. 135.

49   Burgoyne, Robert, *Film Nation: Hollywood Looks at U.S. History* (Minneapolis, 1997). p. 20.

50   Neale: *Genre and Hollywood.* p. 31.

51   Duncan: *Blue-Eyed Child of Fortune.* p. 343.

52   Belton: *American Cinema/American Culture.* p. 168.

53   Burgoyne: *Film Nation.* pp. 20–1.

54   Basinger: *The World War II Combat Film.* p. 15.

55   Huggins: 'The Deforming Mirror of Truth'. p. 38; Burgoyne: *Film Nation.* p. 26.

56   Burgoyne: *Film Nation.* pp. 27 and 29.

57   Also noted by Burgoyne: *Film Nation.* p. 36.

58   Belton: *American Cinema/American Culture.* p. 178.

59   Gilroy, Paul, *There Ain't No Black in the Union Jack* (London, 1987). p. 52; a link made by Burgoyne: *Film Nation.* p. 17.

60   Gilroy: *There Ain't No Black.* p. 52.

61   Tunney, T., '*Gettysburg*', *Sight and Sound*, vol. 4, no. 10 (October 1994). p. 44.

62   Although across various media the South has metaphorical links to defeat – a point made by Jim Cullen in his discussion on Southern rock music, *The Civil War in Popular Culture: A Reusable Past* (Washington, 1995). p. 117.

63   Tunney: '*Gettysburg*'. p. 44.

64   Huggins: 'The Deforming Mirror of Truth'. p. 25.

65   Cullen: *The Civil War in Popular Culture.* p. 155.

66   Huggins: 'The Deforming Mirror of Truth'. pp. 38 and 40.

67   Combs, R., '*Glory*', *Monthly Film Bulletin*, vol. 57, no. 675 (April 1990). p. 106.

68   R.W. Stallman in a discussion of Crane's original novel, 'Notes Toward an Analysis of *The Red Badge of Courage*' in M. Bassan (ed.) *Stephen Crane: A Collection of Critical Essays* (Englewood Cliffs, New Jersey, 1967). p. 135.

69   Cullen: *The Civil War in Popular Culture.* p. 158.

70   Smith, Anthony D., *National Identity* (London, 1991). p. 79.

71   Smith: *National Identity.* p. 78.

72   Pym: 'For the Union Dead'. p. 135; see also Doherty, '*Glory*'. p. 40 and White, A., 'Fighting Black: Zwick on His Feet', *Film Comment*, vol. 26, no. 1 (January–February 1990). p. 22.

5

The Birth of a Nation:
Race, Family, Gender

The Birth of a Nation (D.W. Griffith, 1915) is arguably the most controversial film in the history of cinema. Critical attention for the film has continued consistently since its production, focusing primarily on its particular construction of black characters, but also on its contribution to cinema as art. Despite the film's notoriety amongst Civil War scholars, enthusiasts, historians and film scholars, and the reams of published material available about it, a fresh look at the film in the light of genre and American national identity is pertinent, so this chapter briefly surveys the film's production, its key players and its initial reception in 1915, before reviewing the narrative that caused such significant public responses. I will then go on to investigate the film's generic identity as a hybrid of the epic and the domestic melodrama, and invite certain comparisons and contrasts with the films examined in Chapter 2. It does not necessarily follow, just because *Birth* can be categorised as melodrama, that it will demonstrate the same re-imagination of the American Civil War as the films of Chapter 2. In fact, Griffith's choice of melodrama for his enactment of the war and of Reconstruction leads to a very different imagination of the American nation. The demands of melodrama itself help to provide Griffith with the means to imagine a certain community of American forefathers, revealing a concerted effort to propagate the ideology of white supremacy.

THE HISTORY OF *THE BIRTH OF A NATION*

David Wark Griffith was born in 1875, a mere ten years after the signing of the peace treaty between the Northern United States and the Southern Confederacy at the end of four years of Civil War. By early 1915, when *Birth* was first exhibited in Los Angeles and New York, Griffith had directed or produced well in excess of four hundred films, mostly one- or two-reel films for the Biograph Company. His reputation as a pioneering filmmaker had already spread beyond America, establishing Griffith as a household name at a time when few directors were even credited publicly for their work. He had played a major role in developing the techniques (amongst others) of cross-cutting simultaneous actions, the use of multiple camera set-ups, significant uses of the close-up and the meaningful juxtaposition of varying shot sizes.

Birth is partly modelled on the 1905 novel and stage melodrama *The Clansman* by Reverend Thomas Dixon Jr who was, like Griffith, a Southern man. Dixon's story was never received as a particularly great work of art, in fact as Cary D. Wintz writes in a recent edition of the novel, it was considered at best only 'popular fiction', a low-brow fantasy as opposed to a respected work of literature.[1] It did, however, appeal to certain quarters, such as theatre-goers in North Carolina, who felt that the stage-play was a fair and historically valid picture of the Reconstruction South.[2] This was not a widespread response, as Scott Simmon writes, since the play went on to be the subject of strong reactions throughout the country, and has been linked to race riots that occurred in Philadelphia and Atlanta in 1906.[3] An indication of the reason for this reaction can be found in the novel's opening note 'To the Reader', which plainly states that the narrative concerns 'the Race Conflict' between the white Aryan nation and the black race.[4] Through the medium of film, Dixon's story, initially known by the same title as the novel and play, was made accessible to many millions of Americans, some of whom would have been aware of its source. It is no surprise, then, that Griffith's film caused outrage on a national scale.

Griffith's narrative enlarges upon Dixon's novel and play, adding a pre-war prologue and an enactment of certain events during the Civil War itself. The novel actually begins with the end of the war in a Union military hospital, where the central characters Ben Cameron and Elsie Stoneman first meet. It is also a strange concoction of historical events, melodrama and the supernatural, in which the image of Gus, the black rapist, is found imprinted on the retina of his murdered victim – a part of the story eschewed by

Griffith in the film. According to G.W. 'Billy' Bitzer, *Birth*'s cinematographer, Griffith felt that he was finally directing something that was important and worthwhile in his adaptation of Dixon's novel. No longer was the director simply "'grinding out sausages'" as he was famously quoted saying, but was 'fighting the old war all over again'.[5] Griffith's attention to authentic, historical detail during the filming has become legendary, demanding for example exactly the correct dappled grey horse to carry Robert E. Lee to his surrender. In Bitzer's words, it was as if the production company was back in 1865, adding 'in Griffith's mind we were'.[6]

Indeed, it would appear that it was Griffith's mind that was responsible for much of the narrative of *Birth*, using Dixon's story only as a starting point. Lillian Gish's account of the making of the film states that upon seeing the finished product, Dixon remarked "'this isn't my book at all'".[7] Griffith was re-telling the story, and the history of America, according to his particular imagination of the nation, one that was, like all effective propaganda, based strongly on factual research and documentation. During pre-production the director employed professional historians as well as working himself to research the historical authenticity of the story. According to Lillian Gish, for example, the Civil War photographs of Mathew Brady were consulted with great care to re-stage battles with the utmost accuracy, adding that at the time this technique was an innovation in the cinema.[8]

Under its original title of *The Clansman*, Griffith's film was exhibited at Clune's Auditorium in Los Angeles on 8 February 1915, attended by the director, crew and cast. Assistant cinematographer, Karl Brown, overheard a patron at the cinema saying that Griffith's depiction of the Civil War was "'exactly as grandpa had described it'".[9] Not all audiences felt the same. In their writings, Brown, Bitzer and Gish each express astonishment at the storm of protest that swiftly followed the film's opening and its premières in cities across the nation. As many critical writings about the reception of the film make clear, *Birth* was both a film of its time, reflecting the racist worldview of many white Americans at that moment, but it was also violently and publicly rejected by both black and white Americans after its release and up to the present day.

Across the country at this time there were several carefully organised groups and movements, some interracial, that strove to stand against widespread racism, notably the National Association for the Advancement of Colored People (NAACP). This particular organisation was extremely active in political and cultural campaigns and went on to become deeply involved in the discussions on race in Griffith's film, particularly in their journal, *The Crisis. The D.W. Griffith Papers* contain numerous press articles and minutes of meetings where leading figures in this group, such as Moorfield Storey and Ida B. Wells, gave a public voice to their disgust at *Birth's* deceptiveness and its representation of black people.[10] Although the NAACP managed to have the Los Angeles première of the film delayed, once exhibited, the film continued its run there for several months.[11] They also appealed, successfully, for the more offensive scenes of the film to be cut, including the arrival of slaves in America by ship, the sale of slaves by Northerners to Southerners, a Northern female abolitionist's disgust at the smell of a freed slave[12] and a letter written by Lincoln denying any faith in racial equality.[13] Scott Simmon writes that, despite the claim that a rape scene and castration scene were also removed (alleged by Seymour Stern, a contemporary of Griffith and an enthusiastic supporter of *Birth*), no evidence has been found to substantiate that the scenes existed.[14] Even with its more offensive scenes eliminated, however, *Birth* remained unacceptable to many of its audiences.

Birth was also influential in the renewed public vigour of another political organisation – the Ku Klux Klan – which features strongly in the second half of the film. The Modern Klan (distinct from the Reconstruction Klan suppressed in the late nineteenth century) was already experiencing a revival at the time of *Birth's* exhibition. Leaders of the Klan, however, decided to capitalise on the film's commercial success by printing an advertisement in a local Atlanta newspaper adjacent to publicity for *Birth*. They even staged a public meeting, complete with burning cross, just days before the film's Atlanta release.[15] The Klan was not alone in its enthusiasm for the film. Millions of Americans were prepared to pay the extortionate ticket price of two dollars to see the film, which *Variety* reviewer Mark Vance suggested was at least four times the usual fee for an evening's viewing.[16] One of the most celebrated quotations concerning *Birth* is President Woodrow Wilson's declaration that the film was 'like history written with lightning'.[17] Wilson marvels equally at its horror and (in his opinion) truth. His own historical works were, after all, quoted in a number of the film's intertitles, and so his words of praise were self-promotional at the very least. Wilson's comment was of course retracted when *Birth* faced vehement attacks from some sections of the press and the NAACP.

Simmon adds credence to the argument that *Birth* somehow reflected a widespread racist worldview when he notes that it bears close relation to the attitudes circulating in contemporary academic histories of the early twentieth century – particularly the Dunning School at Columbia University, based on the Reconstruction history by William A. Dunning, representing blacks as a simple and lustful people.[18] Dunning's ideological standpoint is clear from such statements as: 'the ultimate root of the trouble in the South had been, not the institution of slavery, but the coexistence in one society of two races so distinct in characteristics as to render coalescence impossible'.[19] This view of the inferiority of the black race and the horror of miscegenation bears a close resemblance to elements of the Southern literary tradition of the late nineteenth century that propagated the view of a racial hierarchy and fear of miscegenation, and to the views articulated by Griffith through *Birth*. What is important to note is that these views cannot be consigned to the distant past, since Dunning's writings and teachings were instrumental in the proliferation of this ideology right up until the late 1940s.

The continuing presence of racist attitudes is made evident by the backlash from individuals and organisations, struggling to redress common prejudices encouraged by cinema. Written in 1946, over thirty years after the first release of *Birth*, Peter Noble's critique in *Sight and Sound* nods towards Griffith's genius as a filmmaker, but goes on to roundly condemn his racism.[20] Noble's understanding of the film thus acknowledges Griffith's status as an extraordinary pioneer of the cinema, but refuses to condone the film's representation of black people. Griffith himself swiftly replied, denying that he had ever been racist. As in 1915, he felt now that his 'attitude towards the Negroes has always been one of affection and brotherly feeling'.[21] Roy Kinnard explains that Griffith's paternalistic, condescending attitude towards race was the product of the director's upbringing – he was a white Southerner born just years after the South's defeat in the Civil War.[22] He held what has been recognised as a 'hard-core Southern reactionary point of view', one that divided the black race between good and bad, faithful and traitorous.[23] It considered black people incapable of self-government or self-control and saw them as needful of careful, fatherly guidance from the white race. Although these views had been popularised in Southern romances, both in novels and films long before the release of *Birth*, the literary and filmic tradition that actively oppressed and suppressed blacks continued long after the film. Griffith's and his supporters' public defences of *Birth*, recurring into the middle of the twentieth century, prove that racist feelings were not consigned to turn-of-the-century attitudes.

Part of Griffith's self-defence against attack was an appeal to the authenticity of his film. His reply to *Sight and Sound* stated: '[…] I gave to my best knowledge the proven facts, and presented the known truth, about the Reconstruction period in the American South. These facts are based on an overwhelming compilation of authentic evidence and testimony.'[24] In other words, as far as Griffith was concerned, and in his belief system, *Birth* was an accurate depiction of the American South before, during and after the Civil War. To Griffith it was essential to get his facts 'right' because he believed that cinema carried a great responsibility as 'a tool for completing the great goal of history: lifting mankind from animality'.[25] Essentially, Griffith saw film as a potentially moralising and educational force in the hands of filmmakers. Through his depiction of what he saw as truth he might cause his audience to identify with enlightened values and live accordingly – in *Birth* that 'truth' is based upon the racist hierarchy of white over black and the danger of miscegenation, enlightenment being dependent on an acceptance of these contentions. He clearly felt that this was not just his own view, but that it was commonly held by critics and audiences, and thus suffered great consternation at horrified reactions to his film. Perhaps, as Simmon suggests, adverse reactions to *Birth* might not have been quite as strong if Griffith had not claimed it to be historically accurate.[26] It is necessary at this stage, then, to re-visit narrative details of the film, before attempting to more fully question Griffith's ideological stance.

THE STORY

The narrative of *The Birth of a Nation* follows the story of two American families, the Stonemans in the North and the Camerons in the South, who are tragically pitched against one another during the Civil War, then reunited as a white brotherhood after the successful overthrow, by the Ku Klux Klan, of anarchic black political and sexual power. The film follows an epic structure: before the Civil War, during the war, the period of Reconstruction and the restoration of the South to white rule. In a brief prologue the slave traders of the seventeenth century are linked to the abolitionists of the pre-Civil War era, with an intertitle that sets the tone for the entire film: 'The bringing of the African to America planted the first seed of disunion'. The Stoneman family of the North is then introduced in 1860. The father, Austin Stoneman (Ralph Lewis), is a powerful abolitionist in the House of Representatives, and so is associated with the coming disunity in America. As has been often noted, this personality is a caricature of Thaddeus Stevens, the Radical Republican who went on to impose what many Southerners believed to be a harsh Reconstruction programme after the death of Abraham Lincoln (played in the film by Joseph Henabery) in 1865. Stoneman is characterised as both physically crippled (he uses a stick to walk) and morally perverted (he has a mixed-race housekeeper-mistress, Lydia Brown, played by white actress Mary Alden).

Stoneman's daughter, Elsie (Lillian Gish), who adores him, tells him that his sons, Phil (Elmer Clifton) and Tod (Robert Harron), are going to visit their Southern friends, the Camerons, at their plantation in South Carolina. The visit is made up of idyllic scenes of the South where, as an intertitle announces, 'life runs in a quaintly way that is to be no more'. Each member of the Cameron family is a well-defined type with a distinct individuality: Dr Cameron (Spottiswoode Aitken) as a proud but kind gentleman; Mrs Cameron (Josephine Crowell), a matronly and devoted mother; Ben (Henry B. Walthall), a handsome and morally upright son; Margaret (Miriam Cooper), a well-mannered daughter of the South; Duke (Maxfield Stanley) a young and patriotic Southern man; Wade (J. A. Beringer), a playful and carefree adolescent; and Flora (Mae Marsh), an excitable but pure 'Little Pet Sister' who idolises her eldest brother. On their plantation, cotton is picked by the most contented of slaves, whose greatest joy is to dance for the Northern visitors as they tour the estate.

Most of the children of the two families are paired relationally by the Piedmont visit: Duke Cameron and Tod Stoneman develop a friendly rivalry as 'chums', Phil Stoneman and Margaret Cameron begin a romance and Ben Cameron falls in love with the ideal woman – Elsie Stoneman – when he sees her photograph. This pairing of the families' children acts as proof, in the logic of the narrative which brings Northern and Southern characters together on the plantation, that the siblings make up one single family, naturally drawn to one another in the Southern agrarian idyll of Piedmont. The Edenic paradise is then shattered by Lincoln's call for volunteers to enlist in a Union army against the seceding states of the South – blame for the outbreak of war being apportioned to the North. Nothing is mentioned of secession, or the first wartime aggression at Fort Sumter being instigated by the Confederate army. Lincoln, however, is depicted in a tableau – a typical melodramatic device conventionally used to suggest a moment or character of great importance – weeping and praying at his desk. It is thus suggested that Lincoln himself does not desire conflict, but equally he cannot prevent the inevitable.

In the North, Elsie sadly says goodbye to her brothers on their way to war, whilst in Piedmont a parade sees off the Cameron sons. Before leaving, Ben gives a Confederate flag to Flora, pointing out to her its sentiment: 'Conquer we must for our Cause is just.' The cause itself is not overtly stated, allowing it to remain sufficiently vague for the viewer to insert the nature of the cause, and for the film to avoid any threat to the heroic, romanticised construction of the South. In receiving this flag, Flora is metaphorically linked to the defeat of the old South, to come later in the film.

The second part of the narrative jumps forwards two and a half years to Ben reading a letter from Flora as he sits waiting for battle. It is interesting to note that it is the family, and not Ben, that faces hostility first when black Union guerrillas, led by a white officer, raid the home at Piedmont. The first travesty of war then is enacted by the Union army upon innocent women, children and the elderly, not the brave young Confederates who await battle far away. The Union raid on Piedmont is the first scene of actual conflict in the film, taking place on the home soil of the Camerons, in the process of which Dr Cameron is wounded. Soon after, however, the two chums meet on the battlefield only to die in each other's arms, representing war's 'bitter, useless sacrifice', as an intertitle describes. Both families express their grief, but continue to serve their respective war efforts (Elsie becomes a nurse) or struggle to survive (the Camerons sell some of their possessions). Meanwhile, General Sherman's army is seen marching through the South, watched by a cowering Southern woman and her children. It is only Northern aggression that is enacted on screen, culminating in the burning of Atlanta. The Confederacy and the Southern characters are never represented as wartime aggressors, only as honourable soldiers and victims. In accord with the melodramatic mode, a distinction of North and South is made in the terms of corporate villain (the Union army) and collective victim-hero (the Confederate army, the Camerons and the single mother with her children at the hillside).

At the battle of Petersburg, the *mise-en-scène* reveals a tired and hungry Southern army in the 'last grey days of the Confederacy'. Despite this, a spectacular battle takes place complete with heroic charges, explosions, and hand-to-hand combat. Ben, labelled 'The Little Colonel', leads a last-hope charge after pausing to give water to a fallen enemy soldier. Although Ben is shot he raises the tattered Confederate flag and plants it in a Union cannon, before collapsing at the feet of his enemy/friend, Phil Stoneman. The aftermath of the Union victory shows distorted dead bodies, no longer distinguishable as Union or Confederate, strewn across the silent battlefield with the poignant intertitle, 'War's Peace'.

The violence of war ends at this point of the film and the narrative turns to the post-war period, corresponding to the starting point of Dixon's original novel. Elsie discovers Ben in hospital and learns, with Mrs Cameron, that he is to be executed for a bogus accusation of guerrilla activities. The Southern mother appeals to Lincoln, the 'Great Heart', for Ben's release. With a god-like power over life and death, Lincoln agrees. A historical facsimile then depicts, as a tableau, the signing of the Confederate surrender, with General Lee appearing statue-like in the shock of defeat. Ben returns to his home, welcomed through the door by the arms of his mother and Little Pet Sister, and the family begins to re-build their lives. In Washington Lincoln attempts to do the same for the nation, but clashes with Stoneman over Reconstruction policies. The president vows to deal with the South 'as though they had never been away', like a good and just father, but his promise is never fulfilled. On 14 April 1865, Elsie and Phil Stoneman witness his assassination. The death of Lincoln, and Stoneman's perverted ambition to empower the black race, cause the suffering of the South as depicted in the third part of the film.

Woodrow Wilson's words introduce the goal of Northern oppression during Reconstruction, to 'put the white South under the heel of the black South', as Stoneman's mixed-race protégé, Silas Lynch (George Siegmann), is sent to Piedmont to oversee the establishment of black rule. An immediate rivalry is set up between Lynch and Ben, which soon escalates to hatred. Ben's distrust of Lynch, an empowered black man, is justified by a series of scenes showing offences committed by freed slaves, including the uncouth, predominantly black state legislature voting for the right to intermarry between races.

Inspiration from a children's game, in which white children wearing sheets terrify black children, leads to Ben forming the Ku Klux Klan, and the new white 'knights' terrorise the black community. When Elsie discovers Ben's involvement with the Klan she halts their relationship, being committed to her father's goal of political equality between the races. The ultimate tragedy occurs when Flora throws herself from a cliff-edge to escape the advances of a lustful black man, Gus (Walter Long). Ben conducts a ritual to swear revenge by dipping the Confederate flag in Flora's blood and after a swift trial Gus is executed and left on Lynch's doorstep. As Ben calls a gathering of the Klan, Lynch musters his black troops in the streets of Piedmont, where Dr Cameron is arrested for his association with the secret organisation. When Elsie pleads to have Ben's father released, Lynch traps her and attempts a forced marriage. The rest of the Cameron family, in hiding, are attacked by Lynch's troops and Piedmont is soon filled with black revellers. A four-way cross-cut sequence shows the ride of the Klan to

16. *The Birth of a Nation* (D.W. Griffith, 1915): The moment of Lee's surrender to a victorious Grant is captured as a tableau.

save the Camerons, to free Elsie and restore the town to peace. A victorious parade through Piedmont then shows Ben and Elsie reunited. The final part of the narrative resolves the racial conflict of Reconstruction by the failure of the black vote and white power is restored. A double honeymoon for Ben and Elsie, Phil and Margaret, shows the couples gazing off-screen towards a future of peace and happiness. An epilogue reveals the god of war dissolving into an all-white Jerusalem, presided over by a white Christ.

At face value, *Birth* is structurally and thematically an extension of the chase films and revenge narratives of early American cinema. It transplants ideas of the white hero's persecution by a racial 'other' that can be found in countless frontier narratives, already familiar to the film-viewing public in 1915. The climactic ride-to-the-rescue also capitalises on the resolution of numerous tales of captured heroines. In this sense, *Birth* is nothing new. However, its sheer scale as a chase-and-revenge picture on a national level was remarkable, and being placed at a specific historical moment (the Civil War) meant that the tried and tested formula was lent an authenticity lacking from previous films. In addition, Griffith's particular interpretation of the period, as a time of interracial instead of

17. *The Birth of a Nation* (D.W. Griffith, 1915): Cameron discovers that his true battle is racial as he holds the body of his dead sister.

geo-political conflict, gives *Birth* an overtly biased ideological slant on American history.

Donald Bogle suggests that Civil War films across the board are racist: 'The problem [...] has never been that they presented Negroes as slaves – for how else could they be depicted? – but that the films have humiliated and debased them far beyond the callings of the script.'[27] If that is so, it is another reason to take account of the racist tendencies present when conducting an analysis of a Civil War film. However, having said this, and in accord with Russell Merritt, analysis of any film cannot afford to focus entirely on one issue, thus 'belabouring the obvious', since that ignores its many diverse aspects.[28] An analysis of *Birth* that concerns itself, for example, only with the treatment of race may risk ignoring large portions of the film. Instead, an alternative approach that seeks to explore its generic identity, demands that the film be examined in its entirety. *Birth* can be seen to meld both epic and melodramatic genres in its reconstruction of a significant historical event, and an analysis of the relationship between its use of genre and of history may reveal what the film seems to 'say' about American nationhood and identity. This approach is taken below, and in the process I will note a particular interaction between the ideology of nationalism and the genre of melodrama.

GENRE

In terms of its mode, *The Birth of a Nation* is undeniably melodramatic, not least in its codes of acting. Roberta Pearson's work on Griffith's Biograph films[29] identifies the innovative, verisimilar acting style that he developed in his acting troupe before *Birth* was produced, and there are certainly many examples of this sophisticated mode of performance in the film, such as the visit to the slave quarters at Piedmont and much of the combat. The histrionic, more expressive, style, however, is also evident. Lillian Gish, Mae Marsh, Henry B. Walthall and many of the other actors use isolated, strongly stressed gestures to communicate emotion and meaning. The use of extended, still, tableaux, also, corresponds to the histrionic code. *Mise-en-scène*, similarly, expresses the suffering of the South, such as the dilapidated Piedmont house and the Camerons' ragged clothing. Perhaps one of the most significant expressive devices is the white costume of the Klan, a literal uniform as well as a metaphorical utterance of white purity and superiority. These melodramatic usages of costume chart a narrative of suffering, uprising and victory for the collective Southern hero, underscored to equally melodramatic effect by the orchestral accompaniment compiled for the film by Griffith and composer Joseph Carl Breil, in which Wagner's pro-Aryan 'Ride of the Valkyries' complements images of the white 'knights' riding to the rescue of the South.

    Birth has been placed within several generic categories since its release, and the traditions on which it was based further complicate its identity. It is most frequently identified as an epic[30] and as melodrama,[31] but has also been described as part of a historical film genre,[32] historical film melodrama[33] and plantation genre.[34] Jack Spears writes that Civil War films were most popular during the silent era when they were a blend of 'patriotic melodramas and crinoline romances',[35] which could also describe *Birth*. Simmon, likewise, sees *Birth* as the result of a fusion of two filmic traditions, the Civil War film and the 'Southern', a generic category of films concerned with plantation life in the old South, set before the onslaught of war.[36] It is Simmon who seems to suggest that, by 1915, a Civil War genre existed, since the list of Civil War films already made by this stage is extensive, at least ten of which were directed by Griffith during his years with the Biograph Company.

Simmon notes that the common link between these films, apart from the Civil War, is a 'code of family honor'.[37] Indeed, the family is the means by which Griffith tells the story of *Birth*, not only in the families at the centre of the narrative but also in the white brotherhood of the Klan, extending beyond these 'knights' to the white family nationwide. This centralising of the family and personalisation of history is what helps to define *Birth* as domestic melodrama. Lary May states that '[e]very crisis of the film revolved around threats to the family' – each historical moment depicted is reflected in its effects on the Stonemans and Camerons during war and peacetimes.[38] Melodrama conjoins the two spheres of social and personal, giving the family, as Christine Gledhill puts it, 'a symbolic potency'.[39] Those threats and crises that encroach on the opening image of a Southern Eden are external and social, but they are made real, as it were, by superimposing them onto the experience of the family. Like the melodramas examined in Chapter 2, in *Birth* the national upheavals directly influence the families – the family consequently becomes symbolic of the nation, or to be more specific, the white nation. That which harms the nation harms the family; that which unites the nation unites the family. For example, the failing health of Dr Cameron relates to the increasing fragility of the South towards the end of the war and during Reconstruction. Equally, a bill passed to allow interracial marriage leads to two central white female characters suffering the 'dishonour' of approaches from black or mixed-race men.

Of course, the grand scale and spectacle of *Birth* lends to its epic identity – a historically situated story on a national scale, complete with vast panoramic battle scenes. Neale writes that the epic genre emphasises spectacle and is concerned with the interaction of politics with military power, rule and struggle.[40] *Birth* can legitimately fit this broad definition as far as its national story is concerned, and through melodrama these thematic concerns are transposed to a personal level in its central characters. The integration of domestic melodrama with the epic allows for the lives of the central characters to become the means of telling the story of history. The archetypal shot that melds melodrama with epic genre shows an unknown mother with her children, gazing fearfully at the progress of General Sherman's Union army through a valley below. The family helplessly watches the destruction of the nation. The link is thus made between nation and family, and ultimately the so-called 'birth of a nation' is seen in familial terms when white rule returns to the South and the couples are reunited. So *Birth* can be comfortably categorised as a hybrid of two genres, making it 'epic melodrama'. As an aside, this supports the work of a number of genre theorists who assert that genres have been mixed and combined since the earliest years of American cinema.[41]

The parallel of the antebellum South with Eden lends a sense of nostalgia to *Birth*. It re-creates an image of what we are expected to recognise as a better world now lost forever, for which we can only yearn. As previously noted, Dixon's original text was part of a literary tradition, albeit a particularly virulent strain, of the Southern plantation myth, made popular by the 'plantation school' of novelists: Joel Chandler Harris (who created the character of Uncle Remus), Thomas Nelson Page, and of course Harriet Beecher Stowe, whose *Uncle Tom's Cabin* (1852), a kind of 'reversal-of-myth', played such a large part in the debate on slavery. The racism and the stereotypes, as well as the romance, of *Birth* are direct descendants of this literary tradition of the mid- to late nineteenth century in America. The stock characters and elements of the myth included the cowardly white Northerner, the arrogant freed slave, the pure and passive female who is subjected to the threat of rape by the 'bad' black man, and the persuasive evil white carpetbagger.[42] Although this literature did not tend to focus on the Civil War itself, it instead characterised a South that 'seemed to be winning the war that it had lost on the battlefields'.[43] The Southern heroes, in accord with the line of conflict of the war, pitched a moral and literal battle against the 'depraved' blacks and corrupt whites of the North.

Despite this, according to Edward Campbell, the Southern plantation myth in literature was popular across the country and indicated a 'national mood of forgiveness' after the war and even helped to 'heal the war's wounds' by the turn of the century.[44] Clearly, its nostalgic appeal was not restricted only to the Southern imagination. From the stock elements of the myth, there developed the stereotyped black figures of Hollywood cinema, called the 'black pantheon' of mythical types by Black Cinema historian Donald Bogle. Each of them is present in *The Birth of a Nation*: the Tom (the Camerons' faithful male slave), the Coon (the entertaining slaves on the Piedmont plantation), the tragic Mulatto (Stoneman's mixed-race mistress, Lydia), the Mammy (at Piedmont) and the Brutal Black Buck (Gus, the lustful renegade who chases Flora to her death).[45]

The threat of rape to the virginal woman is a convention of both the Southern literary tradition and of melodrama, which 'figures evil as a rapist and virtue as a threatened virgin',[46] and much of *Birth* is structured around threats to women. Specifically here, of course, the particular threat is the black rape of a white woman. Noble calls it a 'pathological obsession', present in American literature since the mid-nineteenth century.[47] In the narrative terms of *Birth*, this is represented in the dual threats to Elsie Stoneman and Flora Cameron by black or mixed-race men, and in Flora's case this leads to suicide instead of bearing the terrible dishonour of rape. The greatest dishonour here, Griffith is saying, is that of miscegenation, a particular anxiety descending from the Southern myth and from socio-cultural attitudes of the seventeenth and eighteenth centuries. Melodrama operates as a most effective means by which to articulate this fear of racial intermarriage because of its tendency to represent social anxieties in a sexual conflict.[48]

Simmon highlights another link between melodrama, Southern myth and the woman. He pinpoints the element of female suffering as a metaphor for the suffering of the South in the Civil War.[49] As has been explored above, national, historical occurrences are, through melodrama, personalised into familial experiences, and the experience of the woman here is thus significant on a national scale. Woman acts as metaphor for the South, something to be adored and preserved at all costs. Although Elsie Stoneman is a Northern woman, she stands for the purity and value of womanhood and thence of the nation itself – as Mary Ann Doane writes, Elsie's photograph which is idolised by Ben Cameron circulates as 'the sign of desire, of racial purity, and of national identity'.[50] Elsie being a moral, well-educated, independent woman is highly valued but needful of guidance and protection. Her personal destiny in the film is intricately linked with the historical and narrative occurrences.

Making the female character so central and so significant sits very comfortably with melodrama, which itself is widely received as a woman's genre (see Chapter 2 for a discussion of this restricted understanding of melodrama). Using the remarkable shot of the mother and children on a hillside, watching the unstoppable march of Sherman's army in the valley below, as an example, Simmon states that Griffith in effect 'rewrites the Civil War as a woman's film'.[51] It should be noted that the title of the film indicates this: use of the word 'birth' refers to an experience indelibly associated with woman. A child is born of the suffering and pain of its mother. The birth of the nation that Griffith depicts is characterised then by national suffering and pain, its mother being the South rather than the entire nation since it is the suffering of the South that is most evidently presented to us. Not only is the Civil War and Reconstruction period of American history translated into a family experience, then, but it is also specifically female.

In this respect, parallels can be identified between *Birth* and the Civil War melodramas examined in Chapter 2. *So Red the Rose* (King Vidor, 1935), taking place exclusively on a Southern plantation, also foregrounds the woman's experience during wartime with the heroine Valette Bedford. *Gone With the Wind* (Victor Fleming, 1939) is the clearest parallel, constructed on a similar epic scale to *Birth*, and giving Scarlett O'Hara a figurative place as representative of the transformation of the old South, just as Elsie Stoneman's conversion to Ben Cameron's Southern white philosophy represents a national awakening. Chadwick goes so far as to write that '[t]he fingerprints of *The Birth of a Nation* were all over *Gone With the Wind*',[52] such as the mourning of the loss of the old South, the wealthy but honourable Southern families, and the Northern attack on the plantation. *Friendly Persuasion* (William Wyler, 1956) and *Ride With the Devil* (Ang Lee, 1999) shift their focus more clearly towards the male experience, although each of the four films concern themselves primarily with family and its survival.

A common narrative device that connects the viewer to his or her ancestors on the screen is that of the inner struggle, what I have termed earlier as the Self Civil War. *Birth* also displays this device, most clearly through Elsie's conversion. When she discovers that her sweetheart is involved in the terrorist Ku Klux Klan, her abolitionist sensibilities, instilled in her by her father, cause her to halt their relationship. However, once she experiences first hand the effects of power and independence on the black race, she quickly realises that Ben's beliefs and fears are well-founded. Elsie is then redeemed and rewarded by her rescue and marriage. She thus becomes representative of the ideological transformation of the family/nation, like Duncan and Valette Bedford, Scarlett O'Hara, the Birdwell family and Jake Roedell, making her acceptable as the ideal American ancestor. Ben Cameron's transformation, similarly, is an awakening to the true conflict of his people, of white against black. On initially returning to Piedmont after the war he coolly keeps his distance from the new black governor, Silas Lynch, but after his sister's death precipitated by black lust his propriety is defeated by a moral demand for justice. Subsequently, Ben returns the South to its rightful white rule and so is constructed as a heroic American ancestor, freeing the nation of black oppression for the future.

THE CIVIL WAR AND ITS SIGNIFICANCE IN *BIRTH*

A number of writers have stated that the Civil War is not the pivotal narrative device of *The Birth of a Nation*.[53] The war is secondary to the more significant threat to the white family, that of miscegenation. Lang writes that in contrast to *Birth*'s opening titles, Griffith encourages 'abhorrence for the black race, not for war'.[54] However, Griffith takes great pains to show the Civil War in his film, and to make it as authentic and accurate as he is able. He notoriously spent the film's entire original budget of $40,000 on the battle scenes alone, so its significance should not be glossed over. Griffith is not simply showing the war – as perhaps he might have had viewers believe – but is using it for a purpose.

To begin with, to many, the Civil War is the critical historical moment of the modern United States of America. Out of the senselessness of its suffering came a new, more mature nation, albeit one which continued in many ways to segregate and oppress. According to Rogin, the Civil War was still being fought in the minds of some contemporaries in 1915: certain extras hired from the South took issue with wearing 'Yankee' uniforms during the battle scenes.[55] Griffith himself grew up hearing his father's stories of the war, many of which may have been embellishments. Jacob 'Roaring Jake' Griffith was wounded fighting for the Confederacy, and his son had 'an almost idolatrous admiration for him', despite the father's reputation for drink and laziness in his later years.[56] Being born so soon after the end of the war and being raised on Southern stories of honour and glory, this period was very significant to Griffith. Awareness of these aspects of the Griffith persona helps to reveal what he understood the Civil War to be about and why he used it to bolster his manifesto for white supremacy. This detail of *Birth*'s history thus feeds into an interpretation of the film itself.

By the time of *Birth*, the war was part of a cultural tradition, a means of entertainment even, as well as a point of historical identity for Americans. Griffith's treatment of the war, however, overtly uses the war as an ideological tool, to create a perfect white American ancestry. Mimi White's essay states that the war is used in *Birth* as a 'purification rite', by which any worrying or morally unacceptable members of the ideal family are eliminated.[57] Her examples to support this proposal include the two 'chums', the younger brothers from the two families, whose repeated embraces can be construed as latent homosexuality and who finally die in each others' arms. But another of the Cameron sons is killed in battle, and his only crime, if anything, is to be rather quiet, and White's implication of an incestuous relationship between Elsie Stoneman and her brother seems rather difficult to substantiate. However, White's description of the war here as 'a rite of purgation' helps to see it as a painful lesson that has direct implications for the white family – the nation as family is turned against itself and must labour to learn what true unity is about in order to emerge stronger than before, purified by its experience and made acceptable as the roots of an ancestral American familyhood.

Although it is quite clear, as Lang states, that it was abhorrence of the black race not of war that Griffith championed in *Birth*, his representation of battle is authentically detailed and emphatic, depicting its effects on both soldier and civilian alike. Four years of war are vividly condensed into a guerrilla attack on the Southern town of Piedmont, a skirmish on the edges of a battle, a view of Sherman's march to the sea, the burning of Atlanta and the battle at Petersburg. Other mention is made by intertitle of incidents and battles, such as the First Battle of Bull Run, and Griffith's historical facsimiles offer almost static tableaux of Lincoln's volunteer draft of 1861 and the signing of the peace treaty at Appomattox Courthouse in 1865. Although a lot of history suffers an ellipsis here, Griffith shows a great deal more of the conflict than most Civil War films, both before and after *Birth* (of course, *Birth* being the longest American film to that date, no other film had had the capacity to show as much of the war).

A definite factor in the visibility of any war in the cinema is the vast cost of staging battles, an exorbitant $40,000 for *Birth* in 1915, and the complexity of its direction. It has been posed that subsequent Civil War films concentrated less on battle scenes for financial reasons,[58] adding further, no doubt, to the tendency to represent the war through other genres. I would like to pose another aspect, or another way of looking at the presence of the war in a Civil War film, the length of time and extent of detail devoted to the enactment of battle. *Birth* devotes an unusually large amount of screen time to a reconstruction of combat. Griffith could have chosen to show minimal combat, and employed instead a large degree of 'telling'. In other words, such a film might have told us about the war through newspaper headlines or perhaps the almost ubiquitous Civil War montage sequence. It might have shown us more of the fate of the family, such as in *Gone With the Wind*, or it may have excised the war altogether as may occur in some Westerns, e.g. *Red River* (Howard Hawks, 1948), picking up the characters' lives after the war is over. The film is rare indeed that has such a great degree of 'showing' combat than *Birth*, the combat films *Glory* and *Gettysburg* aside, which are large-budget films that prioritise battle itself as a central narrative element.

Another form of 'telling' about the Civil War is through symbolic reference. *Young Mr Lincoln* (John Ford, 1939), for example, relates the popular story of Abraham Lincoln's life as a scholar and lawyer, years before his election as president of the United States, and yet it tells us a lot about the Civil War. The games and competitions he is asked to judge in his community's festivities each offer a glimpse of the painful duty Lincoln (played by Henry Fonda) must face when his nation is divided in two and he must act fairly as judge and father to all. Symbolically speaking, Lincoln judging a homemade pie competition is about the Civil War.

Griffith also employs symbolic telling of the war. In the opening scenes of the film, when we see the Cameron family sitting on the porch of their home by its large white pillars, the father, Dr Cameron, is shown petting a kitten while two puppies alternately doze and play at his feet. When the kitten is accidentally dropped onto the puppies an intertitle reading 'Hostilities' appears on the screen. It is tempting to try to read this short sequence on a deeper level than perhaps it was meant, linking the colours of the animals to the white and black races, or to North and South, with the kitten perhaps signifying the destructive carpetbaggers, Austin Stoneman or even the arrival of slaves in America as depicted in the first shots of the film. Paul O'Dell suggests that instead Griffith is using a symbolic means of demonstrating the disturbance to peace and harmony soon to be felt by the characters of the film.[59] Although I would not go so far as to identify a puppy with a race and a kitten with a carpetbagger, the placing of the word 'Hostilities' into the scene, being a term associated with aggression and violence, must operate more than in melodramatic terms only. By its very nature, this word implies the coming of war, or at least the disagreement suggested between Dr Cameron and Ben caused, shortly after, by the newspaper headline announcing the threat of certain Southern states to secede.

However, what Griffith actually shows of the war is of vital importance to an analysis of the film and its ideology. The first we actually see of hostilities is within the walls of the Cameron home itself during the Northern raid of Piedmont. The white women of the family hide in the basement, while those men who have not gone to war, both black and white (and some black women too) engage the Unionists in hand-to-hand combat. Confederate soldiers save the family but not before the Cameron home is set aflame and Dr Cameron is wounded. This is the only time that we see black soldiers engaged in a form of warfare in the film, implying that corrupt or easily led black soldiers were not a part of the 'real' war on the battlefield, and thus the Civil War was a war of white against white. The film *Glory* made around seventy-five years later goes some way towards refuting this implication, presenting the story of a black Union regiment's involvement in the war, effectively transferring the status of enemy from the black race to racism itself.[60]

This scene of the invasion of Piedmont is indicative of how the war is treated by Griffith: Northern aggressors attack an innocent South, the effects are felt by Southerners and the family itself suffers loss and damage. This is perhaps most poignant in the shot previously mentioned of the mother with her children watching the onslaught of Sherman's army. This moment is a damning comment on the North: this is the Union army, a force of Christian men, who are the cause of the Southern family's adversity. Immediately following this shot is the sight of Atlanta in flames. The intertitle reads: 'The torch of war against the breast of Atlanta'. Flames, as in the attack on the Piedmont home, signal war and destruction for which the Union army is responsible. Atlanta is feminised with the use of the physical term 'breast', linking the plight of the South, again, to the suffering of woman. Moments later, Griffith cuts back to the family watching the army move slowly on in the valley. We are left in no doubt as to whom Griffith attributes fault in this war. It is most definitely an indictment of Union tactics and behaviour, making *Birth* a determinedly Confederate view of the Civil War.

Images of the battlefield show what are at face value distinctly male experiences. In a sense the absence of women in these scenes could indicate, as with the Piedmont raid, that the real war takes place here on the battlefield, away from civilians. It is a long way, however, from indicating that the two principal conflicts found in *Birth*, of nation and of race, are defined through gender, i.e. that the national conflict of North and South is a masculinised war and the racial conflict of white and black is a feminised war. Instead the gendered oppositions exist across the melodramatic oppositions of villain and hero throughout the film. During the Civil War, the North is predominantly characterised as masculine villain, through Sherman's attack on Atlanta and the Union attack on Piedmont. The South is characterised as feminine victim-hero, with Ben's collapse in defeat at Petersburg and the metaphorical 'rape' of the Piedmont property.

However, Griffith's treatment of North and South is inconsistent. The first battle scene of the film relays the final meeting of the two chums, the younger Stoneman and Cameron sons, before their death like lovers in each other's arms. It would be unacceptable to describe one as masculine and one as feminine, instead it is a metaphorical image of the destruction of the unified nation. This short scene acts as a microcosm of Griffith's take on the war. The intertitle beforehand, indicating the fate of the two friends, reads: 'War claims its bitter, useless sacrifice'. We then see a son of the North and a son of the South both die on the field. Neither side wins, and that is because they are fighting the wrong battle. As far as Griffith is concerned, the real battle will come later when North and South must unite against their common, masculinised enemy – the black race led by corrupt white men.

The battle of Petersburg, which has Ben pitched against his Northern friend Phil Stoneman, further enacts the destruction of the nation with friends involved in the 'wrong' war. Through the juxtaposition of a number of technical and sentimental elements, the South is further romanticised and idolised, in readiness for the narrative's transition to the conflict proper between white and black. As Ben makes the final charge, a shot is inserted of his family in Piedmont at prayer – as if they have somehow been divinely led to pray for his protection at this very moment. Ben subsequently breaches the gap between the two lines of soldiers and throws his flag into a Union cannon, before collapsing and being dragged to relative safety by his friend in the Union army.

This whole episode personalises the experience of war by placing the film's central characters into an actual historical battle, intercut with views of the family home. The formal construction of the battle summons a meeting of the national and the personal, the collective and the individual, channelling the national experience through the members of the Stoneman and Cameron families. In essence then, this is not only a melodramatic telling of the war, i.e. narrated in the melodramatic mode, but it is also the war seen through the eyes of melodrama, incorporating the moral dilemma of a family at war with itself. It allows for the fact that the central Southern character is male, not female, even though feminine imagery is so prolific and women are themselves so integral to Griffith's impressions of the South. Ben's presence as the representative of the new South is acceptable amongst the many links to woman because he is treated in such a sentimental manner. Together with the death of the chums, Ben's conduct in war constructs a tragic account of the lost cause. What these scenes achieve, in their depiction of the Northern and Southern friends meeting on the battlefield and suffering death or injury, lends intense power to Griffith's overall project to invest identification with the white American ancestor. When this is laid beside the Camerons' experience of masculinised black power and potency, it contributes to an impression of feminised Southern victimhood that is, cathartically, overturned by Ben's formation of the Ku Klux Klan.

One further element of the film that cannot be neglected is its treatment of the figure of Lincoln. Chadwick writes that Lincoln is represented in many Civil War films as a representative of a united nationalism, necessary particularly for the viewing public at times of national disruption, such as the

Second World War or the Cold War.[61] Lincoln is also, as mentioned earlier, one of *Birth's* father figures. As president of the Union during the war and America's leader during the early days of peace, he is in a sense the father of the united nation. Lang describes *Birth's* Lincoln as like 'a father who must make unpopular decisions for the good of the entire family'.[62] An oft-noted example of this is his fatherly gesture of absolution towards Mrs Cameron when she supplicates him for her son's pardon from a false accusation of guerrilla activity. *Birth's* Lincoln also makes it plain to Austin Stoneman that the Southern states after the war are to be treated as if they had never left the Union – rather like the father defending his returned child in the Christian parable of the Prodigal Son. In fact, Griffith seems to treat Lincoln with the kind of awe one would expect in a film about Jesus Christ – he is shown barely moving, often sitting alone or with a silent crowd of political disciples, in prayer or wiping a tear from his eyes. His bowed body appears to carry the weight of the war on its shoulders, in the way that Christ chooses to carry the burden of the sins of humanity.

What revolves around this figure is a kind of 'cult of Lincoln'. When he is assassinated mid-way through the film, and his divine presence is removed, his loss is signalled by an intertitle as the death of the South's one true friend, again like the Christ figure who is a friend to the child, the destitute and the fatherless. In his death he becomes a martyr to the Southern cause, which the film explains is crushed by Reconstruction.[63] Without Lincoln the Southern people, led by Ben Cameron, must awaken to a new paternity that is finally sanctioned at the end of the film by a floating figure of Christ above the New White Jerusalem. Without Lincoln there to condone the union of North and South, the film can only appeal to a higher order, that of God Himself.

Needless to say, prominent and powerful black leaders are absent, such as Frederick Douglass. This is an absence that is characteristic of almost all Civil War films, and as far as I am able to tell went unnoticed critically until he was represented briefly in Zwick's *Glory*. It is quite possible that Griffith intended Lynch's character in *Birth* to be representative of all black abolitionists, encoding them as dangerous, lustful, power-crazy individuals. Since Lynch is then unsuccessful in his advances on Elsie Stoneman, he does not go on to father mixed-race descendants. Griffith does not permit him to be a father at all and so American ancestry remains safely white.

So, despite the tendency across much critical writing about *The Birth of a Nation* to ignore the Civil War, there is a tremendous amount to be said about its place within the film and its contribution towards the message of white supremacy. Ultimately the film's racist substance depends upon a representation of the war as having no direct relationship with the real political causes of the historical conflict, whilst venerating the heroic but tragic white brotherhood that rises up against its proper (black) enemy. In this way the film fights the Civil War afresh, making it one chapter in the story of black suppression, not emancipation as it truly was.

A WHITE NATIONAL ANCESTRY

Earlier, I noted that the family is the channel through which Griffith tells the story of *Birth*, and that this family extends beyond the Stonemans and Camerons (who are eventually linked as one family by the double marriage of its children) to the white nation as a whole. As the family is re-born through marriage, the nation is re-born through the white triumph over black power. This metaphor of family for nation, which is appropriate for a generic mix such as melodrama and epic, is central to an ideology of nation – that of nationalism. Anthony Smith's study of national identity states that 'the metaphor of family is indispensable to nationalism'.[64] Each member of a nation makes up a 'brotherhood', unified together by right of birth (or blood), culture and place.[65] This brotherhood must not be divided, and if its union is threatened from within or without, then that which is different or 'other' must be resisted, if necessary by force, in the name of unity and uniformity. Smith adds that the 'most potent and durable aspects of nationalism' can be found in its cultural symbols, rituals and language, including items such as flags, parades, uniforms and heroic figures.[66] This all sounds remarkably familiar when held up against *Birth*, which presents so many vivid parallels between family and nation. The indivisibility of nation, for example, is part of the ideology that is threatened by the Civil War. Northern brother is forced to fight against Southern brother in an 'unnatural' conflict within the national family. At face value the war is the threat to unity, but in *Birth*, once war is over the threat remains – the threat of black supremacy – suggesting that the war was not the real threat to the nation at all, but simply the means by which the threat emerged.

The means by which Griffith unifies the white nation is through an appeal to an older national heritage, one which is particular to the Camerons of the South, that of their Scottish ancestry. Smith writes that a tool of nationalism is an appeal to 'ancient beliefs and commitments to ancestral homelands and to the generations of one's forefathers'.[67] Again this is the metaphor of family, but this time it is specifically interwoven with ancestry and ancient doctrine traceable to its roots. This concept is most clearly expressed in Ben Cameron's religious ritual at the formation of the Klan, swearing an oath to avenge Little Pet Sister's death, using symbolically loaded items such as the Confederate flag soaked in her blood. The flag is associated with Flora by her repeated use of it as belt or handkerchief, but also it is representative of the Southern nation. Adopted by the Confederate congress as the 'national' flag in 1863, it was known as the 'Stainless Banner', in accord with the Confederate perception of their cause, and was an adaptation of the Scottish St Andrew's cross.[68] This Stainless Banner in Ben Cameron's hands becomes stained with the blood of innocence. Merritt's analysis credits the flag with a strong religious link, in that it resurrects her memory and the lost cause in some kind of transubstantiation, made possible by Ben's ritual.[69] Issuing from the wounds of this young woman, her blood is pure by virtue of her virginity (she preserved her honour through suicide), but also by virtue of birth, because she is part of the ancestral Scottish line that Ben now seeks to reawaken in the imagination of the South, in its new war against the black race. Through this nationalistic ritual, the Civil War has been displaced from its historical and symbolic position as the founding moment of the union of the American states, and replaced by a racial war that heralded the 'true' birth of the nation. The fatherhood of this new nation belongs to both Ben and his Anglo-Saxon forefathers who, in the words of an intertitle, remain 'undefeated'. Notice that the father figures to whom the Klan renews allegiance are not the founding fathers of America, but their forefathers from another land and another culture. The implication is that this appeal to distant ancestors from Europe makes whiteness even purer, even whiter, making their superiority over the African American absolute.

So what is being said in *The Birth of a Nation* about America and American identity? What do the ideological influences of nationalism, racism and Southern mythology feed into in terms of a national identity? What place does the Civil War occupy in this and how does this link with genre? Griffith's avid supporter, Seymour Stern, in trying to answer a different question – why *Birth* continued to suffer attack – stated that the film challenged a distinctly Northern totalitarian ideology. He defended Griffith's depiction of 'good' blacks, saying that this indicated an ideological approach to history, not a racist one.[70] Stern is correct in that *Birth* is ideological, although incorrect in identifying racism as beyond ideology. The film is the result of a complicated interaction of several interlinking ideologies pertinent to the time of the film's production and the creative minds behind it. Clyde Taylor, for example, notes 'the significant feat' that Griffith accomplishes in transplanting the Southern myth onto white American nationalism,[71] by which Griffith re-creates the South as America the nation. Consequently, as Taylor writes, the South and the purity of the white race become the focus of an original national experience instead of the frontier and the taming of the land, a fiction more allied with the Western.

Taylor also highlights the explicit Christian ideology present in the film, particularly, as I have noted above, the loss and restoration of Eden, which 'rehearses Christian eschatology in national terms'.[72] What Taylor is saying here is that this particular narrative has an apocalyptic dimension complete with a 'dark angel' (Stoneman), martyrs (soldiers, Lincoln, Flora, the South), redeemers (Ben, the Klan) and a New Jerusalem in the closing sequence. In using Christian symbolism, distinctions between good and evil and the outworking of retributive justice, Griffith situates his audience as Christian. Not only that, but he thus identifies America as a Christian nation. This is not just because Christian ideology is present in the film, but because the audience is required to identify with the heroic redeemer figures of the narrative, the Klan, whose symbols include the burning cross and the pure white, priest-like robes.

Taylor makes an interesting observation about *Birth* and *Gone With the Wind*, asking if it is a coincidence that so many of America's landmark films concern race. He writes: 'Might it be that some affinity exists between breakthrough productions and national allegories in which the definition of national character simultaneously involves a co-defining anti-type?'[73] Indeed, since the central characters with which American viewers are required to identify are so emphatically coded as white, then that which is black cannot be American. It makes for what Taylor calls 'an epic of White supremacy'.[74] If the point of identification for the audience is the Christian Anglo-Saxon family, then that identity rests on racial distinctiveness. As Mary Ann Doane writes, 'it is the white family which is the microcosm of the nation – the black family is non-existent'.[75] America as a nation and the nation as family are explicitly inscribed as white.

Lary May's observations on the political nature of *Birth* resemble Stern's comment about Griffith's attack on Northern totalitarianism. The three most influential men in the film's production, Dixon, Griffith and Wilson, were each Southern Democrats. *Birth* is the result of a particular political standpoint, that of the Democratic Party of the late nineteenth century, and its ideology concerning the Civil War, i.e. the imposition of a corrupt regime (Reconstruction) on the South by Northern Radical Republicans (represented by Austin Stoneman in the narrative).[76] Stoneman, the loosely based caricature of Thaddeus Stevens, openly opposes Lincoln's war aims and Reconstruction policy, accusing him of taking a too soft-handed approach. His anti-slavery stance made him an enemy to the South, and his caricature in *Birth* thus pitches him as, if not anti-Christ then at least anti-Lincoln, who would defend the immoral crime of miscegenation. No wonder then, as May notes, that Wilson was initially so enthusiastic about the film, being himself the first Southern Democrat president since the Civil War era. One could add that it may also account for some of the adverse reaction to the film at the time of its reception, since America was (and is) not politically uniform.

Griffith's desire, as he prophesied to *The Editor* magazine in 1915, was to see history eventually being taught to school children by moving pictures.[77] He saw cinema as a potentially unbiased form of education without any ideological perspective – suggesting a Gramscian belief in the power of 'common sense'. As Lillian Gish describes in her autobiography, Griffith's goal was to tell the 'truth' about the Southern experience during and after the Civil War.[78] She quotes him saying: 'I'm going to use it [Dixon's novel] to tell the truth about the War between the States. It hasn't been told accurately in the history books. Only the winning side in a war ever gets to tell its story.' In order to do this he had to add the Civil War itself to his adaptation of *The Clansman*, which begins as the war ends, and so ensure audience identification with the white heroes who prove their mettle on the battlefield. Seen in the light of Griffith's prophecy that history would be taught through cinema, the director clearly believed that his version of events was accurate, truthful and unbiased, but in reality the Civil War becomes his ideological tool. He may have been able to see conventional histories of the Civil War as inevitably biased, but he failed to see cinema as such.

However, Griffith's prophecy is uncannily true; much of what we learn about history is from the cinema. Even though *Birth* was first exhibited only fifty years after the Civil War, and many veterans still survived, it was hailed by many as the most realistic, accurate view of that era ever made public. In *Birth*, however, history is being used to propagate Griffith's personal ideologies. Griffith felt that he identified closely with his audience and that his films reflected their views,[79] but *Birth* seems to reflect a great deal more of Griffith's understanding of American identity than that of his contemporaries who protested at the film's content. Whether or not he consciously saw filmmaking as a means to disseminate his ideologies, he certainly approached film as a morally and socially educational tool. Despite his belief that film and history could one day be fused into an unbiased form, *Birth* reconstructs Griffith's worldview on the mistaken understanding that the audiences shared his position. Instead of a consensus, an ideological struggle ensued, taking place in the printed media and the political activity of the NAACP amongst others, and extending into the critical writing of the present in an 'unending dialogue' – a term used by historian E.H. Carr to analogise the writing and re-writing of history.[80]

It is ironic that it is the use of the genre of melodrama in *Birth* that separates it so distinctly from the other Civil War melodramas of Chapter 2 (and many, if not all, of the other representations of the war). In those films, the overtly personified villain was found to be missing. Although certain detestable characters were present, they did not offer a consistent or highly personified threat throughout the narratives. It is true that most Civil War films, from each of the genres, construct the ideal American ancestor as white, but *Birth* is the only film to follow the demands of melodrama, to oppose his heroes with distinctly personified villains. Griffith states through this film that the black man is the binary opposite of the white man, he is the villain, the abhorrence in America's history, who cannot be allowed to be part of the nation's historic familyhood.

It is with this historical family tree that I finally conclude this study of American Civil War films, turning to two of the more recent interpretations of the American Civil War, *Gods and Generals* (Ronald F. Maxwell, 2003), and *Cold Mountain* (Anthony Minghella, 2003), both of which invite interesting comparisons with *The Birth of a Nation*.

NOTES

1   Dixon, Thomas, *The Clansman: An Historical Romance of the Ku Klux Klan*, edited by C.D. Wintz (Armonk, New York, [1905] 2001). p. vii.

2   Inscoe, J.C., '*The Clansman* on Stage and Screen: North Carolina Reacts', *North Carolina Historical Review*, vol. 64, no. 2 (1987). pp. 139–61.

3   Simmon, Scott, *The Films of D.W. Griffith* (Cambridge, 1993). p. 10.

4   Dixon: *The Clansman*. p. xxxiii.

5   Bitzer, G.W., *Billy Bitzer: His Story* (New York, 1973). pp. 89, 107.

6   Bitzer: *Billy Bitzer: His Story*. p. 109.

7   Gish, Lillian, *The Movies, Mr. Griffith and Me*, with Ann Pichot (London, 1969). p. 132.

8   Gish: *The Movies, Mr. Griffith and Me*. pp. 136–7.

9   Brown, Karl, *Adventures With D.W. Griffith* (London, 1973). p. 91.

10   Bowser, Eileen, (ed.) *The D.W. Griffith Papers, 1897–1954* (New York and Kentucky, 1982).

11   Guerrero, Ed, *Framing Blackness: The African American Image in Film* (Philadelphia, 1993). p. 10.

12   Simmon: *The Films of D.W. Griffith*. p. 108.

13   Guerrero: *Framing Blackness*. p. 14.

14   Simmon: *The Films of D.W. Griffith*. p. 105.

15   Simcovitch, M., 'The Impact of Griffith's *Birth of a Nation* on the Modern Ku Klux Klan', *Journal of Popular Film*, vol. 1, no. 1 (Winter, 1972). p. 46.

16   Vance, Mark, '*The Birth of a Nation*', *Variety* (12 March 1915).

17   First reported in the *New York Post*, '*The Birth of a Nation*' (4 March 1915). p. 9.

18   Simmon: *The Films of D.W. Griffith*. p. 111.

19   Dunning, William A., *Essays on the Civil War and Reconstruction* (New York, [1897] 1965). p. 382. A brief outline of Dunning's work can be found in Bruce Chadwick's book on Civil War cinema, *The Reel Civil War: Mythmaking in American Film* (New York, 2002). pp. 30–1.

20   Noble, Peter, 'A Note on an Idol', *Sight and Sound*, vol. 15, no. 59 (Autumn, 1946). pp. 81–2.

21   Griffith, David Wark, '*The Birth of a Nation*: A Reply to Peter Noble', *Sight and Sound*, vol. 16, no. 61 (1947). p. 32.

22   Kinnard, Roy, *The Blue and the Gray on the Silver Screen: More Than Eighty Years of Civil War Movies* (New York, 1996). pp. xiii–xiv.

23   Pines, Jim, *Blacks in Films: A Survey of Racial Themes and Images in the American Film* (London, 1975). p. 12.

24   Griffith: '*The Birth of a Nation*: A Reply to Peter Noble'. p. 32.

25   May, Lary, *Screening Out the Past: The Birth of Mass Culture and the Motion Picture Industry* (New York, 1980). p. 72.

26   Simmon: *The Films of D.W. Griffith*. p. 110.

27   Bogle, Donald, *Toms, Coons, Mulattoes, Mammies and Bucks: An Interpretive History of Blacks in American Films*, 3rd edition (Oxford, 1994). p. 88.

28   Merritt, Russell, 'D.W. Griffith's *The Birth of a Nation*: Going After Little Sister' in P. Lehman (ed.) *Close Viewings* (Tallahassee, 1990). p. 217.

29   Such as Pearson, Roberta, '"O'er Step Not the Modesty of Nature": A Semiotic Approach to Acting in the Griffith Biographs' in C. Zucker (ed.) *Making Visible the Invisible: An Anthology of Original Essays on Film Acting* (Metuchen, New Jersey, 1990). pp. 1–27.

30   Such as the British review in *Bioscope*, 'The Birth of a Nation: An American Odyssey', vol. 28, no. 465 (9 September 1915). pp. 1114–15.

31   For example, Wood, Gerald, 'From *The Clansman* and *Birth of a Nation* to *Gone With the Wind*: The Loss of American Innocence' in D.A. Pyron (ed.) *Recasting: 'Gone With the Wind' in American Culture* (Gainesville, 1983). p. 133.

32   Grindon, Leger, *Shadows on the Past: Studies in the Historical Fiction Film* (Philadelphia, 1994). p. 8.

33   Lang, R., (ed.) *The Birth of a Nation: DW Griffith, Director* (New Brunswick, New Jersey, 1994). p. 8.

34   Guerrero: *Framing Blackness*. p. 11.

35   Spears, Jack, *The Civil War on the Screen and Other Essays* (Cranbury, New Jersey, 1977). p. 12.

36   Simmon: *The Films of D.W. Griffith*. p. 116.

37   Simmon: *The Films of D.W. Griffith*. p. 117.

38   May: *Screening Out the Past*. p. 81.

39   Gledhill, Christine, *Home is Where the Heart Is: Studies in Melodrama and the Woman's Film* (London, 1987). p. 21.

40   Neale, Steve, *Genre and Hollywood* (London, 2000). p. 85.

41   See Neale: *Genre and Hollywood* and Altman, Rick, *Film/Genre* (London, 1999).

42   See O'Brien, K., 'Race, Romance, and the Southern Literary Tradition' in Pyron: *Recasting: 'Gone With the Wind'*. pp. 154–7, for an elaboration on these elements.

43   O'Brien: 'Race, Romance, and the Southern Literary Tradition'. p. 154.

44   Campbell, Edward, *The Celluloid South: Hollywood and the Southern Myth* (Knoxville, 1981). pp. 9–11.

45   Bogle: *Toms, Coons, Mulattoes*. pp. 4–15.

46   Lang: *The Birth of a Nation*. p. 17.

47   Noble: 'A Note on an Idol'. p. 81.

48   Doane, Mary Ann, *Femmes Fatales: Feminism, Film Theory and Psychoanalysis* (New York, 1991). p. 227.

49   Simmon: *The Films of D.W. Griffith*. p. 118.

50   Doane: *Femmes Fatales*. p. 230.

51   Simmon: *The Films of D.W. Griffith*. p. 121.

52   Chadwick: *The Reel Civil War*. p. 190.

53   For example, Lang: *The Birth of a Nation*. p. 17, and White, M., '*The Birth of a Nation*: History as Pretext', *Enclitic*, vol. 5, nos 2–6 (1981/2). p. 21.

54   Lang: *The Birth of a Nation*. p. 12.

55   Rogin, M., 'The Sword Became a Flashing Vision', *Representations*, no. 9 (Winter, 1985). pp. 150–95; also in Lang: *The Birth of a Nation*. p. 271.

56   Barry, Iris, *D.W. Griffith: American Film Master* (New York, [1940] 1965). p. 7.

57   White: '*The Birth of a Nation*: History as Pretext'. p. 22.

58   Kinnard: *The Blue and the Gray on the Silver Screen*. p. xvii.

59   O'Dell, Paul, *Griffith and the Rise of Hollywood* (New York, 1970). p. 14.

60   A point also made by Chadwick: *The Reel Civil War*. p. 284.

61   Chadwick: *The Reel Civil War*. p. 169.

62   Lang: *The Birth of a Nation*. p. 21.

63   Lang: *The Birth of a Nation*. p. 21.

64   Smith, Anthony D., *National Identity* (London, 1991). p. 79.

65 Smith: *National Identity*. p. 76.

66 Smith: *National Identity*. p. 77.

67 Smith: *National Identity*. p. 78.

68 Cook, R., *Civil War America: Making a Nation, 1848–1877* (Harlow, 2003). p. 178.

69 Merritt: 'D.W. Griffith's *The Birth of a Nation*'. p. 227.

70 Griffith: '*The Birth of a Nation*: A Reply to Peter Noble'. p. 34.

71 Taylor, Clyde, 'The Re-Birth of the Aesthetic in Cinema' in D. Bernardi (ed.) *The Birth of Whiteness: Race and the Emergence of US Cinema* (New Brunswick, New Jersey, 1996). p. 21.

72 Taylor: 'The Re-Birth of the Aesthetic in Cinema'. p. 21.

73 Taylor: 'The Re-Birth of the Aesthetic in Cinema'. p. 15.

74 Taylor: 'The Re-Birth of the Aesthetic in Cinema'. p. 19.

75 Doane: *Femmes Fatales*. p. 228.

76 May: *Screening Out the Past*. p. 82.

77 Griffith, David Wark, 'Five Dollar Movies Prophecied', *The Editor* (24 April 1915); also in Bowser: *The D.W. Griffith Papers*, and Geduld, H.M., (ed.) *Focus on D.W. Griffith* (Englewood Cliffs, New Jersey, 1971).

78 Gish: *The Movies, Mr. Griffith and Me*. p. 131.

79 May: *Screening Out the Past*. p. 77.

80 Carr, E.H., *What is History?*, 2nd edition (Harmondsworth, 1987). p. 30.

6

An Enduring Southern Ancestry

This chapter conducts an analysis of two more recent Civil War films: Ronald F. Maxwell's 2003 film *Gods and Generals*, and Anthony Minghella's *Cold Mountain* of the same year. The two films are strikingly dissimilar in their narratives and style, and ideologically they serve different concerns. Whilst both narrate a Southern story, and both are presented in the melodramatic mode, their historical family trees have quite different compositions. *Gods and Generals* is the prequel to Maxwell's *Gettysburg* (1993), and the first of what was planned to be the director's Civil War trilogy, ending with *The Last Full Measure*, covering the final two years of the war. Although *Gettysburg*, based on the novel *The Killer Angels* by Michael Shaara (1974), was initially produced for television and went on to earn itself the highest viewer ratings of any Cable TV programme in the US,[1] *Gods and Generals* performed poorly at the box office. Producer Ted Turner pulled out of support for the final, third film, which was to be based, like *Gods and Generals*, on a novel by Shaara's son Jeff, *The Last Full Measure*. Plans have been put indefinitely on hold at the time of this writing. Maxwell's previous Civil War film, *Gettysburg* is, first and foremost, a combat film, with large portions of screen time given to military movements, preparations for battle and actual warfare. In a sense, it is probably the most visually accurate of Civil War representations in the cinema, having an attention to detail unlike any film that went before it. It is, however, also an epic, concerning itself primarily with an event of national importance and presented on a vast scale. In a similar vein, and like *The Birth of a Nation* and *Gone With the Wind*, Maxwell's second Civil War film *Gods and Generals* runs in excess of three hours, and like these other films of the classical era it is a generic hybrid with the epic, in this case a combination with the combat film and the domestic melodrama.

Released ten years after Maxwell's earlier film, *Gods and Generals* attends to some of the same historical characters as *Gettysburg* (including Joshua Chamberlain and Robert E. Lee), but turns back to an earlier point in the Civil War story, from the outbreak of war in 1861 to the death of Colonel Thomas 'Stonewall' Jackson in 1863, two months before the conflict at Gettysburg. Unlike the earlier film, however, *Gods and Generals* does not solely concern itself with battlefield incidents and preparations. Instead it alternates its narrative between combat and the domestic experience of the war, particularly concentrating on the home and family of one key Southern military figure, 'Stonewall' Jackson.

Through Maxwell's meticulous research through diaries, memoirs and biographies, historical figures such as Jackson and General Lee of the South and Joshua Chamberlain of the North, are depicted facing difficult choices and impossible situations during the conflict. In *Gettysburg* Chamberlain (Jeff Daniels) chooses between defeat and certain suicide when his regiment runs out of ammunition before the Confederate enemy. He chooses to charge forward with bayonets fixed, and is rewarded with victory. This kind of scenario is typical of what Maxwell himself, in his online essay 'Beyond the Myths',[2] describes as each character's 'own internal struggle – his own personal civil war'. In this statement, Maxwell is conforming to a Civil War film tradition noted in Chapter 2's examination of *Friendly Persuasion*, that of the Self Civil War faced by the American ancestor. The message of Maxwell's films, and also of the novels upon which they are based, is in keeping with the representations studied so far; the American individual during the Civil War faces internal conflict that parallels, and at times displaces, the significance of the national conflict. In passing the test of the Self Civil War, he or she passes into the pantheon of worthy American ancestors, and even more so in Maxwell's films with their characters being based on actual historical figures. Although Maxwell asserts that his approach goes 'beyond the myths', then, it does in fact reinforce them. The following analysis locates these myths and situates them within the American tradition of re-writing the Civil War, the drive to 'remember/forget' the past that is noted by Benedict Anderson. Through a consideration of responses to the film from the academic community, and Maxwell's own position on the potential of historical film, a most interesting parallel can be found with the first epic Civil War film, *The Birth of a Nation*.

'ON THE BATTLEFIELDS OF
A NATION DIVIDED'

The theatrical trailer for *Gods and Generals* begins with the Warner Brothers logo in sepia. Like the opening sequence of a number of contemporary Warner films the Warner Brothers insignia is re-coloured to channel audience expectation of the film to follow. Here, sepia signifies the past, and indicates clearly that this will be a historical film. This is briefly followed by the Turner Productions logo which, when used in combination with the preceding sepia image, communicates immediately that this is likely to be a Civil War film, given Ted Turner's consistent preoccupation with this period in American history. *Gods and Generals* is the fourth Civil War film to be commissioned by Turner, each of which uses high production values to re-enact events from the war as authentically as possible. Turner's first commission, *Ironclads* (Delbert Mann, 1991), was based on the clash of Union and Confederate submarines the Monitor and the Merrimack, and his second, *The Hunley* (John Gray, 1999), concerned the manually propelled Confederate submarine. His first collaboration with Maxwell, *Gettysburg*, had Turner himself appearing in a cameo on the battlefields of Pennsylvania.

The trailer continues with a series of rapid dissolves, images and sounds from the film, intercut with what appears to be the tip of a bayonet thrusting through wood, an image that is finally revealed to be the film title. The first image of the trailer, however, is from one of the most memorable scenes of the film. Two men in long shot meet on rocks at the middle of a river as an intertitle states, 'They carried the same Bible'. The shot confirms that this is a Civil War film. From the costumes of the men on screen (indicating their difference) and from the common religion followed by both (indicating their sameness), it can be easily deduced that this will be a narrative of a single nation divided. The titles continue with the words: 'They believed in the same God. One side fought for God's glory. The other for His kingdom on Earth. But for the duration of the war, God refused to take sides.' They are strongly emotive words, speaking of identity through religion and the taking up of arms in the name of God. It is also a statement of the intention of the filmmakers, since, if God refused to take sides, then neither will the film.

A voice-over then operates to further cue audience expectation of the narrative: 'On the battlefields of a nation divided, in the heart of a General who fought in the name of God, in a world turned upside down, Heaven and Hell were never far apart.' The words are accompanied by more shots from the film, including some in the homes of the key characters. From these words and images it is suggested that this will be a generic hybrid – it states that action will take place both on the battlefields and in the heart of one particular man, i.e. it is both action and emotion, both combat and (in the restricted sense) melodrama. Heaven and hell exist in both, and so melodrama will be brought to the fields of battle, and the horrors of combat will be brought into the home. A title then finally confirms what the audience is already likely to suspect: 'A true story of the Civil War'. Thus the filmmakers are announcing that this film is a representation of the truth, one that does not 'take sides'.

Ultimately, *Gods and Generals* does take sides, predominantly because of its attention to the figure of 'Stonewall' Jackson (Stephen Lang). A large portion of the film's four hours are concerned with his military career and his relationships with his wife, his closest friends and his God, even though the source novel alternates its narrative more equally between Jackson and Lee. Inevitably, a closer identification is encouraged with this character than with the central Northern figure, Joshua Chamberlain (Jeff Daniels), who receives considerably less screen time. Therefore, the film cannot prevent a stronger identification with the South than with the North, despite the filmmakers' attempts at fairness.

The film opens with words from George Eliot's *Daniel Deronda* (1876), extolling the vital link between people and their homeland, beginning with: 'A human life, I think, should be well rooted in some spot of a native land, where it may get the love of tender kinship for the face of the earth […]'. It seems a curious choice of quotation, considering that Eliot's novel concerns Zionism, not the American Civil War, yet an important statement is made here. What is being established, albeit somewhat obliquely, is that the characters of this film are men and women with a love for their 'spot' of native land. The Generals of the title, whether Union or Confederate, will be seen to fight over land. This is a remarkable standpoint for the film to take, since the majority of films about the Civil War, as this study has outlined, fail to explore or explain the reasons why the men of the nation fought.

The quotation goes on to end with: 'The best introduction to astronomy is to think of the mighty heavens as a little lot of stars belonging to one's own homestead.' It seems to be a comment bafflingly irrelevant to concerns of the Civil War. However, again the words have a resonance with the idea of home and one's ownership even of the sky above it. The motif of the sky is one that is returned to throughout the film, less to intimate that a man may own the patch of stars above his home, than to suggest that the same sky is shared by all American men and women, both slave and free. Although it is not overtly stated, there is a sense from these opening words that the land of America is the home of all Americans and that the separate armies of the Civil War, ironically, were fighting for the same thing: their home.

The narrative itself follows the story of the war from Lincoln's call for volunteers in April 1861 until the death of Jackson in the summer of 1863. Robert E. Lee (Robert Duvall) turns down an offer to command Lincoln's military force, and instead accepts leadership of the North Virginian regiments for the Confederate army, stating that his desire is that the 'sacred soil' of Virginia be not 'polluted by the foot of the invader'. This declaration sets the tone for the film in terms of the causes of conflict. To Lee, as to the Southern army, the purpose of the war is to resist the federal forces that are attempting to invade and control their land, and has nothing to do with the institution of slavery nor abolitionism.

The film then introduces a Southern family, the Beales, in the Virginian town of Fredericksburg. If the viewer is aware of Civil War history, it will be clear why this town has been chosen, since it was the location of one of the Union's most devastating defeats. Here, widow Jane Beale (Mia Dillon) sews Confederate flags for her two sons leaving for war, inviting comparison with Ben Cameron's gift of the flag to his young sister Flora in *The Birth of a Nation*. Jane and her black servant, Martha (Donzaleigh Abernathy), kiss the young men goodbye with the words 'surely goodness and mercy have followed me all the days of my life'. All that the Confederate flag has come to symbolise in terms of white supremacy is vaulted over in an impression of the good, Christian, Southern family, fighting for the protection of their homes.

A strong devotion to the Christian faith is also found in Thomas Jackson, the military instructor who is called, in both a military and a religious sense, to train new cadets. Before leaving for the Virginia Military Institute he prays earnestly with his wife Anna (Kali Rocha) for peace in the nation. Although to Jackson war is 'the sum of all evil', he is determined to 'fight for his country', meaning Virginia. In reading Bible verses together about the building of a heavenly house, Jackson and Anna invest his war involvement with a religious fervour verging on Holy War. Jackson's character is therefore introduced as, first and foremost, Christian, suggesting that Maxwell intends that this strong relationship with God be a dominant factor in audience identification with a historical figure who is known as much for his single-minded military excellence and firm treatment of his troops as for his faith.

A montage sequence shows civilians of all kinds leaving their professions to join the Confederate army. Jackson, in the first of several rousing and emotive speeches to his men, reiterates their reason for fighting: it is a direct response to the federal threat to Virginia. In a later speech, he tells the troops that this is their 'second War of Independence', likening their situation to that of their American ancestors in the eighteenth century. This theme of self-defence continues to be reiterated throughout the film, notably by Colonel J.E.B. Stuart (Joseph Fuqua), who arrives from the frontier having fought the Apache tribes stating, 'The Apache were defendin' their homes, as we'll be defendin' ours. If we fight as well as the Apache, I pity the Yankee invader.' The comment works both to conform to certain twenty-first-century sensibilities, such as respect for the Native American, and to make it plain that the Southern purpose in fighting the Civil War was related to defence of one's home, as opposed to any other motivation, such as one's right to own a slave.

Combat is seen for the first time forty minutes into the film with a series of small battles. Jackson earns his nickname when a soldier points out that their general sits without fear on his horse, like a stone wall. The general's bravery is rewarded with a 'red badge' in the form of a shot in the left hand, which he holds high throughout the battle, undoubtedly for sensible, medical reasons, but also as a sign of his courage to the men under his command. As would be expected from the director of *Gettysburg*, the authentic detail of the *mise-en-scène* is at times astoundingly convincing, with accuracy of uniforms, weapons and wounds. Through the juxtaposition of alternating long shots and extreme long shots, tracking in opposite directions, a sense of battlefield chaos is effectively constructed.

It is almost an hour of screen time before the film introduces the second central character of the film, the Northern philosophy and literature tutor, Joshua Chamberlain. This character was possibly the most interesting in Maxwell's previous Civil War film, *Gettysburg*, in his remarkable bravery when facing almost certain death with no ammunition. Here, Chamberlain is introduced in the classroom, challenged by a young student about the acceptance of slavery in a society based on the tenets of freedom and equality. Chamberlain, or the film itself, is saved from an awkward moment by a cut to his home, where he tells his wife that he is enlisting in the Union army. Instead of reading Bible verses together, as Jackson and his wife had done, this couple quote a Lovelace poem about the English Civil War to one another, devoting themselves to love, honour and duty. A distinction is made through the two different choices of literature between head (Union) and heart (Confederate), in keeping with a romanticised impression of the old South. It is also a subtle distinction between national identities of North and South: the Northern man reads English poetry and so is linked with America's European past, whereas the Southern man reads the Bible, and so is citizen of a holy nation that exists for all time. Given that Jackson has been established in the first hour of the film as the key protagonist with whom the viewer is encouraged to identify, it is evident that the film is leaning towards an endorsement of the conventional romantic myth of the noble South.

Apart from a number of small skirmishes, the film concentrates on two major Civil War events: the Union attack on Fredericksburg and the Confederate attack on Union forces encamped at Chancellorsville, and both end in a Confederate victory. Throughout this time Jackson struggles with his conscience about involvement in the war, like a Self Civil War of his own, and becomes increasingly emotional over the course of the film. When a five-year-old girl, with whom he has built a close friendship, dies of scarlet fever, he weeps inconsolably. His officers remark that their general has never been seen to cry before, but a doctor replies that Jackson is in fact crying for all the dead of the war. Through a succession of events, after Jackson is sent westwards to Chancellorsville, the Confederates attack an unsuspecting Union encampment, and Jackson becomes separated from the bulk of his army on a reconnoitre. In the dark, his own soldiers fire on him and he is fatally wounded. He develops pneumonia and dies, despite General Lee's conviction that Jackson is somehow invincible. The film ends with Jackson's close companion and cook, a freedman by the name of Big Jim Lewis (Frankie Faison), following his coffin at a procession in Virginia.

Captions then link *Gods and Generals* to the second part of the Maxwell trilogy, *Gettysburg*, by stating that General Lee's encouraging victory at Chancellorsville leads to an invasion of the North where, less than two months later in July 1863, they suffer a terrible defeat on the farmlands of Pennsylvania. A note is made that another film will complete the trilogy, to be called *The Last Full Measure*, a goal that currently appears to be unattainable, and special thanks are given to the many hundreds of Civil War re-enactors that made the film possible.

HYBRIDITY, INTERTEXTUALITY AND MODE IN *GODS AND GENERALS*

It would be useful at this stage to review what has been discovered about the two key genres of this study pertinent to *Gods and Generals*, domestic melodrama and the combat film, and their particular treatment of the Civil

War. Both genres, together with the Western, were found to have a common ideological purpose in the construction and reverence for an honourable, worthy American ancestor, the root of the viewer's historical family tree. The Civil War domestic melodrama tends to use the Southern family as its relational link to the present; the Civil War combat film tends to employ the Northern regiment for the same. In both, in order to avoid casting North or South as a collective villain, the enemy is either ignored or hidden in swiftly edited montages of silhouettes and smoke.

It is the rules of the Civil War domestic melodrama that are most closely followed in *Gods and Generals*, particularly in its close attention to family life. There are three central families represented in the film, the Chamberlains, the Jacksons and the Beales, Jackson's surrogate family in Fredericksburg. Chamberlain's wife is only present in one scene, although he is shown writing a letter home, and so the dominant family relationship he has is instead with his brother, Tom (C. Thomas Howell). This is a relationship that viewers of *Gettysburg* will remember as both comic and moving, with the younger man repeatedly and inappropriately calling his brother by his middle name, Lawrence, and their silent embrace after the Union victory at the end of the film. Joshua Chamberlain is again characterised in *Gods and Generals* as an older brother trying to protect his sibling from harm in a potentially fatal environment. His care for Tom represents his compassion for both the men under his command and the slaves in captivity in the South. However, it is more with Stonewall Jackson's relationship to family that the film concerns itself. Throughout the narrative the intensity of his yearning for his wife and for a child increases, until his emotional breakdown when explaining to his five-year-old Fredericksburg friend that 'all the daddies will come home'. His emotional crisis is part of the moral transformation that is conventional in the Civil War domestic melodrama. Characters in this type of film are forced to face a personal crisis of some sort, their Self Civil War, through which a new moral consciousness is born. Jackson's particular transformation takes him from religiosity and impermeability, through the guilt of involvement in the war, to emotional brokenness. It works to fortify an ideology of the Civil War as a tragedy on a national scale – usually the undercurrent of the Civil War combat film, not the domestic melodrama, which tends to understand the war as a necessary evil in the moral transformation of the national family.

This evil that is present in Civil War domestic melodramas is the de-personalised villain, war itself, the ultimate test faced by the American ancestor. In accord with this convention, *Gods and Generals* has hardly a single villainous type. One scene shows Union soldiers looting Fredericksburg, but unlike *Birth's* violent Union attack on the Camerons' home, these soldiers are easily persuaded not to loot the house by the black servant, Martha, claiming that the property is her own. The house is briefly turned into a makeshift hospital for Union wounded and Martha helps in their care. In such a way, the aggression of the Union attack on the town is subsumed by a reconciliation for the sake of the wounded. The film contains no self-centred, racist quartermasters, no plantation overseers, no slave ringleaders and no mutinous uprisings. As such, it presents itself as the Civil War domestic melodrama *par excellence* with its complete absence of a villain, the effect being that the characters of the film hold no blame or defect and thus are the perfect forefathers of the American viewer.

The absence of enemy is, similarly, essential to the Civil War combat film. In the films of this study such as *Drummer of the 8th* (Thomas H. Ince, 1913) and *Glory* (Edward Zwick, 1989), situated amongst Northern regiments, the Confederacy was barely seen and this was found to conform to a certain Civil War mythology that refused to apportion blame in the conflict. Thus, Northern characters were given most if not all of the films' screen time and any mention of the causes of conflict was avoided. Although *Gods and Generals* alternates its narrative between both Union and Confederate heroes, it does not quite escape any allotment of blame. The trailer articulates a desire to refuse sides in the re-telling of the war, but the narrative begins with news of Lincoln's call for Union volunteers in April 1861. Rather like the first news of hostilities in *The Birth of a Nation*, no mention is made of the initial Confederate aggression at Fort Sumter, nor of the pre-war atmosphere of political and economic unrest. The film then goes on to repeat the Virginian purpose for entering the war: to defend their state against the invasion of federal forces. So, despite what seems to be a sincere attempt at blamelessness, *Gods and Generals* chooses to accentuate Northern aggression over Southern self-defence. This choice is not essentially a manipulation of the truth, but its omission of pre-war conditions encourages an impression of a Northern aggressor.

Since the film enacts many of its events in the American South, unlike other Civil War combat films, it cannot avoid depictions of slavery. Because there can be no overt blame, however, there cannot be any suggestion of Southern guilt in its treatment of slaves. In *Gods and Generals* slavery is sanitised, not exposed, through the lives of two black characters, Jackson's cook, the freedman Jim Lewis, and the Beale family's servant, Martha. These two characters correspond to a stereotype of the conventional plantation mythology of nineteenth-century Southern romantic fiction, faithful blacks akin to the Piedmont slaves of *The Birth of a Nation*. Each is prepared to risk life and limb for either their American homeland or their owner's property, but, in a concession to twenty-first-century sensibilities, would quite like the slaves to be free too.

The treatment of Jim Lewis particularly reveals the film's ideological standpoint on race and slavery. One night on the trail to Fredericksburg, Jackson and Jim stop to pray together for their loved ones. As a heavenly choir sings on the soundtrack, Jim asks God why it is that good Christian men can 'tolerate their black brothers in bondage', and why 'they don't just break them chains'. Jackson looks on kindly and assures Jim that one day the slaves will be free. The two men are joined both by their common faith and by their shared belief in/desire for the emancipation of black slaves. This construction of Jackson acts to consolidate an identification with the Southern hero, and may even encourage a closer identification with the Confederate cause, as if somehow history has gotten it all wrong, when key figures in the Southern army actually wanted emancipation after all.

It is in fact the Northern characters that express a more remarkable, and to today's understanding, accurate position on slavery and emancipation. When Lincoln's Emancipation Proclamation is reported in the press, Chamberlain explains to his brother, Tom, that freeing the slaves was never an original Union war aim (which is true), but that 'war changes things'. He scolds Tom for calling black people 'darkies' because it is a patronising expression, and concludes his lesson saying, 'We have seen more suffering than any man should ever see, and if there is going to be an end to it, it must be an end that justifies the cost...War is a scourge, but so is slavery.' Not only is war a horrific state of affairs, as the film painstakingly explores, but slavery is an equally detestable infringement of human rights. The Northern characters, then, are absolved of any kind of blame in their federal aggression by this wholehearted espousal of the American value of freedom. Although the horror of slavery is neutralised in this film, it is the idea of captivity that is abhorred, in keeping with current dominant ideologies.

The fate of the two black characters is also worthy of mention. Unlike the black soldiers of *Glory*, who die on the battlefield, both Jim and Martha survive to the end of the narrative. This is an important point to make, since part of the project of the Civil War combat film (and all Civil War films) is to construct a worthy American ancestry. The central characters face a test of courage, usually in the form of armed conflict, and are rewarded with glory. Those that die become part of a pantheon of American heroes, those that survive are thus free to live on and procreate. In the survival of both Jim and Martha, then, the heroes of the past become the ancestors of the present generation, and with those ancestors being black the American historical family tree ceases to be all-white. Although these two characters do not participate in armed combat, i.e. they do not literally fight for their country like the soldiers of *Glory*, and they are not central characters, their acceptance into American historical familyhood is worthy of note.

Being one of the key elements of the combat film, armed conflict operates as a climactic component of *Gods and Generals*. Maxwell makes regular use of his trademark aerial perspectives, swift tracking shots of armies on the attack and close shots that reveal the incredible attention to historical detail in costume and weaponry. Sound also contributes to the authentic construction of battle, notably the sound of stray bullets whizzing past shadowed bodies at night outside the town of Fredericksburg. The authenticity does not stop there, however, as much of the dialogue of the film was based on letters, diaries and records of speeches by such figures as Jackson. A kind of stilted turn of phrase that is evident in the dialogue is suggestive of a language over a century old. In terms of the set, Maxwell meticulously reconstructed classrooms, homes and battle formations according to surviving buildings and photographs. Together with the incorporation of actual events and historical figures, these factors contribute to a convincing accuracy in this 'true story of the Civil War'.

Common to each of the genres examined in this study, the melodramatic mode is employed as a means of externalising and expressing the tests, rites of passage and emotional journeys of Civil War heroes, through performance, *mise-en-scène* and music. As found in many of the films of this study, the melodramatic mode is not necessarily an unreal or exaggerated representation of events, in fact it translates the Civil War into an emotional reality through its stylistic elements. The use of *mise-en-scène* for example is often used to signify a contrast between war and peacetime through changes in colour, lighting and set. Put to use in the Civil War combat film, the melodramatic mode also serves to subjectify the soldier's experience of war, such as the voice-over in *The Red Badge of Courage* (John Huston, 1951) or the use of slow motion and distorted sound in *Glory*. *Gods and Generals* avoids such overt subjective devices, and yet manages to portray the fear and shock of the battle experience through performance. Soldiers are often seen praying, weeping or struggling frantically with ammunition. A Union soldier with one arm blown off asks politely but tremulously for permission to leave the field, which is given by his stunned officer. Moments such as these operate to authenticate the emotional, as well as physical, reality of Maxwell's Civil War reconstruction. There are, however, four key scenes that I would like to highlight in their significant adoption of the melodramatic mode and their imagining of the Civil War.

The first is the aftermath of the first small battle of the film. Jackson and his officers walk slowly through the darkened field, surveying the bodies of their fellow soldiers. Melancholy strains of music foreground the soundtrack as smoke clears to reveal a lone drum rolling by and a family photograph lying on its side. Thunder rolls in the skies as Jackson states, 'I will never forget these men. We must never forget them.' It is a poignant and melodramatic reminder of the tragic loss of life incurred by the Civil War. A second example occurs during the attack on Fredericksburg, when a similar lesson of the tragedy of war is given to the Union army. A group of Irish Union soldiers, firing from a stone wall, are pitched against fellow countrymen in the Confederacy. The film has already made it clear that Irishmen can be found on both sides of the conflict. Chamberlain's invaluable first officer, Kilrain (Kevin Conway), has stated earlier, 'We left [Ireland] together to escape the tyranny, and we end up shootin' one another in the land of the free.' Now these men are seen engaging in this very conflict, during a scene of harrowing authentic detail. Alternating shots show the Union Irish noticing their former 'brothers' and, with Celtic music swelling emotively, one soldier bursts into tears as he reloads and fires. Scenes such as this are as poignant and powerful as Josh's emotional display in *Friendly Persuasion* when he fires on the Confederate enemy. It is an example of the filmmakers' mission to refuse sides in the conflict as well as emphasise the inherent sadness of a nation-family at war with itself.

What the melodramatic mode is helping to achieve here is the sense of the sameness of those involved in the Civil War, whether Union or Confederate. This is encapsulated in a third example of the melodramatic mode which occurs during the Union attack on Fredericksburg and effectively links each of the film's central characters to one another through an actual, and phenomenal, event. The repeated motif of the sky has been used throughout the film, such as the opening words from George Eliot, Jackson praying to the heavens with Jim, and when the very skies thunder at the tragedy of life lost. Then, during the night outside Fredericksburg, soldiers on both sides of the conflict shield themselves from enemy bullets with the bodies of their fellows. An eerie silence heralds the manifestation of the *aurora borealis*, the 'Northern lights', in the sky above the men. A strange calm falls on Union and Confederate soldier alike, as each gazes at this wonder in the sky. It is true that the Northern lights were seen at this time, but their presence is a masterstroke of the melodramatic mode, as if the sky itself is expressing the pain of war and the true goodness of the men fighting it. It also acts to draw the characters back into communion, since all gaze at the same sky above, just as all carry the same Bible and worship the same God.

Finally, in a scene reminiscent of *The Red Badge of Courage*, a fourth instance of the melodramatic mode can be found. A Union soldier and his Confederate counterpart shout to each other across the Rappahannock River, the same location of Henry Fleming's conversation with a Confederate who kindly warns him to stay in the shadows, or risk getting a 'red badge'. The scene is the same that opened the theatrical trailer of *Gods and Generals*. The two soldiers call each other Billy Yank and Johnny Reb, one expressing a desire for tobacco, the other for coffee. Most of the scene is comprised of a single medium shot that lasts almost a minute, with no dialogue and no music, as the two men stand like brothers at the mid-point of the river, exchanging gifts, before silently returning to their posts. What Maxwell constructs here is a melodramatic silence reminiscent of the house-burning episode of *So Red the Rose* and the trek to Tara through the devastated battlefields in *Gone With the Wind*. Although the films make regular use of the mode's sentimental musical score, they also register moments, like these, of intense emotion or significance with the use of silence. This is perhaps one of the most moving scenes of *Gods and Generals*, and acts together with the scenes mentioned above to represent the sameness of North and South, their brotherhood and the family of America.

Maxwell does, however, employ the melodramatic mode in a way that contrasts with his efforts to depict all Americans as one, in the final battle of the film, which enacts the Confederacy's surprise attack of a Union encampment at Chancellorsville. As the first Confederate flag is seen cresting the hill outside the Union camp, Wagnerian choral chanting seems to state that this is an army of God, bringing death, destruction and justice. One cannot help but compare it to the advance of King Arthur and his knights in John Boorman's *Excalibur* (1981) or, more significantly, the ride of the Ku Klux Klan in *The Birth of a Nation*. It is difficult to say whether this is demonstrative of a failure to live up to the intent to refuse the taking of sides, or perhaps an implication of the national and historical significance of the moment: a Confederate victory in a war ultimately won by the Union.

MAXWELL'S CIVIL WAR: EDUCATING THE YOUNG PEOPLE OF AMERICA

The critical reception of *Gods and Generals* did not differ from hundreds of Civil War films before it: critics have complained about its manipulation of historical facts and its sentimentality. Historian Patrick Rael published an essay on the internet site *History News Network*,[3] entitled '*Gods and Generals* is Good Hollywood – Don't Go See It', linking his response to the endorsement of *Birth* by Dorothea Dix in 1915, who wrote that Griffith's film was 'history vitalized. Go see it, for it will make a better American of you.'[4] Rael complains that Maxwell's film offers up only 'tamed' historical figures and loyal slaves with modern sensibilities, and predicts that it will appeal only to 'Civil War buffs'. *North and South* magazine, the American journal for Civil War academics and enthusiasts, published a compilation of responses from historians who berated the film for its tediousness, its historical inaccuracy and its conformity to lost cause mythology. History professor Robert Brent Toplin declared, '[i]f D.W. Griffith, […], could rise from the dead and attend a screening, he would probably find much to appreciate in *Gods and Generals*'.[5] The magazine's editor, Keith Poulter, even summed up the sentimentality of the film as 'Disney does Dixie'.[6]

An analysis of *Gods and Generals* would be incomplete without attending further to these parallels with *The Birth of a Nation*. It has been noted above that both films make strong use of the melodramatic mode, and of conventions of the epic film and domestic melodrama genres. This in itself is not remarkable; *Gone With the Wind* does the same, and each of the films examined throughout this study are presented in the melodramatic mode. *Birth* and *Gods* both also alternate their narratives between a national and familial story, ultimately turning much of their attention to the Southern experience in the war. It is this choice of focus that causes some of the problems that have been the complaint of Maxwell's detractors. Because Maxwell cannot ascribe any guilt to his Southern heroes for the institution of slavery, the film inevitably re-writes one corner of history. He chooses to depict only faithful black slaves in order to protect the integrity of a gallant South, and so inadvertently invites comparison with *Birth* and *Gone With the Wind*. The film instils the Confederacy with such affection that the giving of a flag by a mother to her sons cannot help but be compared to Ben Cameron's gift to his little sister. In the same vein, the Valkyrie-like approach of the Confederates to battle on their enemy could be obliquely interpreted as a sanctification of the Klan's ride to the oppressed South's rescue.

Perhaps the most significant comparison is in the treatment of Jackson. Like the conventional representation of Abraham Lincoln, epitomised in *Birth*, Jackson is constructed as a saviour-figure, an icon to his men and a perfect example of the heroic American ancestor. He is even seen praying to God with a shawl about his shoulders, a common image of Lincoln. Like the Lincoln of *Birth* he weeps for the dead, and like the Lincoln of *The Littlest Rebel* (David Butler, 1935) he is kind to children and holds the fate of his nation in his hands. In this similarity Jackson takes on the Christ-like status apportioned to Lincoln by these and other films. In his first battle Jackson is shot in his left hand, in his last battle he is wounded in the right hand, thus by the time of his death he has received the stigmata that act as signs of his sacrifice for his people. His accidental fatal wounding is even at the hands of his own men, like Judas's betrayal of Christ. Together with his repeated Biblical quotations, Jackson represents a martyred saviour-figure on a par with the Lincoln of Civil War cinema. As many historians have noted, Stonewall was indeed made a key icon for the South in his death, 'the pre-eminent Confederate martyr', as Robert Cook puts it.[7] In *Gods and Generals* he operates as no less than this, as a device to reclaim honour for the South, and for all Southern descendants, who are able to see their own glorious ancestor on screen. Needless to say, to depict any kind of anti-Lincoln figures, such as *Birth*'s Austin Stoneman, would too overtly detract from a continued reconciliation of the national family.

The final line of comparison can be found in the director's personal goal in the exploitation of historical film. Maxwell has been very active in public discussions of his Civil War films, both in defending them against accusations of inaccuracy or downplaying racial issues, and in promoting historical films as educational tools. What he goes to great pains to emphasise is the 'truth' of his Civil War films. An interview with *The Washington Times* cites him stating: 'We are telling the truth here'.[8] In a strange parallel of Griffith's post-*Birth* publicity, Maxwell, who is open about his Christian faith, conducted interviews with Christian and educational organisations concerning the nature of his film and its values. A three-part review of *Gods and Generals* published online by World Net Daily assured readers: 'If you've ever fretted or complained how revisionists continue to rewrite American history, how schools teach more fiction about America's glorious past than they teach fact, you must hit the theatre this weekend.'[9] Maxwell's interview with the reviewer, Rebecca Hagelin, found him making the following comments:

> We are all very susceptible to the power of the media. The media, particularly films, have a powerful influence on our lives. Films have the ability to tell stories

with such authority that the stories they tell can pass as truth, whether or not they are truth. I have a moral obligation to exercise responsibility in my telling of history. The telling of history is the life and death of a people. An inaccurate portrayal can be the death of a culture over the years.

This is a perspective shared by a host of historians concerning the 'mangling' or 'deforming' of history, accomplished through many a historical film. However, there is an implicit claim made here that Maxwell's films tell historical truth. The implication of this is confirmed in the second part of the review in which Hagelin writes:

> [...] his words remind me why an accurate portrayal of history is especially important for our children during these troubled times: 'In the climate we live in since Sept. 11, we can take great solace and find peace in knowing that America has a history of strong character – we can handle even terrorism if we know our past.'[10]

It is exactly this hope, that the children of today can learn the 'truth' of their ancestors, and thus about themselves, through (Maxwell's) Civil War films that is at once both commendable and hazardous. It would appear that what Maxwell is hoping for is that the educational sector will take up his film as a tool to educate the young people of America about themselves. This possibility is made even more evident by responses such as that of *The Cincinnati Enquirer*, which described *Gods and Generals* as 'school-friendly', with 'only a few instants of graphic gore'.[11] High school teachers across the US responded to the film with enthusiasm. In fact, lesson plans which incorporate *Gods and Generals* into high school history classes can be easily found by browsing the internet.

18. *Gods and Generals* (Ronald F. Maxwell, 2003): Stonewall Jackson as Southern Christ-figure.

Like D.W. Griffith, Maxwell has gone to extreme pains to construct an authentic and carefully researched construction of the Civil War, and like Griffith he desires to see it exploited for its educational value. Both directors appear to view the medium of film as a potentially unbiased form, in the right hands, that is able to teach young Americans about themselves, and both seem to believe that the key educational aid in this pedagogic philanthropy is the American Civil War. Just as hundreds of directors, authors and artists have demonstrated, the Civil War is understood as a means of affirming the American people of today by linking them to the American people of the past. Their films are part of the pedagogic industry to remember/forget the past, constructing an American familyhood reaching back to the 1860s. Maxwell's film in particular, like the original novel upon which it is based, has elements that set it apart from most Civil War films – it invites black individuals to join the American family tree – and so in this respect it deserves congratulations. To use a film as educational material, however, is a different matter. It might be more pertinent, perhaps, to teach our children how to take a critical stance towards cinema and written histories alike, rather than accept either as a simple statement of truth.

COLD MOUNTAIN: MORE THAN A 'ROAD MOVIE WITH A LOVE STORY'

Like Maxwell's film, *Cold Mountain* can also be seen to conform to the traits of the domestic melodrama, although it might just as usefully be addressed as an epic romance. Confederate soldier Inman (Jude Law) deserts the battlefield in order to return to his sweetheart in the South, Ada, played by Nicole Kidman, a similarity to Homer's *Odyssey* that did not escape the attention of several reviewers, both of the film and the source novel of the same name by Charles Frazier. The narrative concerns itself equally with Inman's trials on his journey and Ada's struggle as an educated lady in a hostile environment. Like Jake in *Ride With the Devil*, Inman's desire is to return home – Ada is his home, as he states to mountain woman, Maddy (Eileen Atkins), on his travels – and like the protagonists of the War-Westerns of this study he is not complete until he is united with a woman. *L.A. Weekly*'s online article by Ella Taylor describes the film as 'a road movie with a love story',[12] recognising that the film is less concerned with the Civil War than it is with the eventual joining of the heterosexual couple. Its overt concern with romance is highlighted in the lengthy sex scene, undoubtedly the most protracted of all Civil War films. Taylor's assessment of the film is not entirely reasonable, an issue that I shall return to below.

The film was not received positively across the critical establishment for a number of reasons, one being the absence of black characters. In the UK, the *Guardian*'s review[13] accuses the film of 'socio-political myopia', there being barely a single black face in the film. Although this is not strictly accurate, there are some important conclusions to be drawn about the film's construction of the American ancestor. One black soldier is seen fighting for the Union during the single episode of combat at the film's beginning, and at one point he fights a Native American Confederate soldier, being a concession to the presence of soldiers on both sides of the conflict not being white. The two soldiers, in hand-to-hand combat, fleetingly gain eye contact. The moment is so brief that it is not clear whether it is designed to ask the question why these men might be involved in what to all appearances seems to be a white man's war. Later a slave family is seen on the run, only to be slaughtered off-screen, and an establishing shot of a plantation home-cum-hospital shows black slaves picking cotton. Beyond these, an occasional glimpse of a black servant or slave is made at intervals during the film. Slavery is never overtly discussed, except for Ada's statement in voice-over, that she is glad to 'escape' Charleston and its 'world of slaves and corsets and cotton', and later a neighbour's comment that Ada has decided to free her father's slaves. An interview with the black director Spike Lee makes an interesting point about this absence: 'We're going backward if *Gone With the Wind* is more progressive than *Cold Mountain*. *Gone With the Wind* was made in 1939. In 2004 we're not even in it? We're going backward. I don't understand it.'[14] What this comment indicates is that even the most contemporary of Civil War films continue to hail the white American ancestor, not his black counterpart, *Glory* and *Gods and Generals* aside. Considering that the resolution of *Cold Mountain* is the revelation of Ada having borne a child to Inman, and since the family of the Civil War domestic melodrama is representative of the nation, the film clearly depicts the birth of a new, white nation, the most apparent ideal of which is the capacity to overcome any hardship for the sake of love.

A clear example of the absence of the black ancestor, and indeed of the black hero, can be found by the viewer with some knowledge of the battles of the Civil War. The first event of *Cold Mountain* is the infamous Battle of the Crater in July 1864, in which Union General Ulysses S. Grant ordered that a tunnel be made underneath the 'no-man's land' between enemy trenches and a mine be exploded beneath the Confederate troops defending

Petersburg. At this point Inman is hunched in a Confederate trench, gazing at a photograph of Ada, much as Ben Cameron is seen to do with a photograph of Elsie Stoneman in *The Birth of a Nation*, longing to be with a woman he barely yet knows. The explosion from beneath the trenches that is then reconstructed is one that led to one of the most disturbing of Union losses when their own troops became trapped in the crater of their own making, where they were effectively slaughtered by the Confederate soldiers above. The incident on film incorporates the use of pyrotechnics, special and digital effects technology, the latter of which is becoming more frequent in films depicting combat, notably when one soldier's uniform is flayed from his body by the blast. According to historical accounts,[15] Confederate troops opened fire on black Union troops caught in the crater, killing around 600 black men. *Cold Mountain*, however, chooses to depict a predominantly white presence in the crater, reinforcing a remembrance of the conflict as a white man's war. This is not, of course, a manipulation of the facts, there were more white soldiers than black caught in the crater. However, the choice to avoid presenting such a notorious moment of black genocide is indicative of a trend found throughout the film.

For a large portion of the film, *Cold Mountain* follows a non-linear structure, being composed of multiple flashbacks (in keeping with the structure of the *Odyssey*) to specific moments in Inman's desertion and journey back to *Cold Mountain*, and Ada's efforts to run a farm after her father's death. Ada's voice links the episodes together, principally in the form of letters to Inman, a device that can be found in the source novel. The film is composed very much in the melodramatic mode, most notably in its use of colour, lighting and music. Flashbacks to the antebellum days and the growth of affection between Ada and Inman tend to be bright, sunny and colourful, until the death of Ada's preacher-father (Donald Sutherland) in their garden in the rain. Episodes during the war, of Inman's desertion and journey, and Ada's harsh existence, are predominantly dark or bleached of vibrant colour, with many of the latter scenes filmed in the wintry environment of Romania. There is a dominant concern with the land and with nature, not unlike that found in films such as *Gone With the Wind* and, to an extent, *Gods and Generals*, which lends a sense of the natural to Inman's and Ada's love for each other across the expanse of land that separates them. The film, one can argue, is more concerned with this romance than it is with the conflict itself. It is a foregrounded semantic element that is more prominent even than the romances found in *Gone With the Wind* and *So Red the Rose*, so prominent in fact that it confirms

Cold Mountain as a domestic melodrama with a strong bias towards historical romance.

The use of nature is central to the construction of this romance, particularly animals and birds. When Inman is first seen in the trenches outside Petersburg, a wild rabbit causes much amusement as it is chased for food. Later, after the explosion, a horse emerges from a burning trench and trots away. Both the rabbit and the horse stand for something that Inman seeks, freedom to be with Ada. Animals throughout the film are there as more than a means to construct an authentic rural America, they act to comment upon characters and the narrative. Ada's fear and inadequacy as a lone woman on her farm is illustrated when she is terrorised by a cockerel. Her journey to self-sufficiency by the end of the film is then demonstrated by her skinning a dead lamb, then placing its fleece upon an orphaned lamb for it to be accepted in the herd. The rhythm of the natural world is something that Ada must learn, as she must also do away with her beloved piano and the trinkets of her former Charleston existence. This natural rhythm is, similarly, Inman's lesson when Maddy, the old mountain woman who restores him to health on his journey, explains that all of nature has a purpose, whilst she caresses then slaughters a lamb at her feet. These episodes, amongst others, reinforce the naturalness of Ada's and Inman's relationship. One might also wonder if there is a suggestion that war itself owns a place in this natural system, but since the causes and purposes of the war are never entertained in the film it is difficult to speculate.

Not all natural motifs are dealt with in such an ambiguous manner. A flashback later in the film shows the lovers attempting to free a white dove from Ada's father's chapel. Such associations of peace and freedom are rather clichéd but suggest also a releasing of Ada from her mannered, cultured Southern lifestyle, with the dove's white plumage paralleling the white frills and bonnet of Ada when she first arrives at Cold Mountain – a vision of beauty, purity and fascination for the farming community. It has little to communicate concerning another kind of freedom, that of the slave population of the South. Although the use of the white dove is over-emphatic, birds are used in another way that is altogether more interesting. Friends Sally and Esco (Kathy Baker and James Gammon) help Ada to see into her future by leaning her back over their well, holding a mirror to see the water below. In the reflection Ada sees Inman returning to her from the war, surrounded by crows. This vision is fulfilled at the end of the film when Inman is shot and killed, encircled by crows, and so nature's prophecy comes to pass. This kind of metaphysical plot device is not, strangely, that uncommon. Sally Bedford, the mother of Valette in *So Red the Rose*, has a clairvoyant gift that is passed on to her daughter. Thomas Dixon's story of *The Clansman* has the black rapist's face imprinted on the retina of his dead white female victim. Scarlett O'Hara dreams of being lost in the mist, where she in fact finds herself at the end of *Gone With the Wind*. It is a narrative element that I have never seen commented upon in any study of Civil War films, and it might seem ill-fitting in a historical reconstruction. However, it is used exclusively, as far as I am able to tell, in domestic melodramas of the Civil War. The implication may be that it is a device that is designed to appeal to one demographic in particular, the female viewer. It is also, however, in keeping with a category of films that deals regularly with the forces of fate and destiny. The viewer knows the 'end of the story' of the Civil War, and so cues such as prophetic signs and clairvoyant dreams contribute to the inevitability that is already known, the sense of a war that was unavoidable.

CAUGHT UP IN 'SOMEONE ELSE'S WAR'

As a domestic melodrama one might expect *Cold Mountain* to conform to the trait found in the category to avoid full characterisation of a villain. As a contemporary Civil War melodrama, however, it does provide such a character, similar to *Ride With the Devil*'s maniacal Pitt Mackeson. As was explored in the analysis of *Ride With the Devil*, there is evidence that some Civil War films are now incorporating the fully characterised villain, returning to the convention of traditional melodrama that uses the dichotomy of hero and villain to inscribe moral co-ordinates for the viewer. In the case of the Civil War narrative, however, and in respect for the perpetual Civil War myth, hero and villain must not be found across the opposition of North and South. In keeping with this careful negotiation of villainy, the antagonists of *Cold Mountain* are found amongst the Southern population of Ada's home. The villainous group here is led by Teague (Ray Winstone), a greedy, violent ex-landowner who sets up his own Home Guard. He desires both Ada and the farm she struggles to make productive with fellow labourer Ruby (Renée Zellweger), and his bullying tactics hold the people of the region in a grip of fear.

The performance of Ray Winstone, a British actor, immediately sets him apart for the viewer who is familiar with his star persona: a violent, vicious rapist and criminal, as constructed from roles in films such as *Scum* (Alan

Clarke, 1979), *The War Zone* (Tim Roth, 1999) and *Love, Honour and Obey* (Dominic Anciano and Ray Burdis, 2000). In contrast to Jude Law's blond, sculpted, masculine beauty, Winstone is overweight and grizzled. He is also accompanied by a long-haired albino accomplice, Bosie (Charlie Hunnam, another British actor) who, like Mackeson of *Ride With the Devil*, has a lust for torture and murder.[16] When Ada's neighbour Sally harbours her own sons who have deserted from the army, this man murders Sally's husband with a sword and tortures her to such an extent that it causes her to become mute. Not only do these men resort to sadistic violence for their own ends, thus clearly constructing them as villains, but also amongst them is this man that is 'other', the albino Bosie. His whiteness, which is 'too white', is encoded as freakishness (the character in the novel is merely fair and sickly). Bosie is 'abnormal', and this visual sign points to his psychological abnormality, a device that is common in Hollywood depictions of albinism, and something that is resisted publicly by organisations such as NOAH, the National Organization for Albinism and Hypopigmentation. It seems ironic that a twenty-first-century film which depicts the era of the American Civil War should replace the 'othering' of the black man with the 'othering' of a too-white white man, incorporating within him characteristics of the brutal black buck.

Ultimately, this band of villainous types must be punished or destroyed, and it is Inman who finally dispenses this justice, but at the cost of his own life when he is fatally wounded by Bosie. The villains of *Cold Mountain* then, like Mackeson in *Ride With the Devil*, are there to admit a psychopathic tendency in the American character, an abhorrence, yet they are disposed of through death, sending the clear signal that good will win out. Since Inman's brief return to Cold Mountain before his death grants him one night with Ada, the goodness of the hero lives on through his child and he remains a venerable ancestor. The villains, in their deaths and failure to procreate, have their line halted, and so they are barred from entry to the historical family tree. As noted above, like *Ride With the Devil*, the villainous characters and the heroes are all Southern, and as progressive as this might seem, it is a device to engage the viewer in a dramatic moral conflict that avoids the opposition of North and South.

Is Inman, however, truly the hero that he is implied as being? This is a man who, when handed over to the Home Guard by a deceitful farmer as a deserter, declares that he will not go back to the army to be killed for a cause that he does not believe in. What could have been construed in an earlier film as cowardice, is explained as moral superiority over today's understanding of the lost cause. In *The Undefeated* (Andrew V. McLaglen, 1969), the man who refuses to fight is branded a coward, and he is excommunicated, refused entry to the historical family tree. In such a film as *The Undefeated*, it is taken for granted that the war was a necessity, and it was therefore the duty of all, both North and South, to fight. Years on in *Cold Mountain*, it is the hero who turns his back on conflict since he has a higher calling, to make love not war. It is a sign of our changing attitudes to warfare, and may even be an omen of a changing relationship with the Civil War itself. The conflict in this film is made peripheral in the affirmation of the heterosexual romance and contemporary anti-war sensibilities. In this respect, *Cold Mountain* is a world apart from most Civil War films. *The Red Badge of Courage*, for example, shows the process within the 'Youth' Henry Fleming from cowardice to courage, and he is seen rejoining the national conflict, eventually earning himself the respect of all around him. McBurney of *The Beguiled* (Don Siegel, 1971), played by Clint Eastwood, demonstrates his cowardice by firing on vulnerable enemy soldiers before running rampant with the affections of a Southern girls' boarding school – sins for which he is ultimately punished through murder. Even John Dunbar's journey westwards, away from the war, to the frontier in *Dances With Wolves* is a reward for his battlefield bravery, and sees him still in the service of the army. Inman, however, is the first protagonist to turn his back on the war for personal, even selfish, reasons, and yet he goes on to demonstrate positive moral characteristics such as mercy, generosity and love. It is tempting to suggest that this is only possible at all by the backgrounding of concerns with the national conflict itself, making the war simply a tragic backdrop to the story of lovers – Romeo and Juliet meet Odysseus and Penelope.

19. *Cold Mountain* (Anthony Minghella, 2003): The Southern villain represented as monster.

It is important, however, to examine the political consequences of a hero that deserts from the war. Despite reviews and criticisms that highlighted the film's blithe ignorance of the deep significance of the Civil War to American audiences, one reviewer saw it as more faithful to history than other films depicting the war. Mackubin Thomas Owens, for the *National Review*, wrote that *Cold Mountain* is 'anti-*Gods and Generals*' because 'it describes a South at odds with the lost cause – a South divided against itself'.[17] The film is, according to Owens, a more faithful rendering of the historical situation, which found hundreds of thousands of Southerners rejecting the political and military position of the Confederacy. He concludes his review stating that the characters of Inman, Ada, Ruby and Teague are 'as much a part of the story of the Confederacy as Robert E. Lee and Stonewall Jackson'. This perspective on the film is a means by which to re-evaluate several episodes found in its narrative where the romantic myth of the South is gradually broken down, two of which are most revealing.

On Inman's travels he becomes the reluctant companion of a corrupt minister, Veasey (Philip Seymour Hoffman), who has been run out of his town for getting a black girl pregnant. On finding a farmer struggling to remove a dead bull from a river, another employment of the animal motif, the two fugitives offer their help. They are rewarded with an invitation to the farmer's home, which appears to be a hovel-cum-brothel, where the men are accosted by a group of lustful women. The sequence has none of the playful comedy of a similar scene in *Friendly Persuasion*, when Josh and his father visit an all-female household to sell produce, instead the experience is threatening and seedy, ending in their arrest by the local Home Guard. The episode shows much that Code-era Hollywood could not: sexual intercourse with children looking on, dirt, sweat, bodily functions. In accord with his heroic construction, Inman just barely resists the sordid temptation in respect for Ada, but that is not what is specifically important about the scene. What is relevant, politically speaking, is that these characters are Southerners. They are poverty-stricken, immoral, desperate, and willing to hand over their fellow countrymen for financial survival. They do not conform to the honourable Southern ancestor, reiterated throughout twentieth-century cinema and literature, and ever-present in other contemporary films such as *Gods and Generals*.

Another sequence follows after Inman has escaped arrest, when he comes across a young widowed mother, Sara (Natalie Portman) and her sick baby at a lone farmhouse. When Inman offers her his pistol, she rejects it and all 'metal' forged by men for violence. At her request, he lies with her in her bed with an arm around her body, but does not have any sexual contact with her. The following morning the farm is overrun with Union foragers, one who maliciously leaves the baby on the ground open to the elements and then attempts to rape Sara. Inman kills two of the men, but although the remaining Union soldier has tried to protect the vulnerable baby, he is shot dead by Sara. This is no mere case of mistaken identity, this is a mother driven to hysterical action by loneliness and fear, despite her loathing for this man's war, murdering a merciful, starving soldier in cold blood.

In the case of both of these examples, the characters cannot be understood as villains as such. They are individuals caught in 'someone else's war', so to speak, poor farmers, vulnerable women, people who encourage not a little sympathy from the viewer, who place more priority in survival than in the Confederate cause. As such, they expose a fissure in the myth of the old South. This sets the film apart from countless Civil War films that have gone before in that it also causes a fracture in the ideological project that is ubiquitous in this film category: they survive. These characters, in particular the lustful women at the farmhouse and Sara the widow, all have children. They are therefore, unavoidably, part of the American historical family tree. Their characteristics are more representative of a real history than of a myth. How interesting it is, then, that such diversions from the common myth of the American Civil War should be found in a film that foregrounds a romantic journey of the sort found in Greek mythology. It is evident that *Cold Mountain* is not simply a romantic love story as Ella Taylor's review states; it is a narrative that appears to play to the heterosexual audience, yet covertly cuts to the core of the Civil War experience away from the battlefields.

It is perhaps down to this modification of the Civil War myth and of the South that director Anthony Minghella had such difficulty in finding a studio to support the venture. In an interview with the *Guardian* newspaper,[18] Minghella explained this reluctance: 'That tells you there isn't really an appetite for ambitious movie-making out there.' What exactly he sees as 'ambitious movie-making' may have nothing to do with his challenge to Civil War mythology, but one is tempted at the very least to suggest that to some studios or producers, *Cold Mountain* simply does not work hard enough to venerate the American ancestor, albeit an ancestor who is represented mostly by white, good-looking stars. Minghella does himself no favours in the eyes of the American viewer by stating later in the interview:

> To be honest, I could care less about Union soldiers and Confederate soldiers. I kept thinking about the Cultural Revolution in China. What was interesting

to me about this material was the war away from the battlefield, and the abuses that accrue when there's chaos in the land and people are empowered to police when the men are gone.

The first of Minghella's comments here could easily mislead. Whilst he may not be principally concerned with the Union versus the Confederacy, his film is very much concerned with the effects of war. In particular, it is remarkable in its treatment of women. Women are seen to survive torture, to run a farm as efficiently as a male workforce, to live in harmony with nature, to show generosity beyond measure and to kill to protect their own. Even Ada, whose personal Self Civil War might seem initially to be one of how to survive deprivation, can be found at the end of the film violently beating Teague with the butt of a rifle. Ada, Ruby, Sally, Sara and Maddy are each vivid tributes to the women who fought to survive the Civil War, bereaved, starving and lonely. It is appropriate then that Minghella chooses not to emphasise the sectional conflict, since each of these women are from the South, and a narrative drawing comparison between Union and Confederacy would inevitably construct a veneration of the Southern woman. Instead, the critical viewer might even understand the film as one that re-writes the master narrative of the Civil War – a narrative that in Hollywood terms has so far been almost exclusively written by men – in which the part of the woman is to sew a flag for her sweetheart and weep over his coffin. It is Ruby, after all, who, on the news that Teague and his men have shot her deserting father, says: 'Every piece o' this is man's bullshit! They call this war a cloud over the land, but they made the weather and then they stand in the rain and say, shit! It's rainin'!'

Cold Mountain is also a testament to the men of the war who were driven to extreme measures, selling deserters for money, stealing a single woman's last pig for food, and, of course, walking away from warfare when its cause no longer seems 'just'. Without the romantic narrative, which is a necessary narrative motivation taken from the source novel and which no doubt was intended to draw the greater proportion of audiences, this film might have been one of the most harsh indictments of the American Civil War yet filmed.

In comparison to Maxwell's second Civil War film, which was not able to earn enough at the box office to cover budget, *Cold Mountain* made a profit of around $80 million. Whether this was thanks to the appeal of a love story or the presence of two top-billing stars cannot be said, but *Cold Mountain* is an anomaly in the Civil War film pantheon. Its deft ignorance of race and slavery aside, and notwithstanding its re-affirmation of the white national family at its end, this film allows the possibility that the American Civil War did not purge the nation of its flaws, that not every American ancestor is truly worthy or honourable.

NOTES

1   From author's correspondence with Jeff Shaara, author of *Gods and Generals* (1996) and *The Last Full Measure* (1998).

2   Ron Maxwell's Official Website, www.ronmaxwell.com/beyond myths.html.

3   Rael, Patrick, '*Gods and Generals* is Good Hollywood – Don't Go See It', *History News Network*, http://hnn.us/articles/1280.html (24 February 2003).

4   Dix, Dorothea, *Boston Globe* advertisement for *The Birth of a Nation* (9 April 1915), in Bowser, Eileen, (ed.) *The D. W. Griffith Papers, 1897–1954* (New York and Kentucky, 1982).

5   Poulter, Keith, 'Briefings: Historians Respond to *Gods and Generals*', *North and South*, vol. 6, no. 3 (April 2003). p. 88.

6   Poulter: 'Briefings: Historians Respond'. p. 91.

7   Cook, Robert, *Civil War America: Making a Nation, 1848–1877* (Harlow, 2003). p. 173.

8   Collier, Peter, 'Committed Storyteller', *The Washington Times* (22 February 2003). p. D01; also on Ron Maxwell's official website, www. ronmaxwell.com.

9   Hagelin, Rebecca, 'Among "Gods and Generals" – Part I' (18 February 2003) http://www.worldnetdaily.com/news/article.asp?ARTICLE_ ID=25616.

10   Hagelin: 'Among "Gods and Generals" – Part II', http://www.worldnet daily.com news/article.asp?ARTICLE_ID=25720.

11   McGurk, Margaret A., '*Gods and Generals* Shows South's Side', *The Cincinnati Enquirer* (21 February 2003); also http://www.cincinnati.com/freetime/ movies/reviews/ 02212003_godsandgenerals.html.

12   Taylor, Emma, 'Song of the South', *LA Weekly* (18 December 2003). http://www.laweekly.com/news/features/song-of-the-South/2129/

13   Interview with Andrew Pulver, the *Guardian*, 'Down from Cold Mountain' (11 December 2003).

14   Interview with Spike Lee, http://www.foxnews.com, no longer archived. Can now be found at http://www.findarticles.com/p/articles/mi_qn4196/ is_20040220/ai_n10948159

15   See for example Cook: *Civil War America*. p. 178.

16   Jonathan Rhys Meyers, who plays Mackeson in *Ride with the Devil*, is an Irish actor. Hollywood's attraction to British and Irish villains is clearly not on the wane.

17   Owens, Mackubin Thomas, 'Lost on *Cold Mountain*: The Anti-*Gods and Generals*', the *National Review* (7 January 2004), http://www.national review.com/owens/owens/200401070906.asp.
18   Interview with Andrew Pulver, the *Guardian*, 'Down from Cold Mountain' (11 December 2003).

Conclusion:
To Remember/Forget

I began this exploration into American Civil War films with a quotation from the late Shelby Foote about the nature of the conflict of 1861 to 1865. Foote stated in an interview that 'the Civil War defined us as what we are, and it opened us to what we became, good and bad things'.[1] In this comment can be found the belief that is at the foundation of each of the films examined in this study, that the Civil War is about the making of a nation and its identity. According to Foote, in order for American individuals to more fully understand their personal identity, they should seek first to understand the Civil War and learn how and why that identity was born. Even if stories of that past are fictional, because of their very situation during the Civil War they become stories of origin and identity, linking the Americans of today to the Americans of yesterday. As Bhabha has written, the concept of nation itself is 'Janus-faced', being comprised of what occurred in the past and what can be hoped for in the future from the perspective of the present.[2] Just as an understanding of nation links both the past and the present, an understanding of national identity does the same. This is exactly the function of Civil War films, which are constructions or imaginings of the birth of the American nation, for the purpose of propagating a certain national identity in the present.

The questions of this book have revolved around this imagining of American national identity. In investigating what kind of identity is constructed in Civil War films, I have considered how genres have participated in adaptations of the war, and similarly how the war has wrought changes to genres. I have questioned how true to genre selected films are, in order to ascertain adaptations essential to persistent understandings of the Civil War. For example, the absence of the villain was considered in Civil War domestic melodramas, consistent with the demands of an ideology that imagines the war as a conflict suffered by a family in which no blame can be found. I also identified the employment of the melodramatic mode across the range of genres in their imagining of the Civil War, and the resultant materialisation of tests and ideals in the American ancestor. This final chapter reviews the principal questions of my investigation and summarises my findings. It proposes that there are three dominant, interrelated ideals to be found in the three genres studied, working together to comprise one overarching ideological project: the education of the American nation about its identity.

It follows that if the melodramatic mode is 'a coherent mode of imagining and representing',[3] then its employment in the production of a Civil War film makes it a coherent mode of imagining and representing the Civil War. Since the melodramatic mode is so consistently used in Civil War films, it is difficult to imagine the war without the mode. In fact, it could be said that narrative and mode together make a 'Civil War imagination' with its own recognisable images, sounds and occurrences. Additionally, Brooks describes the mode's task as to distinguish and emphasise 'basic ethical and psychic truths' to a modern, secular world.[4] It is, to Brooks, adopted to make materially evident a set of moral absolutes or ideals that act, one could say, as a form of education. In the Civil War imagination, such 'truths' can be identified as aspects or values of the American ancestor, generated for the proliferation of a certain American national identity. Each of the three genres analysed in this study reveals its own fundamental ideal or truth that is part of this secular education of the American nation.

THE AMERICAN FAMILY WILL SURVIVE

In the analysis and comparison of Civil War domestic melodramas *So Red the Rose*, *Gone With the Wind*, *Friendly Persuasion* and *Ride With the Devil*, the central fictional families were found to be representative of the American nation as a whole. The films each adapted the central generic convention of melodrama, as a means of embodying and resolving moral oppositions, by re-writing the Civil War as a process of moral transformation for individuals in the family. In this way, characters had to face their own personal 'Self Civil War', an inner struggle caused or exacerbated by the national conflict. In surviving this crisis, the characters achieved a new moral maturity and worldview, reflected in changes within the films' melodramatic mode.

Valette Bedford in *So Red the Rose*, for example, makes the journey from a petulant Southern belle to a woman of integrity and wisdom, a transformation embodied particularly in her change of costume from a white, frilly crinoline, to the simple, modest dress of a farmhand. Ada Munroe in *Cold Mountain* makes a very similar journey, gradually letting go of the corsets and frills of Charleston in exchange for the life of a self-sufficient survivor. Jake Roedel in *Ride With the Devil* is seen to transform from an independent and idealistic youth, to a man with responsibilities and the maturity that comes from experience, signified by the cutting of his hair. Each of these characters prove themselves to be morally upright Americans in their compassion for others (even Scarlett O'Hara cares for her friend Melanie during a difficult childbirth) and in their devotion to family. In this last respect, the Civil War's threat to the family is seen to cause the most pacifist of characters, the puritan father in *Friendly Persuasion*, to symbolically turn his 'ploughshare into a sword' by taking his hunting rifle to find his lost son, and Southern belle Ada turns to violence when she attacks Teague in *Cold Mountain*.

The films were also found to subvert the melodrama's demand for a 'highly personalised villain',[5] bar a small selection of villainous types that could not be construed as representative of either North or South. Since the characters' struggles were fundamentally personal, and since Civil War mythology demands the absence of blame, consistent villains will rarely be found in these domestic melodramas. Neither will overt references to causes of the Civil War or intelligent debates about the issue of slavery, unless to emphasise a character's inherent moral goodness, such as Jake Roedel's eventual respect and affection for the ex-slave Holt in *Ride With the Devil*.

So a coherent construction of American national identity can be found in Civil War domestic melodramas, one that embodies certain moral ideals that are a combination of generic convention and Civil War mythology. That national identity exists in the representative American family which forms the roots of a historical family tree. Through the family's struggles and survival, the historical family is seen to survive, and all that is good and upright within it can be understood as the genetic characteristics of the present-day American. The lesson of these films is that the American nation was and is a family, and that family will always survive whatever challenges it must face.

ALL THREATS ARE OVERCOME BY UNITY

Escape from Fort Bravo, How the West Was Won, The Undefeated and *Dances With Wolves* were each studied in Chapter 3 in relation to the conventions of the Western, a genre that self-consciously deals with notions of American identity. The War-Western was found to replace the internal crisis of the American ancestor in Civil War domestic melodramas with an external struggle, fought principally at the Western frontier.

The films adopt certain iconographic and narrative demands of the Western, such as the line of conflict across the frontier and the embodiment of opposing values across that geographical axis. However, because the central characters are each somehow involved in the Civil War, their identity is initially constructed as either Union or Confederate, and so is not defined by the dichotomy of East and West. Like the changes found in the Civil War domestic melodrama, the opposition of North and South must be eradicated to conform to the higher authority of Civil War mythology. There must be no internal or domestic collective enemy in the Civil War, only brothers who learn to forget their differences and unite against an external enemy. The Western provides this external threat by placing the characters at the frontier where they adopt the new, united identity of 'Americans', leaving behind their identity of Union or Confederate, in the face of a 'non-American' enemy along a new axis of conflict. For example, Captain Roper and his escaped soldiers in *Escape from Fort Bravo* join forces to fight their common enemy, the savage Indians. All allegiances to the Union or the Confederacy are forgotten in the face of an external threat. The same communion occurs in *The Undefeated*, when Union Colonel Thomas and Confederate Colonel Langdon unite their groups to resist both the Eastern government and the Mexican revolutionaries.

The War-Western was also found to adapt the character of the Westerner from the lone and independent 'man who knows Indians' into a veteran of war who knows the horror of armed conflict and desires to settle and raise a family. This change is a consequence of his adapted identity from soldier of war to defender of a united nation. Characters such as Zeb in *How the West Was Won* and John Dunbar in *Dances With Wolves* choose their bride in the West and in so doing symbolically begin the reproduction of the new nation. The construction of American national identity in the War-Western, then, is founded on the identification of what is not-American as a threat, the eradication of that threat by the newly united American group, and the continuation of that communion by the heterosexual joining of partners.

The lesson that the War-Western teaches the viewer is that, through unity, the American nation can resist all external threats.

BEING PREPARED TO DIE FOR WHAT IS RIGHT

The Drummer of the 8th, *The Red Badge of Courage*, *The Horse Soldiers* and *Glory*, investigated in Chapter 4, are part of the sub-genre of the combat film. Establishing the definition of the combat film as one which has a high percentage of on-screen combat, these films were evaluated for their conformity to expectations of a category that tends to concentrate on wars of the twentieth century.

One of the key conventions of the combat film, the reconciliation of the all-male group towards a joint goal, is strongly evident in films such as *The Horse Soldiers* and *Glory*, with individuals aligning personal values for the sake of the whole. Colonel Marlowe, in *The Horse Soldiers*, lets go of his hatred of the medical profession for causing his wife's death in order to leave his past behind and complete his mission. Trip in *Glory* must also repent of his bitterness as an escaped slave to join with the black regiment in fighting for their double cause: the emancipation of the black race and the gaining of respect as men in a white man's war. In each case the military goal of the troop or regiment is primary, and the heroes' acceptance of that goal is part of their journey towards a confirmed masculinity.

The achievement of a new masculinity is a central component of the combat film, and these Civil War narratives explore it fully, with Billy of *The Drummer of the 8th* attaining manhood by his involvement in the war, and Henry the 'Youth' in *The Red Badge of Courage* bravely joining the ranks of fighting men. Interestingly, Stonewall Jackson in *Gods and Generals*, a film that was described as part-combat film, part-domestic melodrama, and Robert Shaw of *Glory*, are both seen to mature into a more sensitive masculinity, one that appreciates compassion and tenderness as much as courage and duty. It is, perhaps, a consequence of changing understandings of masculinity that sees these more recent screen heroes demonstrating the kind of 'feminised' values that at one time would have been drilled out of the men during training. Whatever the resultant expression of masculinity, however, when one of these sons of America dies in service, his death acts to immortalise a certain readiness to die for what he believes to be right. Thus a tension exists between the glory of fighting for a just cause and the tragedy of life lost.

The all-male fighting group in these Civil War combat films, then, functions to represent a certain spirit inherent in the American character. Through a similar form of unity to that found in the War-Western, the individuals align themselves to a common goal which is, simply, to fight. Their cause is rarely expounded, since this would threaten the blamelessness of each side in the conflict. In achieving this goal, the heroes are rewarded by achieving manhood, the reward having been conditional on either dying or being prepared to die. The central problematic that exists here is that the survivors of conflict in these films, the men who are able to go on and father a new generation, are exclusively white, whereas amongst the 'sons' who die and can never be fathers are the only central black characters to be found in the category. Although other combat films do depict black Civil War veterans, such as *Buffalo Soldiers* (Charles Haid, 1997), these tend to be set post-war, and are as rare as films that portray black soldiers actually fighting the war. Thus, what emerges is the adoration of the white American soldier, fighting a war that ostensibly seems to have nothing to do with race. Since the causes of the war are seldom entertained, the lesson of the Civil War combat film is that the American white ancestor was brave, thoroughly masculine and ready to die for his nation.

FAMILY, UNITY AND SELF-SACRIFICE IN OTHER GENRES

The three ideals summarised above of family, unity and self-sacrifice are the central pillars of an ideology of the American nation found in the three genres that most frequently represent the Civil War. Were this study to be extended to explore the reliability of these findings, perhaps other ideals might be found in different film genres. But it is worth a brief glance at a small selection of films not yet considered to ask whether the same ideals of family, unity and self-sacrifice can be found.

Although most of the films considered in this study present the war as a most serious and tragic event, there are several comic Civil War films. Buster Keaton's *The General* (1927), for example, was a showcase for Keaton's brand of physical and witty comedy, using the Civil War as a backdrop to the protagonist's antics. Johnnie Gray (Buster Keaton) is a railway engineer on the locomotive 'The General', and so his career is too valuable to the South for him to be allowed to enlist. His Southern sweetheart, Annabelle (Marion Mack), construes this as cowardice on Johnnie's part, but he goes on to rescue both his locomotive and Annabelle when they are abducted by enemy soldiers. The film's representation of combat turns the tragedy of death into comedy, as Johnnie joins the Southern army but each soldier he talks to is shot dead. Ultimately, he becomes a hero, he leads the troops home and is made a lieutenant. The narrative demonstrates the masculine test of the combat film in which the protagonist must prove his courage through a readiness to sacrifice his own life. His reward, as found in the Self Civil Wars of the domestic melodrama, comes in the form of his sweetheart's love. The general affirms the bravery of the fighting man and so corresponds to the ideological project of praising the qualities of the Civil War ancestor.

Another genre that presents the Civil War, usually in a single act of its narrative, is the biopic, following the life or career of a historical figure such as Abraham Lincoln. *They Died With Their Boots On* (Raoul Walsh, 1941) narrates the career of George Armstrong Custer, the infamous general who died during the Indian Wars. Custer (Errol Flynn) is presented as a vain, eccentric but loveable and courageous Union officer, whose impulsive and costly leadership tactics manage to bring victory to the North in several battles. The military blunders that are the source of Custer's notoriety are translated into moments of genius and bravery. As well as this, Custer's home life is given the treatment of the melodramatic mode, making him a passionately romantic husband to his wife, played by Olivia de Havilland. Through this reinscription of a historical figure, the film can be clearly identified as a mythification of Custer, imagining him as an all-American, single-minded hero, a man of the stuff that made America great. It conforms again to the ideology of a brave, masculine American parent, one who is as fervently dedicated to a military life as he is to his family.

One film that seems to stand out from conventional Civil War narratives is *The Beguiled* (Don Siegel, 1971). Instead of presenting Union and Confederacy as both equally heroic and equally blameless, the North and South of this film are equally corrupt. A wounded Northerner, McBurney (Clint Eastwood), is nursed back to health at an all-female Southern boarding school, but his presence introduces sexuality and violence to the women's lives. He uses his masculinity and the women's desire for romance, and in some cases for sex, to seduce them and divide their loyalties to one another (and to the South), leading to their amputation of his leg and eventual murder. The film has strong psychoanalytical associations as well as disturbing themes of entrapment, paedophilia, incest, betrayal and perversion. *The Beguiled* takes the metaphorical association of the Union raid as sexual attack, and literalises it. At least three of the women, in fact, welcome this intrusion, in contrast to films such as *The Birth of a Nation* or *So Red the Rose*.

This brief summary suggests that *The Beguiled* may well be the first film to reject the ideological project of ancestral reverence. McBurney has sexual contact with one, and possibly two, of the girls at the school, and so his line may continue. Also, the perversion that he displays is equally present in the school's headmistress, Martha (Geraldine Page), who was in an incestuous relationship with her brother before the narrative begins. In a lustful dream Martha even imagines herself in a threesome with McBurney and the innocent older girl, Edwina, who has fallen in love with him. Martha is, in a sense, part of a perverted American family. To reinforce this perversion of the myth of an honourable and just South, a small group of Confederate soldiers stops at the school, ostensibly to offer protection from Union troops, but actually motivated by lust. Although the men are sent on their way by Martha, their very identity as Confederate soldiers is an outright challenge to the myth of the honourable Reb. The means of escape from this alarming impression of nineteenth-century Americans is McBurney's murder, with a meal of poisonous mushrooms, which is both punishment for his crimes and an attempt to halt his genealogy so that he cannot be an American ancestor. In the execution of their plan to murder McBurney, the women participate in a unity that rids the future of his abhorrent presence. Since the man has had sexual contact with girls in the school, however, this cannot be guaranteed. The film's use of sepia cinematography as the film opens and closes looks like an attempt to remove the narrative from the present by sheer historical distance, keeping the warped characters safely in the past but, in a sense, the damage has already been done. Firstly, the opening sepia images are genuine photographs from the Civil War era, including one of Abraham Lincoln and others of battlefield carnage. The first moving image is of the young girl, Amy, picking mushrooms in a wood, also in sepia. The use of the sepia association between actual historical images and cinematography insinuates a covert authentication of the narrative. Secondly, McBurney's line may continue as a result of his sexual contact with two of the women. McBurney, Martha, the girls who participate in the murder and the group of lustful Confederates could all therefore be regarded as a foretaste of the worrying characteristics found in several characters in *Cold Mountain*.

Leaving *The Beguiled* and *Cold Mountain* aside for a moment, what these brief reviews of other Civil War films can suggest is that the key ideals in the American ancestor are present across the generic landscape. They contribute to an overall ideological project to construct an imagined *historical* community, allowing Anderson's description of nation as 'imagined community'[6] to expand across time from the Civil War to the present.

THE EDUCATION OF AMERICA

Benedict Anderson's metaphor for the concept of nation as an 'imagined community' sees a comradeship or brotherhood existing in the minds of a nation's members. If this concept is combined with Bhabha's understanding of nation, as 'Janus-faced', looking back to the past and forward to the future, an interesting synthesis can be made. The way that a nation imagines its past representatives, as some kind of brotherhood, born in a specific moment in history, has a direct influence on the way that the nation imagines its present and its future. This is the assumption on which the vast majority of Civil War films appear to be based. The Civil War is about the making of the united American nation, and it is the point in history when modern American identity was born. Therefore, the characters from Civil War films are the ancestors of the imagined American family. What the films achieve is the propagation of an ideology that confirms commitment to family, unity of values and bravery as qualities of the American of today, by virtue of his relationship with the American of yesterday. There is therefore a coherent and dominant ideological project at the root of Civil War films.

It was proposed in my introductory chapter that there is a case for arguing that the existence of a common ideology across American film genres may be restricted to the classical Hollywood era.[7] It was also asked whether Civil War films reflect the multiple and conflicting ideologies of a pluralistic western world.[8] In response, there is certainly a common ideological goal to be found across Civil War film genres, which is the deliberate forging of a relationship between the American viewer and his praiseworthy ancestor. It is not an ideology, however, that is restricted to the classical Hollywood era, since its presence can be found in some of the most recent Civil War films produced. Although the nature of that ancestor moves gradually, and extremely slowly, away from a 'white lovefeast'[9] to include the rare Native American or African American, the project remains largely the same.

The inclusion of new members to the family, however, is the single most convincing evidence that the ideologies of Civil War films may be plural: the changing representations of race and the gradual acceptance of non-white ancestors into the American pantheon is clear to see as the twentieth century progresses. Primarily the black soldiers of *Glory* (even though they do not survive the war), but also characters such as the Native American, Blue Boy, in *The Undefeated*, Holt in *Ride With the Devil*, and Jim and Martha in *Gods and Generals*, should each be singled out as exceptions to the ubiquity of the white bias of Civil War ancestry. It is important to note, however, that the Civil War film has not yet been made that has its *central* character a black or Native American individual who survives the war, goes on to father the children of the future, and stands to represent the whole of the American nation, not only its ethnic population.

It would appear then, that the cinematic construction of the American Civil War is, broadly speaking, aimed at the white audience of America, produced to teach the nation about its heritage and its identity. Its white bias and its preoccupation with the metaphor of family can be recognised as part of what Anderson identifies as the goal to educate the nation to 'remember/ forget' the Civil War. The purpose of Civil War films is not simply to remember what is held in common and to forget what caused division, but also to teach each new generation of Americans to accept a coherent myth of origins. Many historians and commentators regularly remind us of the dangers of this. Robert Brent Toplin, for instance, although he argues for the validity of historical film, quite rightly states '[s]tudents are learning history from the dramas they see on the screen, and, unfortunately, they are often subjected to a deeply flawed portrayal of the past'.[10] One might understand one of these 'flaws' to be the propagation of the myth of origins that I have explored through the pages of this book.

The work of the most prolific of contemporary directors of Civil War films, Ron Maxwell, takes some noteworthy departures from the myth, whilst conforming to it in other respects. The characters of *Gods and Generals*, even though many are real historical figures, carry as much mythical significance as Ben Cameron and Elsie Stoneman in *The Birth of a Nation*. In fact, each of Maxwell's Civil War films continues in the long tradition of this category of filmmaking: to attribute honour and glory, without blame, to all involved in the conflict. Although his latest film does foreground two African Americans, making a most important contribution to the American family tree, his films situate their lives in second place behind the more dominant celebration of the white American ancestor.

Maxwell's personal sense of responsibility in his reconstructions of the Civil War, because of the perceived power of historical films, cannot fail to draw comparison to comments from D.W. Griffith concerning the educational potential of cinema. Griffith's prediction stated: 'The time will come, and in less than ten years [...] when the children in the public schools will be taught practically everything by moving pictures. Certainly they will never be obliged to read history again.'[11] He saw cinema as being the ultimate educator with no opinion or bias, simply the re-creator of history, and *The Birth of a Nation* would have, no doubt, been the first film on the syllabus. Maxwell, similarly, seems to see his films as the unbiased 'truth' that should be handed on to the American people of today. Anderson's identification of this project – the 'pedagogic industry' that works to remember/forget the Civil War[12] – can thus be recognised in Civil War films released up to the present day, and there is no reason to believe that this may cease in the future.

There may be only a small number of historical films exhibited in any year, but they continue to secure high production values and, at times, respectable box office returns, and the Civil War remains one of the most common historical referents in Hollywood. Although each new film may appear to offer a new perspective on the war, the conscious or unconscious aim of its makers is to demonstrate the endurability of all that is good in the American character, and the presence of multiple genres simply broadens the appeal to the diverse American public. The ongoing dialogue in critical journals and histories about these films seeks to expose and counter the drive to remember/forget the American Civil War, striving instead to reveal a monstrous side to the nation's ideological make-up that, even now, seeks to either write the black race out of the American family or out of American history altogether. Some individuals and institutions still strive to disseminate an ideology of white supremacy, barely changed from the philosophy of *The Birth of a Nation*. After all, it is still possible to order reasonably priced videos of *Birth* from the Indiana Historical Research Foundation, the organisation that promotes the history, ideology and memorabilia of the Ku Klux Klan.[13]

This practice can be recognised as part of the master narrative of American History, identified by Nathan I. Huggins, which works to exclude the truths of race and slavery because of the problem they present to the establishing pillars of the American nation: liberty and equality.[14] With the black race excluded from American familyhood, as it is in *The Birth of a Nation* and many films since, including *Cold Mountain*, these twin values can be remembered and celebrated with a clear conscience. The true causes of the Civil War, being so closely related to issues of race and slavery as well as a breach of national unity at political and economic levels, become irrelevant. In a statement that reveals the success of this educational project, Jeanine Basinger writes '[p]erhaps we do not care to see our Civil War depicted in any way but as what it is: a quarrel in the family over material matters'.[15] The real Civil War has thus been largely forgotten in the cinema, and replaced by a myth of the birth of the nation, an era to which the white American viewer can turn to satisfy a 'quest for personal roots'.[16] Only in a handful of films is there an attempt to remember a different history, a counter-history which remembers that some of those forefathers were Native American, black or even, as in the case of *The Beguiled* and *Cold Mountain*, dishonourable whites. What should be asked, then, is whether *Glory*, *Gods and Generals* and *Cold Mountain* will be the final word in appealing to the American public to remember a different history of the Civil War. Will *Cold Mountain* be the last Hollywood film to consciously dishonour the American Civil War ancestor, whilst allowing him or her to survive the war without any distancing devices that couch the character safely in the past?

It has not been the aim of this thesis to draw D.W. Griffith, or any film director for that matter, as a monster. Griffith's contribution to cinema cannot be underestimated and reaches far beyond *The Birth of a Nation*, and even he, in his own way, attempted an apology for this film. The Barnet Bravermann Collection, now part of The Griffith Papers, cites the director in his latter years saying that if *Birth* were to be re-made, it should only be shown to 'film people and film students'.[17] For the sake of the 'Negroes', who he saw as having progressed so much socially, he stated, 'it is best that *The Birth of a Nation* in its present form be withheld from public exhibition'. He recognised that his film was harmful, even though he may not have truly understood why, and relegated it to the rarefied heights of film studies. In a kind of prophetic fulfilment, today's new viewers of *Birth* are mostly film students, watching the film predominantly as a piece of groundbreaking cinema, and this at least must continue. The unending dialogue about *The Birth of a Nation* and other Civil War films must be exactly that, unending, for the vital reason that critical enquiry can work to expose the way that cinema has participated in the imagining of a blameless and thoroughly honourable American national identity.

NOTES

1   *American Civil War*. Prod. Ken Burns, Prod. Co. Florentine Films, Dist. Co. PBS/Turner Home Entertainment, 1990, USA.
2   Bhabha, Homi K., 'Narrating the Nation' in H.K. Bhabha (ed.) *Nation and Narration* (London, 1990). p. 3.

3   Brooks, Peter, *The Melodramatic Imagination: Balzac, Henry James, Melodrama and the Mode of Excess* (New York, 1995). p. vii.

4   Brooks: *The Melodramatic Imagination.* p. 15.

5   A term from Brooks: *The Melodramatic Imagination.* p. 16.

6   Anderson, Benedict, *Imagined Communities*, 2nd edition (London, 1991). p. 6.

7   From the position taken in Wood, Robin, 'Ideology, Genre, Auteur', *Film Comment*, vol. 13, no. 1 (January–February, 1977). p. 47.

8   From the position taken in Collins, Jim, *Uncommon Cultures: Popular Culture and Post-modernism* (London, 1989). p. 90.

9   As Thomas Cripps describes the united group in *The Undefeated* in Cripps, Thomas, 'The Absent Presence in American Civil War Films', *Historical Journal of Film, Radio and Television*, vol. 14, no. 4 (1994). p. 372.

10   Toplin, Robert Brent, *Reel History: In Defense of Hollywood* (Lawrence, Kansas, 2002). p. 9.

11   Griffith, David Wark, 'Five Dollar Movies Prophecied', *The Editor* (24 April 1915) in E. Bowser (ed.) *The D.W. Griffith Papers, 1897–1954* (New York and Kentucky, 1982); also in H.M. Geduld (ed.) *Focus on D.W. Griffith* (Englewood Cliffs, New Jersey, 1971).

12   Anderson: *Imagined Communities.* p. 201.

13   See www.kkklan.com.

14   Huggins, Nathan I., 'The Deforming Mirror of Truth: Slavery and the Master Narrative of American History', *Radical History Review* (Winter, 1991). pp. 24–47.

15   Basinger, Jeanine, *The World War II Combat Film: Anatomy of a Genre* (Middletown, 2003). p. 75.

16   Tosh, J., *The Pursuit of History*, revised 3rd edition (Harlow, 2002). p. xv.

17   Bowser: *The D.W. Griffith Papers.* 1982.

Selected Filmography

American Civil War. Dir. and Prod. Ken Burns, Prod. Co. Florentine Films, Dist. Co. PBS/Turner Home Entertainment, 1990, USA.

Beguiled, The. Dir. Don Siegel, Prod. Don Siegel, Prod. Co. Malpaso, Dist. Co. Universal, 1971, USA. Main cast: Clint Eastwood (John McBurney), Geraldine Page (Martha), Elizabeth Hartman (Edwina), Jo Ann Harris (Carol), Darleen Carr (Doris), Mae Mercer (Hallie).

Birth of a Nation, The. Dir. D.W. Griffith, Prod. D.W. Griffith and Harry E. Aitken, Prod. Co. Epoch, Dist. Co. Epoch, 1915, USA. Main cast: Henry B. Walthall (Ben Cameron), Mae Marsh (Flora Cameron), Miriam Cooper (Margaret Cameron), Lillian Gish (Elsie Stoneman), Robert Harron (Tod Stoneman), Wallace Reid (Jeff), Donald Crisp (Gen. Ulysses S. Grant), Joseph Henabery (Abraham Lincoln), Raoul Walsh (John Wilkes Booth), Eugene Pallette (Wounded Union Soldier), Walter Long (Gus).

Cold Mountain. Dir. Anthony Minghella, Prod. Albert Berger, William Horberg, Sydney Pollack, Ron Yerxa, Prod. Co. Miramax Films/Mirage Enterprises/Bona Fide Productions, Dist. Co. Miramax Films, 2003, USA. Main cast: Jude Law (W.P. Inman), Nicole Kidman (Ada Monroe), Renée Zellweger (Ruby Thewes), Eileen Atkins (Maddy), Brendan Gleeson (Stobrod Thewes), Philip Seymour Hoffman (Veasey), Natalie Portman (Sara), Giovanni Ribisi (Junior), Donald Sutherland (Rev. Monroe), Ray

Winstone (Teague), Kathy Baker (Sally Swanger), James Gammon (Esco Swanger), Charlie Hunnam (Bosie), Jack White (Georgia).

Dances With Wolves. Dir. Kevin Costner, Prod. Jim Wilson and Kevin Costner, Prod. Co. Tig Productions/Majestic Films International, Dist. Co. Orion Pictures, 1990, USA. Main cast: Kevin Costner (Lt. John J. Dunbar), Mary McDonnell (Stands With a Fist), Graham Greene (Kicking Bird), Rodney A. Grant (Wind in His Hair), Floyd Red Crow Westerman (Chief Ten Bears), Tantoo Cardinal (Black Shawl), Robert Pastorelli (Timmons), Charles Rocket (Lt. Elgin), Maury Chaykin (Maj. Fambrough), Jimmy Herman (Stone Calf), Nathan Lee Chasing His Horse (Smiles a Lot).

Drummer of the 8th, The. Dir. Thomas H. Ince, Prod. Thomas H. Ince, Prod. Co. Broncho/New York Motion Picture Co., Dist. Co. Mutual Film Corp., 1913, USA. Main cast: Cyril Gardner (Billy), rest of cast not credited.

Escape from Fort Bravo. Dir. John Sturges, Prod. Nicholas Nayfack, Prod. Co. MGM, Dist. Co. MGM, 1953, USA. Main cast: William Holden (Capt. Roper), Eleanor Parker (Carla Forester), John Forsythe (Capt. John Marsh), William Demarest (Campbell).

Friendly Persuasion. Dir. William Wyler, Prod. William Wyler, Prod. Co. Allied Artists, Dist. Co. Allied Artists, 1956, USA. Main cast: Gary Cooper (Jess Birdwell), Dorothy McGuire (Eliza Birdwell), Anthony Perkins (Josh Birdwell), Marjorie Main (Widow Hudspeth), Richard Eyer (Little Jess), Robert Middleton (Sam Jordan), Walter Catlett (Professor Quigley), Phyllis Love (Mattie Birdwell), Mark Richman (Gard Jordan).

General, The. Dir. Buster Keaton, Prod. Buster Keaton and Joseph M. Schenk, Prod. Co. United Artists/Buster Keaton Productions Inc., Dist. Co. United Artists, 1927, USA. Main cast: Buster Keaton (Johnnie Gray), Marion Mack (Annabelle Lee), Glen Cavander (Capt. Anderson).

Gettysburg. Dir. Ronald F. Maxwell, Prod. Robert Katz and Moctesuma Esparza, Prod. Co. Turner Pictures/Esparza-Katz Productions, Dist. Co. New Line Cinema/Mayfair, 1993, USA. Main cast: Tom Berenger (Lt. Gen. James Longstreet), Martin Sheen (Gen. Robert E. Lee), Stephen Lang (Maj. Gen. George E. Pickett), Richard Jordan (Brig. Gen. Lewis A. Armistead), Jeff Daniels (Col. Joshua Lawrence Chamberlain), Sam Elliott (Brig. Gen. John

Buford), C. Thomas Howell (Lt. Thomas D. Chamberlain), Kevin Conway (Sgt 'Buster' Kilrain), Maxwell Caulfield (Col. Strong Vincent), Royce Applegate (Brig. Gen. James L. Kemper), Brian Mallon (Maj. Gen. Winfield Scott Hancock).

Glory. Dir. Edward Zwick, Prod. Freddie Fields, Prod. Co. TriStar Pictures, Dist. Co. Columbia TriStar, 1989, USA. Main cast: Matthew Broderick (Col. Robert Gould Shaw), Denzel Washington (Trip), Cary Elwes (Cabot Forbes), Morgan Freeman (John Rawlins), Jihmi Kennedy (Sharts), Andre Braugher (Searles), John Finn (Sgt Mulcahy), Donovan Leitch (Morse), Cliff De Young (Col. Montgomery), Raymond St Jacques (Frederick Douglass), Richard Riehle (Quartermaster).

Gods and Generals. Dir. Ronald F. Maxwell, Prod. Ronald F. Maxwell, Prod. Co. Antietam Filmworks/Turner Pictures, Dist. Co. Warner Bros, 2003, USA. Main cast: Stephen Lang (Lt. Gen. Thomas 'Stonewall' Jackson), Jeff Daniels (Lt. Col. Joshua Lawrence Chamberlain), Robert Duvall (Gen. Robert E. Lee), Keith Allison (Capt. James J. White), Mira Sorvino (Fanny Chamberlain), Kevin Conway (Sgt 'Buster' Kilrain), C. Thomas Howell (Sgt Thomas Chamberlain), Frankie Faison (Jim Lewis), Mia Dillon (Jane Beale), Donzaleigh Abernathy (Martha), John Prosky (Brig. Gen. Lewis Armistead), Joseph Fuqua (Maj. Gen. J.E.B. Stuart).

Gone With the Wind. Dir. Victor Fleming, Prod. David O. Selznick, Prod. Co. MGM/Selznick International, Dist. Co. MGM, 1939, USA. Main cast: Vivien Leigh (Scarlett O'Hara), Clark Gable (Rhett Butler), Leslie Howard (Ashley Wilkes), Olivia de Havilland (Melanie Hamilton), Thomas Mitchell (Gerald O'Hara), Hattie McDaniel (Mammy), Everett Brown (Big Sam), Oscar Polk (Pork), Barbara O'Neil (Ellen O'Hara), Victor Jory (Jonas Wilkerson), Butterfly McQueen (Prissy), Ona Munson (Bell Watling).

Horse Soldiers, The. Dir. John Ford, Prod. John Lee Mahin, Martin Rackin, Prod. Co. Mahin-Rackin/Mirisch Corp., Dist. Co. United Artists, 1959, USA. Main cast: John Wayne (Col. John Marlowe), William Holden (Maj. Henry 'Hank' Kendall), Constance Towers (Hannah Hunter), Althea Gibson (Lukey).

How the West Was Won. Dir. Henry Hathaway, John Ford and George Marshall, Prod. Bernard Smith, Prod. Co. MGM/Cinerama Productions

Corp., Dist. Co. MGM, 1962, USA. Main cast: Spencer Tracy (Narrator), Debbie Reynolds (Lilith Prescott), Carroll Baker (Eve Prescott), Lee J. Cobb (Lou Ramsey), Henry Fonda (Jethro Stuart), Carolyn Jones (Julie Rawlings), Karl Malden (Zebulun Prescott), Gregory Peck (Cleve Van Valen), George Peppard (Zeb Rawlings), Robert Preston (Roger Morgan), James Stewart (Linus Rawlings), Eli Wallach (Charlie Gant), John Wayne (Gen. William T. Sherman), Richard Widmark (Mike King), Harry Morgan (Gen. Ulysses S. Grant), Russ Tamblyn (Reb).

Red Badge of Courage, The. Dir. John Huston, Prod. Gottfried Reinhardt, Prod. Co. MGM, Dist. Co. MGM, 1951, USA. Main cast: Audie Murphy (Henry Fleming, the Youth), Bill Mauldin (Tom Wilson, the Loud Soldier), Douglas Dick (Lieutenant), Royal Dano (Tattered Man), John Dierkes (Jim Conklin, the Tall Soldier), Andy Devine (Cheerful Soldier), Arthur Hunnicut (Bill Porter).

Ride With the Devil. Dir. Ang Lee, Prod. Ted Hope, Robert Colesberry, James Schamus, Prod. Co. Hollywood International Multimedia Group/Maplewood Productions/Good Machine/Universal, Dist. Co. Universal, 1999, USA. Main cast: Tobey Maguire (Jake Roedel), Skeet Ulrich (Jack Bull Chiles), Jewel (Sue Lee Shelley), Jeffrey Wright (Daniel Holt), Simon Baker (George Clyde), Jonathan Rhys Meyers (Pitt Mackeson), John Ales (Quantrill).

So Red the Rose. Dir. King Vidor, Prod. Douglas MacLean, Prod. Co. Paramount, Dist. Co. Paramount, 1935, USA. Main cast: Margaret Sullavan (Valette Bedford), Randolph Scott (Duncan Bedford), Walter Connolly (Malcolm Bedford), Elizabeth Patterson (Mary Cherry), Janet Beecher (Sally Bedford), Robert Cummings (George Pendleton), Harry Ellerbe (Edward Bedford), Daniel Haynes (William), Clarence Muse (Cato).

They Died With Their Boots On. Dir. Raoul Walsh, Prod. Robert Fellows, Prod. Co. Warner Bros, Dist. Co. Warner Bros, 1941, USA. Main cast: Errol Flynn (George Armstrong Custer), Olivia de Havilland (Elizabeth Bacon Custer), Arthur Kennedy (Ned Sharp), Charles Grapewin (California Joe), Anthony Quinn (Crazy Horse), Sydney Greenstreet (Gen. Winfield Scott), Gene Lockhart (Samuel Bacon), Hattie McDaniel (Callie).

Undefeated, The. Dir. Andrew V. McLaglen, Prod. Robert L. Jacks, Prod. Co. Twentieth Century Fox, Dist. Co. Twentieth Century Fox, 1969, USA.

Main cast: John Wayne (Col. John Henry Thomas), Rock Hudson (Col. James Langdon), Lee Meriweather (Margaret Langdon), Tony Aguilar (Juarista Gen. Rojas), Roman Gabriel (Blue Boy), Marian McCargo (Ann Langdon), Merlin Olsen (Cpl Little George), Big John Hamilton (Mudlow).

Bibliography

Alster, L. (1990) '*Glory*', *Films and Filming*, no. 425, pp. 46–7

Altman, R. (1999) *Film/Genre*, London: British Film Institute

Anderson, B. (1991) *Imagined Communities*, 2nd edition, London: Verso

Baird, R. (1993) '"Going Indian" Through *Dances With Wolves*', *Film and History*, vol. 23, nos 1–4, pp. 91–102

Barry, I. (1965 [1940]) *D. W. Griffith: American Film Master*, New York: Museum of Modern Art

Basinger, J. (1993) *A Woman's View: How Hollywood Spoke to Women, 1930–1960*, London: Chatto and Windus

Basinger, J. (2003) *The World War II Combat Film: Anatomy of a Genre*, Middletown: Wesleyan University Press

Bassan, M. (ed.) (1967) *Stephen Crane: A Collection of Critical Essays*, Englewood Cliffs, New Jersey: Prentice-Hall

Belton, J. (1992) *Widescreen Cinema*, Cambridge, Massachusetts: Harvard University Press

Belton, J. (1994) *American Cinema/American Culture*, New York: McGraw Hill

Bercovitch, S. (1975) *The Puritan Origins of the American Self*, New Haven and London: Yale University Press

Bhabha, H.K. (1990) 'Narrating the Nation' in Bhabha, H.K. (ed.) *Nation and Narration*, London: Routledge, pp. 1–7

Bioscope (1915) 'The Birth of a Nation: An American Odyssey', vol. 28, no. 465, 9 September, pp. 1114–15

Bitzer, G.W. (1973) *Billy Bitzer: His Story*, New York: Farrar, Straus & Giroux

Blake, M. (1991) *Dances With Wolves*, New York: Chivers

Bogle, D. (1994) *Toms, Coons, Mulattoes, Mammies and Bucks: An Interpretive History of Blacks in American Films*, 3rd edition, Oxford: Roundhouse Publishing Ltd

Bordwell, D., J. Staiger and K. Thompson (1985) *The Classical Hollywood Cinema: Film Style and Mode of Production to 1960*, London: Routledge

Bowser, E. (ed.) (1982) *The D.W. Griffith Papers, 1897–1954*, New York and Kentucky: Museum of Modern Art and University of Louisville

Brooks, P. (1995) *The Melodramatic Imagination: Balzac, Henry James, Melodrama and the Mode of Excess*, New York: Columbia University Press

Brown, K. (1973) *Adventures With D.W. Griffith*, London: Faber

Burgoyne, R. (1997) *Film Nation: Hollywood Looks at U.S. History*, Minneapolis: University of Minnesota Press

Buscombe, E. and R. Pearson (eds) (1998) *Back in the Saddle Again: New Essays on the Western*, London: BFI

Campbell, E. (1981) *The Celluloid South: Hollywood and the Southern Myth*, Knoxville: University of Tennessee Press

Carr, E.H. (1987) *What is History?*, 2nd edition, Harmondsworth: Penguin

Carroll, N. (1998) 'The Professional Western: South of the Border' in Buscombe, E. and R. Pearson (eds) *Back in the Saddle Again*, London: BFI, pp. 46–62

Catton, B. (2004) *The Civil War*, Boston: Mariner Books

Chadwick, B. (2002) *The Reel Civil War: Mythmaking in American Film*, New York: Vintage Books

Collier, P. (2003) 'Committed Storyteller', *The Washington Times*, 22 February, p. D01

Collins, J. (1989) *Uncommon Cultures: Popular Culture and Post-modernism*, London: Routledge

Combs, R. (1990) 'Glory', *Monthly Film Bulletin*, vol. 57, no. 675, April, pp. 105–7

Cook, R. (2003) *Civil War America: Making a Nation, 1848–1877*, Harlow: Pearson Education Ltd

Costner, K., M. Blake and J. Wilson (1990) *Dances With Wolves: The Illustrated Story of the Epic Film*, New York: New Market Press

Crane, S. (1985 [1895]) *The Red Badge of Courage and Other Stories*, Oxford: Oxford University Press

Cripps, T. (1963) 'The Reaction of the Negro to the Motion Picture *The Birth of a Nation*', *Historian*, no. 25, pp. 344–62

Cripps, T. (1994) 'The Absent Presence in American Civil War Films', *Historical Journal of Film, Radio and Television*, vol. 14, no. 4, pp. 367–76

Cripps, T. (1996) 'The Making of *The Birth of a Race*: The Emerging Politics of Identity in Silent Movies' in Bernardi, D. (ed.) *The Birth of Whiteness: Race and the Emergence of U.S. Cinema*, New Brunswick: Rutgers University Press, pp. 38–55

Crowther, B. (1963) '*How the West Was Won*', *New York Times*, 1 April, p. 54

Cull, N. (1999) 'Richard Nixon and the Political Appropriation of *Friendly Persuasion*', *Historical Journal of Film, Radio and Television*, vol. 19, no. 2, pp. 239–46

Cullen, J. (1995) *The Civil War in Popular Culture: A Reusable Past*, Washington: Smithsonian Institution Press

Davis, C. and H.L. Gates Jr (eds) (1985) *The Slave's Narrative*, New York: Oxford University Press

Davis, William C. (1996) *The Lost Cause: Myths and Realities of the Confederacy*, Kansas: University Press of Kansas

DeBona, G. (2003) 'Masculinity on the Front: John Huston's *The Red Badge of Courage* (1951) Revisited', *Cinema Journal*, vol. 42, no. 2, pp. 57–80

Dix, D. (1915) *Boston Globe* advertisement for *The Birth of a Nation*, 9 April in Bowser, E., *The D.W. Griffith Papers, 1897–1954*, New York and Kentucky: Museum of Modern Art and University of Louisville, 1982

Dixon, T. (2001 [1905]) *The Clansman: An Historical Romance of the Ku Klux Klan*, edited by C.D. Wintz, Armonk, New York: M.E. Sharpe

Doane, M.A. (1991) *Femmes Fatales: Feminism, Film Theory and Psychoanalysis*, New York: Routledge

Doherty, T. (1990) '*Glory*', *Cineaste*, vol. 17, no. 4, pp. 40–1

Duncan, R. (ed.) (1992) *Blue-Eyed Child of Fortune: The Civil War Letters of Colonel Robert Gould Shaw*, Athens, Georgia: University of Georgia Press

Dunning, W.A. (1965 [1897]) *Essays on the Civil War and Reconstruction*, New York: Harper and Row

Dyer, R. (1997) *White*, London: Routledge

Eliot, G. (1995 [1876]) *Daniel Deronda*, London: Penguin

Elsaesser, T. (1972) 'Tales of Sound and Fury: Observations on the Family Melodrama' in Gledhill, C. (ed.) (1987) *Home is Where the Heart Is: Studies in Melodrama and the Woman's Film*, London: British Film Institute, pp. 43–69

Ferro, M. (1988) *Cinema and History*, trans. N. Greene, Detroit: Wayne State University Press

Foote, S. (1986) *The Civil War: A Narrative*, New York: Vintage Books

Gallagher, T. (1986) *John Ford: The Man and His Films*, Berkeley and Los Angeles: University of California Press

Georgakas, D. (1991) '*Dances With Wolves*', *Cineaste*, vol. 18, no. 2, pp. 51–3

Gercken, R. (2002) 'Misinterpreting *Gone With the Wind*', *Cineaste*, vol. 27, no. 3, pp. 60–1

Gillett, J. (1962/3) 'How the West Was Won', Sight and Sound, vol. 32, no. 1, Winter p. 41

Gilroy, P. (1987) There Ain't No Black in the Union Jack, London: Unwin Hyman

Gish, L. (1969) The Movies, Mr. Griffith and Me, with Ann Pichot, London: W.H. Allen

Gledhill, C. (ed.) (1987) Home is Where the Heart Is: Studies in Melodrama and the Woman's Film, London: British Film Institute

Greenfeld, L. (1997) 'The Origins and Nature of American Nationalism in Comparative Perspective' in Krakau, K. (ed.) The American Nation – National Identity – Nationalism, New Brunswick: Transaction Publishers, pp. 19–53

Griffith, D.W. (1915) 'Five Dollar Movies Prophecied', The Editor, 24 April in Bowser, 1982 (also in Geduld, H.M. [ed.] [1971] Focus on D.W. Griffith, Englewood Cliffs, New Jersey: Prentice-Hall)

Griffith, D.W. (1947) 'The Birth of a Nation: A Reply to Peter Noble', Sight and Sound, vol. 16, no. 61, pp. 32–5

Grindon, L. (1994) Shadows on the Past: Studies in the Historical Fiction Film, Philadelphia: Temple University Press

Grob, G.N. and G.A. Billias (eds) (1982) Interpretations of American History: Patterns and Perspectives, Volume I – to 1877, 5th edition, New York: The Free Press

Guerrero, E. (1993) Framing Blackness: The African American Image in Film, Philadelphia: Temple University Press

Gunning, T. (1989) 'The Cinema of Attractions: Early Film, its Spectator and the Avant Garde' in Elsaesser, T. and A. Barker (eds) (1990) Early Cinema: Space, Frame, Narrative, London: BFI, pp. 56–62

Hagelin, R. (2003) 'Among "Gods and Generals" – Part I', 18 February, http://www.worldnetdaily.com/news/article.asp?ARTICLE_ID=25616; and Part II: ID=25720

Hall, S. (1996) 'How the West Was Won: History, Spectacle and the American Mountains' in Cameron, I. and D. Pye (eds) The Movie Book of the Western, London: Studio Vista, pp. 255–61

Hammond, H.E. (ed.) (1964) We Hold These Truths…a Documentary History of the United States, Bronxville, New York: Cambridge Book Company

Hammond, M. (2002) 'Some Smothering Dreams: The Combat Film in Contemporary Hollywood' in Neale, S. (ed.) Genre and Contemporary Hollywood, London: BFI, pp. 62–76

Horwitz, T. (1999) Confederates in the Attic: Dispatches from the Unfinished Civil War, New York: Vintage Books

Huggins, N.I. (1991) 'The Deforming Mirror of Truth: Slavery and the Master Narrative of American History', Radical History Review, Winter, pp. 24–47

Inscoe, J.C. (1987) 'The Clansman on Stage and Screen: North Carolina Reacts', North Carolina Historical Review, vol. 64, no. 2, pp. 139–61

Jacobs, L. (1968) The Rise of the American Film: A Critical History, New York: Teachers College Press

James, C. (1991) 'Frugging With Wolves', New York Times Reviews, 13 January, p. 13

Kasdan, M. and S. Tavernetti (1998) 'Native Americans in a Revisionist Western: Little Big Man (1970)' in Rollins, P.C. and J.E. O'Connor Hollywood's Indian: The Portrayal of the Native American in Film, Lexington: University Press of Kentucky, pp. 121–36

Kinematograph Weekly (1954) 'Fort Bravo', vol. 444, no. 2436, 4 March, p. 23

Kinnard, R. (1996) The Blue and the Gray on the Silver Screen: More Than Eighty Years of Civil War Movies, New York: Birch Lane Press

Kitses, J. (1969) Horizons West, London: BFI

Klinger, B. (1997) 'Film History Terminable and Interminable: Recovering the Past in Reception Studies', Screen, vol. 38, no. 2, pp. 107–28

Lambert, G. (1952) 'The Red Badge of Courage', Sight and Sound, vol. 21, no. 3, January–March, p. 124

Lang, R. (ed.) (1994) The Birth of a Nation: D.W. Griffith, Director, New Brunswick, New Jersey: Rutgers University Press

May, L. (1980) Screening Out the Past: The Birth of Mass Culture and the Motion Picture Industry, New York: Oxford University Press

McGurk, Margaret A. (2003) 'Gods and Generals Shows South's Side', The Cincinnati Enquirer, 21 February; also http://www.cincinnati.com/freetime/movies/reviews/02212003_godsandgenerals.html

McPherson, J. (1990) Battle Cry of Freedom: The American Civil War, Harmondsworth: Penguin

Merritt, R. (1972) 'Dixon, Griffith, and the Southern Legend,' Cinema Journal, Fall, vol. 12, no. 1, pp. 26–45

Merritt, R. (1990) 'D.W. Griffith's The Birth of a Nation: Going After Little Sister' in Lehman, P. (ed.) Close Viewings, Tallahassee: Florida State University Press, pp. 215–37

Monthly Film Bulletin (1954) 'Escape from Fort Bravo', vol. 21, no. 243, April, p. 52

Monthly Film Bulletin (1959) 'The Horse Soldiers', vol. 26, no. 311, December, pp. 154–5

Monthly Film Bulletin (1962) 'How the West Was Won', vol. 29, no. 347, December, pp. 166–7

Monthly Film Bulletin (1969) 'The Undefeated', vol. 36, no. 430, November, pp. 237–8

Motion Picture Herald (1962) 'How the West Was Won', vol. 228, no. 11, 28 November, p. 700

Neale, S. (1979/80) 'The Same Old Story: Stereotypes and Difference', *Screen Education*, Autumn/Winter, vols 32–3, pp. 33–7

Neale, S. (2000) *Genre and Hollywood*, London: Routledge

Neale, S. (2002) *Genre and Contemporary Hollywood*, London: BFI

New York Post (1915) '*The Birth of a Nation*', 4 March, p. 9

New York Times Reviews (1935) '*So Red the Rose*', 28 November

New York Times Reviews (1963) '*How the West Was Won*', 1 April, p. 54

New York Times Reviews (1970) '*The Undefeated*', 5 February, p. 33

Noble, P. (1946) 'A Note on an Idol', *Sight and Sound*, vol. 15, no. 59, Autumn, pp. 81–2

Nowell-Smith, G. (1977) 'Minnelli and Melodrama', *Screen*, vol. 18, no. 2, pp. 113–18

O'Brien, K. (1983) 'Race, Romance, and the Southern Literary Tradition' in Pyron, D.A. (ed.) *Recasting: 'Gone With the Wind' in American Culture*, Gainesville: University Presses of Florida, pp 153–66

O'Dell, P. (1970) *Griffith and the Rise of Hollywood*, New York: A.S. Barnes and Company

Ostwalt, C. (1996) '*Dances With Wolves*: An American *Heart of Darkness*', *Literature Film Quarterly*, vol. 24, no. 2, pp. 209–16

Owens, M.T., 'Lost on *Cold Mountain*: The Anti-*Gods and Generals*', the *National Review*, 7 January 2004

Pearson, R.E. (1990) '"O'er Step Not the Modesty of Nature": A Semiotic Approach to Acting in the Griffith Biographs' in Zucker, C. (ed.) *Making Visible the Invisible: An Anthology of Original Essays on Film Acting*, Metuchen, New Jersey: Scarecrow Press, pp. 1–27

Pines, J. (1975) *Blacks in Films: A Survey of Racial Themes and Images in the American Film*, London: Studio Vista

Poulter, K. (2003) 'Briefings: Historians Respond to *Gods and Generals*', *North and South*, vol. 6, no. 3, April, pp. 87–95

Prats, A.J. (1998) 'The Image of the Other and the Other *Dances With Wolves*: The Refigured Indian and the Textual Supplement', *Journal of Film and Video*, vol. 50, no. 1, pp. 3–19

Pressly, T.J. (1962) *Americans Interpret Their Civil War*, New York: The Free Press

Pye, D. (1996) 'Masculinity in the Westerns of Anthony Mann' in Cameron, I. and D. Pye (eds) *The Movie Book of the Western*, London: Studio Vista, pp. 167–73

Pye, D. (1996) 'Genre and History: *Fort Apache* and *The Man Who Shot Liberty Valance*' in I. Cameron and D. Pye (eds) *The Movie Book of the Western*, London: Cassell Illustrated, p. 173.

Pym, J. (1990) 'For the Union Dead: *Glory*', *Sight and Sound*, vol. 59, no. 2, Spring, p. 135

Pyron, D.A. (ed.) (1983) *Recasting: 'Gone With the Wind' in American Culture*, Gainesville: University Presses of Florida

Pulver, A. 'Down from Cold Mountain' in the *Guardian*, 11 December 2003

Rahill, F. (1967) *The World of Melodrama*, University Park and London: Pennsylvania State University Press

Ray, R.B. (1985) *A Certain Tendency of the Hollywood Cinema, 1930–1980*, Princeton, New Jersey: Princeton University Press

Reeves, N. (1999) *The Power of Film Propaganda: Myth or Reality?*, London: Cassell

Renan, E. (1990) 'What is a nation?' tr. Martin Thom, in Bhabha, H.K. (ed.) *Nation and Narration*, London: Routledge, pp. 8–22

Rogin, M. (1985) 'The Sword Became a Flashing Vision', *Representations*, Winter, no. 9, pp. 150–95

Ross, L. (1952) *Picture*, New York: Random House

Sarf, W.M. (1991) 'Oscar Eaten by Wolves', *Film Comment*, vol. 27, no. 6, November–December, pp. 62–70

Saunders, J. (2001) *The Western Genre: From Lordsburg to Big Whiskey*, London: Wallflower Press

Shain, R.E. (1976) *An Analysis of Motion Pictures About War Released by the American Film Industry 1930–1970*, New York: Arno Press

Shivas, M. (1963) '*How the West Was Won*', *Movie*, no. 6, January, pp. 28–9

Simcovitch, M. (1972) 'The Impact of Griffith's *Birth of a Nation* on the Modern Ku Klux Klan', *Journal of Popular Film*, vol. 1, no. 1, Winter, pp. 45–54

Simmon, S. (1993) *The Films of D.W. Griffith*, Cambridge: Cambridge University Press

Slotkin, R. (1992) *Gunfighter Nation: The Myth of the Frontier in Twentieth-Century America*, New York: Harper Perennial

Smith, A. and T. Loe (1992) 'Mythic Descent in *Dances With Wolves*', *Literature Film Quarterly*, vol. 20, no. 3, pp. 199–204

Smith, A.D. (1991) *National Identity*, London: Penguin

Smith, H.N. (1970) *Virgin Land: The American West as Symbol and Myth*, Cambridge, Mass.: Harvard University Press

Spears, J. (1977) *The Civil War on the Screen and Other Essays*, Cranbury, New Jersey: A.S. Barnes and Company

Spehr, P.C. (1961) *The Civil War in Motion Pictures: A Bibliography of Films Produced in the United States Since 1897*, Washington: Library of Congress

Spufford, F. (2003) 'Shooting Down the Myth of Jesse James', London *Evening Standard*, 13 January, p. 44

Staiger, J. (1992) *Interpreting Films: Studies in the Historical Reception of American Cinema*, Princeton: Princeton University Press

Stallman, R.W. (1967) 'Notes Toward an Analysis of *The Red Badge of Courage*' in Bassan, M. (ed.) *Stephen Crane: A Collection of Critical Essays*, Englewood Cliffs, New Jersey: Prentice-Hall, pp. 128–40

Stowe, H.B. (1998 [1852]) *Uncle Tom's Cabin*, edited by J.F. Yellin, Oxford: Oxford University Press

Taylor, C. (1996) 'The Re-Birth of the Aesthetic in Cinema' in Bernardi, D. (ed.) *The Birth of Whiteness: Race and the Emergence of US Cinema*, New Brunswick, NJ: Rutgers University Press, pp. 15–37

Thompson, J.B. (1984) *Studies in the Theory of Ideology*, Cambridge: Cambridge University Press

Thompson, J.B. (1990) *Ideology and Modern Culture: Critical Social Theory in the Era of Mass Communication*, Polity Press: Cambridge

Thompson, K. and D. Bordwell (1994) *Film History: An Introduction*, New York: McGraw-Hill

Thomson, D. (1999) 'Riding With Ang Lee', *Film Comment*, vol. 35, no. 6, November/December, pp. 4–6, 8–9

Thomson, O. (1999) *Easily Led: A History of Propaganda*, Stroud: Sutton Publishing Limited

Tibbetts, J.C. (1999) 'The Hard Ride: Jayhawkers and Bushwhackers in the Kansas-Missouri Border Wars – *Ride With the Devil*', *Literature and Film Quarterly*, vol. 27, no. 3, pp. 189–95

Toplin, R. Brent (2002) *Reel History: In Defense of Hollywood*, Lawrence, Kansas: University Press of Kansas

Tosh, J. (2002) *The Pursuit of History*, revised 3rd edition, Harlow: Longman

Tsouras, P. (2006) *Dixie Victorious: An Alternate History of the Civil War*, Newbury: Greenhill Books

Tulloch, H. (1999) *The Debate on the American Civil War Era*, Manchester and New York: Manchester University Press

Tunney, T. (1994) '*Gettysburg*', *Sight and Sound*, vol. 4, no. 10, October, pp. 43–4

Turner, F. (1893) 'The Significance of the Frontier in American History' in Taylor, G.R. (ed.) (1972) *The Turner Thesis: Concerning the Role of the Frontier in American History*, Lexington, Mass: D.C. Heath and Co., pp. 3–28

Vance, M. (1915) '*The Birth of a Nation*', *Variety*, 12 March

Variety (1956) '*Friendly Persuasion*', 26 September

Variety (1962) '*How the West Was Won*', 7 November

Variety (1989) '*Glory*', 13 December

Vera, H. and A. Gordon (2001) 'Sincere Fictions of the White Self in Cinema: The Divided White Self in Civil War Films' in Bernardi, D. (ed.) *Classic Hollywood, Classic Whiteness*, Minneapolis: University of Minnesota Press, pp. 263–80

Walker, M. (1996) '*Dances With Wolves*' in Cameron, I. and D. Pye (eds) *The Movie Book of the Western*, London: Studio Vista, pp. 284–93

Warshow, R. (1954) 'Movie Chronicle: The Westerner' in Kitses, J. and G. Rickman (eds) (1998) *The Western Reader*, New York: Limelight Editions, pp. 35–47

Washington, B.T. (1995 [1901]) *Up From Slavery*, Oxford: Oxford University Press

White, A. (1990) 'Fighting Black: Zwick on His Feet', *Film Comment*, vol. 26, no. 1, January–February, pp. 22–6

White, M. (1981/2) '*The Birth of a Nation*: History as Pretext', *Enclitic*, vol. 5, nos 2–6, pp. 17–24

Williams, L. (1998) 'Melodrama Revised' in Browne, N. (ed.) *Refiguring American Film Genres: History and Theory*, Berkeley: University of California Press, pp. 42–88

Wollen, P. (1972 [1969]) *Signs and Meaning in the Cinema*, London: Secker & Warburg

Wood, G. (1983) 'From *The Clansman* and *Birth of a Nation* to *Gone With the Wind*: The Loss of American Innocence' in Pyron, D.A. (ed.) *Recasting: 'Gone With the Wind' in American Culture*, Gainesville: University Presses of Florida, pp. 123–36

Wood, R. (1977) 'Ideology, Genre, Auteur', *Film Comment*, vol. 13, no. 1, January–February, pp. 46–51

Woodrell, D. (1987) *Woe to Live On*, New York: Holt

Wright, E. (1967) 'The American Character' in Wright, E. (ed.) *American Themes: Selections from History Today*, Edinburgh: Oliver and Boyd Ltd, pp. 1–37

Wright, J.H. (1974) 'Genre Films and the Status Quo', *Jump Cut*, no. 1, May–June, pp. 1, 16, 18

Wright, W. (1977) *Sixguns and Society: A Structural Study of the Western*, Berkeley and Los Angeles: University of California Press

Young, S. (1930) *I'll Take My Stand: The South and Agrarian Tradition by Twelve Southerners*, New York: Harper and Bros.

ADDITIONAL WEBSITES

http://www.foxnews.com/story/0,2933,112130,00.html – 'Spike Lee on the Super Bowl, Oscars and Morality', by Jesse Washington, *Associated Press*, 21 February 2004 (accessed 02/05/04)

http://hnn.us/articles/1280.html – '*Gods and Generals* is Good Hollywood – Don't Go See It', by Patrick Rael (accessed 25/04/03)

www.kkklan.com – Official website of the Indiana Historical Research Foundation (accessed 15/04/03)

http://www.laweekly.com/news/features/song-of-the-south/2129 – 'Song of the South', by Ella Taylor, *LA Weekly*, 18 December 2003 (accessed 18/12/03)

www.ronmaxwell.com/beyondmyths.html – 'Beyond the Myths' on Website of Ronald F. Maxwell (accessed 01/04/03)

http://www.tappedin.org/pipermail/ssf/2003q1/000966.html – Transcript of *Gods and Generals* Forum, 26 March 2003

Index